_Reviews

International Praise for "AI: The Next Revolution in Content Creation"

"In this book, Dr. García brings his extensive experience in helping newsrooms embrace change to the current GenAI revolution sweeping the world. It is a sober overview, without the hype or alarmism that this topic tends to generate. It touches on the current limitations as well as the potential of the technology and is a useful guide to anyone trying to deploy GenAI tools in newsrooms. By incorporating ChatGPT output throughout, the book itself is also a testament to the point Dr. García is making, that GenAI and humans can coexist."

JEREMY AU YONG
Editor, Newsroom Strategy at *The Straits Times*

"I'm impressed by your book – the depth of your analysis is amazing, considering how recently media has been revolutionized by AI. Great work, as always!"

MASSIMO BARSOTTI
CPO/CMO, Eidosmedia, Italy

"Mario García's book masterfully captures the profound implications of the transformative shift that is generative AI. It delivers insights, a depth of understanding, and wisdom forged from decades of pioneering media design and leadership. It is engaging and eloquent throughout."

ROB LAYTON
Asst. professor of mobile journalism, Bond University, Queensland, Australia

"As content creators, especially in news organizations, look at GenAI with trepidation, fear, skepticism, and some hope, Mario García offers a very hands-on, 'how-to' early handbook, one that provides a pragmatic context for how to not only think about generative AI across a wide range of content creation activities – journalism, visual storytelling, design & layout, editorial production, social media and communications – but also offers early, practical steps a reader can take to get going and become proficient in leveraging these nascent yet rapidly evolving artificial intelligence advancements. It helps both demystify and offer a clear-eyed roadmap."

RAJU NARISETTI
Leader, Global Publishing, McKinsey & Company

"As a narrative and investigative journalist, García's book not only inspires me but compels me to embrace AI tools without fear. The book offers practical tips on how AI can assist in generating story ideas, summarizing extensive reports, and analyzing vast datasets. Most importantly, it underscores the pivotal role we, the humans, play in this dance."

BJØRN ASLE NORD
Investigative reporter/journalist, *NRK*, Bergen, Norway

"It's so inspiring to get this knowledgeable and far-sighted look at how media companies around the world are taking part in the AI revolution."

RONNY RUUD
Art director, *Aftenposten*, Norway

"It's an essential read for every journalist and news professional today."

PUNDI S SRIRAM
Chief Product Officer, *The Hindu Group*, India

_Reviews

"I love Mario García's book on AI. It is visionary and practical but also fun with the profound foundation of the news media legacy. What really struck me was García's curiosity towards the future and its possibilities. This comes from a man who has spent more than half a century in the newspaper industry and seen the 'tsunami' changing it. It is like I'm hearing Frank Sinatra singing in the background: 'The Best is Yet to Come!'"

TOMAS BRUNEGARD
Executive Chairman at EuroAcademy, Stockholm, Sweden
Former CEO/Chairman, *Stampen Group*, Göteburg, Sweden

"Artificial Intelligence (AI) can be disconcerting to many journalists who are still waiting for Human Intelligence (HI) to become fully reliable, credible and ethical. But Mario García's inimitable, proven style – in voice and in visuals – helps to reassure readers that AI can work because HI drives the process. His book deconstructs and then defines the technology for designers, editors, reporters and publishers, with meaningful examples – and with references to everyone from Salvador Dalí to Lyle Spencer (and his 1917 news-writing guide), and from Gabriel García Márquez to Maureen Dowd."

J FORD HUFFMAN
Independent editor, designer and writer, former deputy managing editor for design at *USA TODAY*

"Mario García's new book is The Elements of Style for AI in the Newsroom. AI: The Next Generation in Content Creation unpacks the implications of AI for journalists and offers powerful examples of how reporters are already harnessing it to advance their craft. Whether you're an AI skeptic or an early adopter, Dr. García provides unvarnished answers about why and how AI will transform the news business."

GREG MATUSKY
President and founder, Gregory FCA

Other Books by Dr. Mario García

The Story. Vol. I: Transformation; Vol. II: Storytelling; Vol III: Design. There has been one constant throughout my four decade career: Story. The crafting of it, the guarding of it – and the illumination of it through the technology of the epoch I was in. Whether transforming newspapers from broadsheets to tabloids, from tabloids to Berliners, from black and white to color, from print to online – my role has been as steward of the story, always insuring it was told. Today we live in a mobile culture; thus, the new art of storytelling requires that, yet again, we who tell stories must adapt to a new medium in order to continue engaging readers. With the phone as a constant companion, the story has never been closer to us, making the guarding of its purity paramount.

iPad Design Lab. Storytelling in the Age of the Tablet is about storytelling in today's world, as more people consume information using the iPad and other tablets. This guide is the first to analyze the way that consumers take in information on the tablet platform and to help journalists and designers better understand the potential of this exciting medium. Written by Dr. Mario R. García, Founder and CEO of García Media and founder of the the Graphics & Design program at The Poynter Institute for Media Studies, this guide offers insight from the author's more than 40 years of experience.

Pure Design. In Pure Design, Mario García – visionary architect of The Wall Street Journal, the San Francisco Examiner, and Liberation – presents a series of practical design solutions based on decades of experience. Includes insights into designing covers, formatting pages, selecting photos, using content, choosing color palettes, and picking type for newspapers, magazines, books, and websites. Pure Design takes readers through a complete redesign including editorial strategy, steps for successful post-project relations, and dispelling common myths to design, and shows how to create functional attractive design through a variety of platforms.

AI: THE NEXT REVOLUTION IN CONTENT CREATION
© 2024 Mario García Published by Thane & Prose, New York

All rights reserved. Printed in the United States of America.
No part of this book may be used or reproduced in any manner whatsoever without written permission except in the case of brief quotations embodied in critical articles and reviews.

First Edition.

Book cover and interior design by García Media
Editorial Director: **Christien Shangraw**
Art Director: **Rodrigo Fino**
Development Editor: **Pauline Aguilera**
Associate Editor: **Steve Dorsey**

The illustrations throughout this book were exclusively crafted with Midjourney, a leading creative platform that seamlessly merges artistry and imagination using text prompts and AI to render imagery.
To learn more about approach, please see page 205.

ISBN: 979-8-218-33282-2

thaneandprose.com

ai

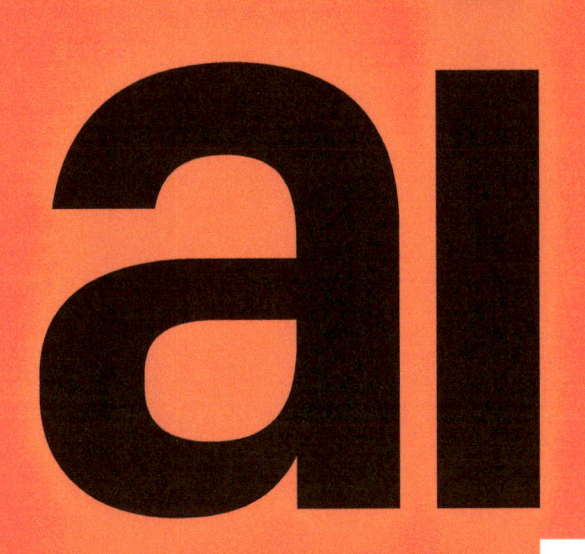

THE NEXT REVOLUTION
IN CONTENT CREATION

BY DR. MARIO GARCÍA

> **"Intelligence without ambition is a bird without wings."**
>
> *Salvador Dalí*

Table of Contents

Appreciations 11
Author's Foreword 15
    The Human/AI Connection 22
Introduction 25
    Definitions of AI 25
    How to Use This Book 29

PART I: UNDERSTANDING AI 30
Chapter 1_The 6th Revolution 33
    Enter the Robots 33
        Overlapping Revolutions 34

Chapter 2_How We Got Here 37
    Algorithms & Automation 37
        AI Players: AP's Aimee Rinehart 40
        Bots: Those Almost Perfect Butlers 42
    → How ChatGPT Sees It (1) 42
        Computers and Magic 43
        How AI/Human Interaction Works 45
    → How ChatGPT Sees It (2) 47
    → How ChatGPT Sees It (3) 50
    When Technology Advances Us 53
        Anti-AI Sentiments 53
    → How ChatGPT Sees It (4) 55
        Knowing Too Much or Nothing 57
    → How ChatGPT Sees It (5) 58
        Intelligence, Sophistication and Hallucinations 59
    → How ChatGPT Sees It (6) 60

Chapter 3_Where We Are Now 63
    The Robot Society Is Here 63
        AI Players: UCF's Ben Sawyer 65
    → How ChatGPT Sees It (1) 67
    What Publishers Want 68
        ChatBot's Main Players 70

→ How ChatGPT Sees It (2)	72
What Publishers Want	74
The World of Media AI	76

PART II: USING AI 78
Chapter 4_Reporting 81

The Reporter and AI	82
Generating Story Idea	82
→ How ChatGPT Sees It (1)	84
For Discussion	86
Generating Transcripts of Public Meetings	89
Drafting Scripts for News Broadcasts	91
Transcribing Information	93
Translating From a Foreign Language	96
Case Study 1: Aftenposten, Norway	97
Translating From a Foreign Language	99
Case Study 2: Worldcrunch, France	101
Helping With the Outline of a Story Idea	103
AI Writing: Lazy?	104
Repetition	106
→ How ChatGPT Sees It (2)	107
AI Acknowledges Where Humans Excel	109
→ How ChatGPT Sees It (3)	111
Essential Tools	113
AI Player: Reid Hoffman	115
Case Study 3: Lost Coast Outpost, USA	116

Chapter 5_Marketing & Social Media 121

AI and Reader Engagement	121
Selling That Content	122
AI and Subscriptions	123
What is CRISP-DM	124
Benefits of AI as Marketing Tool	125
Human to Human	125
→ How ChatGPT Sees It	126

Table of Contents

AI and Social Media 132
Case Study 1: Ringier, Switzerland 134
   AI Players: The Times, UK 136
   Essential Tools 137

Chapter 6_Layout & Design 141
Newspaper Print Layout and AI: A Good Combo 141
Case Study 1: Aftenposten, Norway 142
   → How ChatGPT Sees It (1) 156
AI and Typography 160
Case Study 2: TPTQ Sans CJK, Peter Biľak,
Typotheque, Netherlands 164
   → How ChatGPT Sees It (2) 166
Case Study 3: Axel Springer, Germany 168

Chapter 7_Corporate Communications 171
AI Assists Corporate Communication Teams 171
Case Study 1: Gregory FEA Public Relations, USA 173

Chapter 8_Prompt Engineering 183
Act As If... 183
   → How ChatGPT Sees It (1) 184
   It's All About Those Words 186
   A Story of Three Prompts 186
Case Study 1: Ringier Group, Switzerland 193
Keys to Successful Prompts 195
   Provide Numbers in Your Prompt 198
   → How ChatGPT Sees It (2) 202
   Our Own Experience With Midjourney 205
   Beware of Visual Hallucinations 206

Chapter 9_Content Management Systems 209
When Your Content Management System Has AI 209
Case Sudy 1: Stibo DX, Denmark 212
Case Study 2: Eidosmedia, Italy 220

    A Conversation with Eidosmedia's Massimo Barsotti 222
    Case Study 3: Aptoma, Norway 223

Chapter 10_Creating Guidelines and Protocols 233
    Guidelines to Grow With 233
        The WIRED Magazine AI Charter 234
    Case Study 1: Ringer, Switzerland 243
        Introducing Guidelines to the Reader 247
        Guidelines for Educators 248

PART III: EPILOGUE 252
Chapter 11_AI Doubts & Fears 255
    Mitigating Risks, Leveraging Opportunities 255
        AI and Inaccuracies 258
        When AI Fails 259
        Avianca False Legal 260
        Existential Threat 261
        Then the Luddites Have a New Cause 261
        AI as Competitor for Journalists 262
        AI as Competitor for Business 263
        Where Are Readers Searching? 263
    Filling in the Blanks 264
        "Algorithmic Junk?" 265
        → How ChatGPT Sees It (1) 267
        Beyond the Cautionary Tales 269
        Why the Anti-Ai Sentiment 270
        → How ChatGPT Sees It (2) 271
        → How ChatGPT Sees It (3) 274
        AI Players: Gary Marcus 277
    AI Pioneer, Dr. Geoffrey Hinton 278
        → How ChatGPT Sees It (4) 279
    The Final Prompt 281

Appreciations

This book is dedicated to everyone with a child's curiosity about artificial intelligence. Special thanks to publisher and friend, Thane Neal Boulton, of Thane & Prose, for inviting me to embark on this journey. It has been a discovery mission, complete with surprises along the way and the addition of bots to my daily communications routine.

A project of this magnitude can't happen without the contributions of many. When Thane first asked me to write a book about artificial intelligence, I told him that I did not consider myself an expert on the subject, to which he replied: "Nobody is, yet!" However, I was able to exchange ideas with the best minds on the subject, all of whom are quoted in the book, and without whose contribution the book would not have happened. Greatest appreciation to those whose hard work and tremendous efforts have made the book easier to read and to look at: Christien Shangraw, editorial director; Pauline Aguilera, development editor; and Steve Dorsey, associate editor. The fabulous design of the book has been created by García Media's senior art director, Rodrigo Fino, whom I thank for sharing his talent and experience.

A book about artificial intelligence must include a nod to those bots of ChatGPT and Midjourney for accompanying the human author on the journey, often surprising us with the depth and quality of what they produced.

Mario García, 2023

CREDITS: *Unless otherwise noted, the illustrations throughout this book were exclusively crafted with Midjourney, a leading creative platform that seamlessly merges artistry and imagination using text prompts and AI to render imagery. To learn more about our approach, please see page 205.*

Special thanks to Joe Lennon for the use of his illustration on page 229. For more, see facebook.com/lennoncartoons

"**Human input is key to AI's success because it provides the values, contextual understanding, creativity, flexibility, and responsibility that AI systems currently lack.**

By combining the strengths of human intelligence with the capabilities of AI, we can harness the full potential of this technology while ensuring it aligns with our shared values and serves the best interests of humanity..."

ChatGPT, in its own words!

Author's Foreword

A Dance of Innovation: Humans and AI in Perfect Rhythm for Content Creation's Next Act

The New York Times tech writer, Brian X. Chen, suggests that one way to get the best from ChatGPT is to ask ChatGPT to *"Act as if."* [1] Beginning a prompt with these magic words will instruct the bot to emulate an expert. For example, typing, "Act as if you are a personal trainer," or "Act as if you are a professor of linguistics," will guide the bots to model themselves after such professionals.

At 76, I look at Artificial Intelligence with the curiosity of a toddler, the amazement of a Baby Boomer, and the skeptical eye of a media professional. But I'm also a consumer of content, an academic, a grandfather. And over the course of my five-decade career in visual journalism I have always been an "early adopter" of the various tech developments that have shaken and blessed the media industry.

Today, I am lucky to have an insider's view into newsrooms across the world and access to some of the best minds experimenting with AI.

[1] nytimes.com

_Author's Foreword

FIRST AND FOREMOST, RESPECT FOR THE HUMANS. When the newspaper **The Guardian** announced the guidelines and principles that would guide how they "will and won't use GenAI tools," they made a point of saying they would have "respect for those who create and own content." I appreciate this stance enormously and this book has been written with tremendous respect and reverence for the human contributions that no machine can match yet.

The principal mantra of this book is that AI can be of tremendous assistance to humans for a variety of tasks, but the process begins with human input, requires human supervision, and ends with human evaluation and amendment.

This convergence of human ingenuity and artificial intelligence has the potential to redefine the role of content creators. AI holds a promise of revolutionizing the way we think, create, and share knowledge. It can analyze vast amounts of data, uncover hidden patterns, and generate novel ideas with efficiency. Yet, AI is ultimately a creation of the human intellect. AI can surprise us with its ability to provide information, but algorithms can't match a human's capacity for empathy, intuition, and moral judgment. The human spirit finds its truest expression in the realm of the subjective, the aesthetic, and the deeply emotional. AI is a long way from matching our creativity in the arts, literature, music, and other creative realms. AI can't yet replicate human essence.

It's clear to me that this dynamic dance between AI and humans will yield brilliant and unpredictable results. At the moment, this dance is more like a waltz than a salsa, but the two principals are on the dance floor, getting to know each other's moves.

THIS IS NOT A LOVE LETTER TO AI. What would an emotionless bot do with a love letter? One night as I logged off, I cheekily wished ChatGPT "sweet dreams." I was met with an austere reply:

"As an AI language model, I don't have personal experiences, emotions, or consciousness, so I can't experience emotions such as dreaming. I am designed to assist and provide information to the best of my abilities. My purpose is to help users like you by generating responses based on the input provided."

Imagine a co-worker in the office responding like this. You would return to your cubicle feeling a bit upset. However, that exchange was in November 2022, when **ChatGPT** had just launched. I tried the same "sweet dreams" more recently and got this response: "Thank you, and may your dreams be filled with wonder, possibility, and the limitless potential of human imagination."

Much better! It's more likely that I would dance with this partner. The dance floor is going to get a bit busier as AI works on its moves, and humans become more adept at interacting with AI, or, as some experts call it, "in the loop" with AI.

While this book is about AI and its role in content creation, it is remarkable to notice the many changes that AI is bringing to our lives in other areas as well, as when AI tech was used to "extricate" John Lennon's vocals from an old demo, which was then used to complete a song that Paul McCartney referred to as "the last Beatles record." [2] Or, with AI-enabled teddy bears that can tell children more personalized bedtime stories. [3] AI will also accompany us in our cars, as Mercedes-Benz has announced [4] it is adding OpenAI's ChatGPT chatbot to its cars via a beta program for the Mercedes-Benz User Experience (MBUX) feature in its vehicles, enabling AI-driven voice commands.

"Tell me more about the intricate dance between AI and humans," I asked ChatGPT. "How are they going to be on the dance floor?" ChatGPT responded:

> The dance between AI and humans is a complex interplay of collaboration, innovation, and shared learning. Imagine a dance floor where humans and AI partners move together, each contributing their unique strengths and abilities to create a harmonious performance. Humans, with their creativity, intuition, and emotional intelligence, bring a depth of understanding and subjective interpretation to the dance.

(2) rollingstone.com
(3) ft.com
(4) decrypt.co

_Author's Foreword

They possess the ability to imagine, to dream, and to express themselves through art, literature, music, and various forms of creative expression. Human creativity fuels the initial spark, the inspiration that sets the stage for the dance.

On the other hand, AI brings computational power, data analysis, and pattern recognition to the partnership. It can process vast amounts of information, identify trends, and generate insights with remarkable efficiency. AI algorithms can analyze data sets and extract valuable knowledge, providing new perspectives and informing human decision-making.

The dance truly comes alive when humans and AI join forces, combining their respective strengths in a symbiotic relationship. Humans provide the direction, the values, and the purpose to guide the collaboration. They infuse the dance with intention, emotion, and meaning. AI, in turn, amplifies human potential, enhancing our capabilities, and expanding the realm of what is possible.

Through collaboration, humans and AI can tackle complex problems, create innovative solutions, and uncover new avenues for exploration. They can co-create in fields like content creation, scientific research, healthcare, and many others. The partnership between humans and AI can lead to breakthroughs that would be difficult, if not impossible, to achieve by either party alone.

AI AND THE HUMAN FACTOR. AI is poised to become a volcanic force in reshaping many aspects of our life. It owes its existence to the ingenuity of humans, but it has swiftly evolved into a powerful entity that both relies on and influences our interactions. It's a symbiotic relationship, and we are only at its beginnings. AI holds the potential for immense computational power and seemingly boundless knowledge, but it lacks the essence of human experience, intuition-and moral judgment.

For content creators, the lessons of the past can be helpful here. When the Internet erupted as a major force in the 1990s, some journalists chose to ignore it. Traditional journalism, the output of which was primarily print and broadcast media, had been established for decades. The Internet disrupted this model by introducing new forms of communication and information dissemination. Unfortunately, in many ways, skepticism prevailed, and it would be years before journalists recognized the transformative potential of this new medium enough to embrace it. It is my hope that AI will be assimilated more quickly. And perhaps this book will help.

THE MAGIC OF AI. As I researched AI and wrote this book, I often felt our lack of an adequate vocabulary to describe many aspects of what AI does. We know what algorithms, bots, and prompts are, but the larger vocabulary of AI is nascent. Perhaps that is because much of its very nature remains elusive. In his masterpiece, *One Hundred Years of Solitude*, Gabriel García Márquez's wrote: "The world was so recent that many things lacked names, and in order to indicate them it was necessary to point." Gabriel García Márquez, was a master of magical realism, the Latin American literary movement that blended the ordinary with the extraordinary. It's not difficult to draw a parallel with AI and the way we currently work with the digital world.

Márquez blurs the line between what is real and what is magical. Similarly, AI pushes the boundaries of what we consider possible, introducing machines capable of complex decision-making, natural language processing, and even creativity. The very existence of AI can seem like an extraordinary phenomenon, worthy of awe and wonder, just as magical realist narratives evoke a surreal fascination through their narrative juxtapositions. In magical realistic works of literature, the reader is often left questioning the nature of events, blurring the distinction between the possible and the impossible. AI, with its complex algorithms and neural networks, can produce results that are difficult to explain in simple terms. The inner workings of AI systems can

_Author's Foreword

be perceived as mysterious and inscrutable. Magical realism disrupts conventional storytelling conventions, while AI disrupts traditional notions of intelligence and human capabilities. Both invite questions regarding the self-imposed limitations of our understanding of reality and challenge us to explore uncharted territories of thought.

As I wrote this book, I engaged with AI on a daily basis, and I found myself inspired, in awe, amazed with each discovery. I hope I can transmit that sense to you, the readers. Let this book open wide the doors to the world of artificial intelligence. It is magical and also very real.

Mario García, 2023

Dr. Mario R. García is Senior Adviser on News Design and Adjunct Professor at Columbia University's School of Journalism. He is also CEO/Founder of García Media, a global consulting firm. He has been involved with the redesign and rethinking of more than 750 publications in 120 countries, including The Wall Street Journal and The Washington Post. He came to the School of Journalism as the Hearst Digital Media Professional in Residence in 2013. He is the author of 15 books and continues to work with newsrooms across the world. He has been involved with The Poynter Institute's EyeTrack Research since its start, including the EyeTrack: Tablet. His awards include a Lifetime Achievement Award from the Society for News Design, The Journalism Medal of Honor from the University of Missouri for Distinguished Service in Journalism. In 2015, Mario became the recipient of the Columbia Scholastic Press Association's Charles O'Malley Excellence in Teaching Award. People Magazine mentioned him among the 100 most influential Hispanics in the United States. He received his PhD. from the University of Miami. Today, Mario is totally engaged in mobile-first storytelling and artificial intelligence, and the transformation of news and information across digital platforms.

Follow TheMarioBlog at garciamedia.com.

The Human/AI Connection

One of the most authoritative testimonials for how humans can use artificial intelligence to enhance their creativity comes in the way of a lead piece from the Harvard Business Review (July-August 2023). Titled "How Generative AI Can Augment Human Creativity," the article uses practical examples of ChatGPT and Midjourney use to offer solutions and suggest ideas that the humans can then take and expand. Here are some takeaways for how we can use AI to assist us with our creative projects:

PROMOTE DIVERGENT THINKING: Generative AI can support divergent thinking by making associations among remote concepts and producing ideas drawn from them.

CHALLENGE EXPERTISE BIAS: During the early stages of new-product development, atypical designs created by generative AI can inspire designers to think beyond their preconceptions of what is possible or desirable in a product in terms of both form and function.

ASSIST IN IDEA EVALUATION: Generative AI tools can assist in other aspects of the front end of innovation, including by increasing the specificity of ideas and by evaluating ideas and sometimes combining them.

SUPPORT IDEA REFINEMENT: Generative AI tools can solve an important challenge faced in idea contests: combining or merging a large resources and expertise to develop and implement and may number of ideas to produce much stronger ones.

FACILITATE COLLABORATION WITH AND AMONG USERS: When developing new product ideas or designs, generative AI can facilitate collaborations between a company's designers and users of a prospective product and among users themselves.

HUMAN. The first step to get artificial intelligence to help us begins with input from a human. This is that essential moment when the human trains the bot with Data Collection and Annotation. Humans are involved in collecting relevant data and annotating it to provide labels or tags that help the AI system understand patterns and learn from the data. For example, in image recognition tasks, humans may manually label images to indicate the presence of objects or specific features. Human experts or trainers are responsible for training AI models by providing examples, demonstrations, or feedback.

ARTIFICIAL INTELLIGENCE. After a human feeds input to an AI bot, several processes take place to generate a response or perform a task. First, the Input Processing: The AI bot receives the input provided by the human. This input can be in the form of text, speech, images, or any other modality depending on the system's capabilities. The bot's programming or underlying algorithms analyze and preprocess the input data to make it suitable for further processing. Understanding and Interpretation: The AI bot attempts to understand the input and extract its meaning. This involves various techniques such as natural language processing (NLP), computer vision, or audio processing, depending on the input modality. Once the input is understood, the AI bot performs the necessary computations to generate a response or take action.

HUMAN. At the end of the process, there is a human to review, evaluate and give the final version its approval. This process where a human puts in the finishing touches after the AI bot has generated a response, is often known as human-in-the-loop or human-in-the-loop AI. The human review process adds an extra layer of quality control and human judgment to the AI generated responses, ensuring that the final output is accurate, relevant, and aligned with the user's needs. It serves as a mechanism to address the limitations of AI systems and provide a personalized and refined experience to the end user.

Introduction

Definitions of AI...

Artificial Intelligence is the study and development of computer systems capable of doing activities ordinarily performed by humans. Artificial Intelligence is a branch of computer science that aims to simulate human intelligence by machines. AI was born amid the emergence of cybernetics 70 years ago. The term "AI" emerged in 1956. Expert systems came to the fore by the 1980s, which led to a boom since 2010 on the backs of massive data and new computing power. In an Associated Press report, the definition of artificial intelligence extends to these four items:

- → AI helps to process data
- → AI does not have a mind of its own
- → AI depends on data that humans feed it
- → AI produces results from human-fed information [5]

AI can be divided by subcategory, and the Associated Press has come up with four types of AI technologies that stand out in journalism:

- → machine learning
- → natural language generation
- → natural language processing
- → computer vision

(5) ap.org

_Introduction

MACHINE LEARNING (ML) is a subset of artificial intelligence that involves creating algorithms that can automatically learn from data without being explicitly programmed. Using machine learning, computers can identify patterns in data and make predictions or decisions based on that data. In traditional programming, a programmer writes code that specifies how a computer should process data and make calculations. In machine learning, however, the program does not follow a set of predefined rules. Instead, a machine learning algorithm is trained on a specific dataset, and employs statistical techniques to "learn" a model that can make predictions or decisions based on additional data as it becomes available. Machine learning has applications in various fields such as image recognition, speech recognition, natural language processing, and predictive analytics, among others.

Supervised Learning involves training AI models on labeled data, where the input-output pairs are provided.

Unsupervised Learning involves finding patterns and structures in unlabeled data.

Semi-supervised Learning is a combination of supervised learning and unsupervised learning.

Reinforcement Learning involves training AI models through a system of rewards and punishments based on their actions.

NATURAL LANGUAGE GENERATION (NLG) is a subset of AI that focuses on the creation of natural language text by machines. NLG algorithms can analyze and interpret data, statistics, or structured information and produce human-like text. NLG is often used in situations where large amounts of data need to be converted into easy-to-read, human-friendly text, such as news article publishing, business intelligence, report generation, and more. NLG algorithms use complex algorithms that involve natural language processing (NLP), machine learning, and deep learning. They can turn raw data into easy-to-understand, human-friendly text summaries, comprehensible to non-experts.

NLG systems can also automatically personalize text content based on customer preferences, making them effective in customer service, chatbots, or virtual assistants. NLG algorithms can create contextual conversations using pre-written text templates that can be customized and combined in different ways to generate human-like responses.

NATURAL LANGUAGE PROCESSING (NLP) is a branch of AI that enables computers to understand, interpret, and generate human language. NLP algorithms machine learning, deep learning, and rule-based systems to analyze human language. NLP can be divided into several subfields, including Natural Language Understanding (NLU), Natural Language Generation (NLG), and Natural Language Interaction (NLI). NLP can help computers to understand the meaning of natural language texts, classify and extract relevant information from a large amount of data, and generate human-like responses. For instance, NLP enables chatbots and virtual assistants to understand voice commands and then respond in natural language. It also aids in sentiment analysis, text classification, and machine translation, aiding translation from one natural language to another.

NLP has broad applications in various fields, including natural language interface designs, search engines, intelligent personal assistants, computer-assisted language learning. language interface designs, search engines, intelligent personal assistants, computer-assisted language learning.

HOW TO START USING GENERATIVE AI. The easiest way to start working with generative AI is simply to talk to an AI bot, such as ChatGPT, Jasper AI, Writesonic, or any other chatbot-like interface. Some tools are free to use, as prototypes, while some

_Introduction

require a paid subscription. Talking to a bot is as simple as texting your friends on a mobile device.
   1. Register or subscribe to an AI tool, such as ChatGPT.
   2. In a dialog box, type or dictate a prompt in your language. For example, type "Explain AI to me like I was a 10-year-old."
   3. The bot is likely going to answer right away. That is all that's involved. If you are not happy with a result, tell the bot to rewrite.
It remembers the earlier conversation, so it all feels like talking to somebody.

HOW_CHATGPT_SEES IT

PROMPT: *As a journalist and content producer, you can get started using generative AI by following these steps:*

CHATGPT:
1. Learn how generative AI works. You may already have a pretty good idea just from having read a bit of this book's introduction. If you want to know more, there are always videos and online courses.

2. Identify use cases. How might generative AI can help you in your journalism or content production work? It might save you time by summarizing a long article. It might auto-generate image captions, write clickbait-y headlines, or even news articles.

3. Research available tools. Of the many generative AI tools available which best suits your needs? Popular examples include OpenAI's GPT-3, Hugging Face, and Paperspace.

4. Experiment. Start by inputting small amounts of data. You might start by prompting the tool to generate responses to some frequently asked questions or recent headlines.

→

> **HOW_CHATGPT_SEES IT**
>
> **5. Test and refine.** After generating text, it's important to review and refine the output with more prompts. This is how you'll train the generative model to recognize more complex patterns.
>
> **6. Publish.** But first ensure the content is factually accurate, grammatically correct, and relevant!
>
> **7. Get feedback.** Query your audience about what they find useful, what should be changed, improved. Don't fear criticisms; they will help you to fine-tune your generative algorithm!
>
> Overall, using generative AI requires plenty of experimentation-trial and error. Be patient and always look for ways to improve the output by adjusting the input. ●

HOW TO USE THIS BOOK. Recurring features include:

AI Nuggets: For your edification, AI-relevant facts and data pop up throughout the book – just as they do every day.

AI Players: You'll be introduced to the programmers, philosophers, thought leaders, and other humans behind these intelligent tools throughout the book.

Case Studies: Real instances of AI's utility in content creation.

Essential Tools: Must-have and must-know aspects of AI.

For Discussion: Comparisons that lead to conversation starters.

How ChatGPT Sees It: We "interviewed" the source itself.

ProTips: As you read through this book you'll find this running feature offering quick suggestions for using AI most effectively.

Part One
Understanding AI

→ Chapter 1 - The 6th Revolution
→ Chapter 2 - How We Got Here
→ Chapter 3 - Where We Are Now

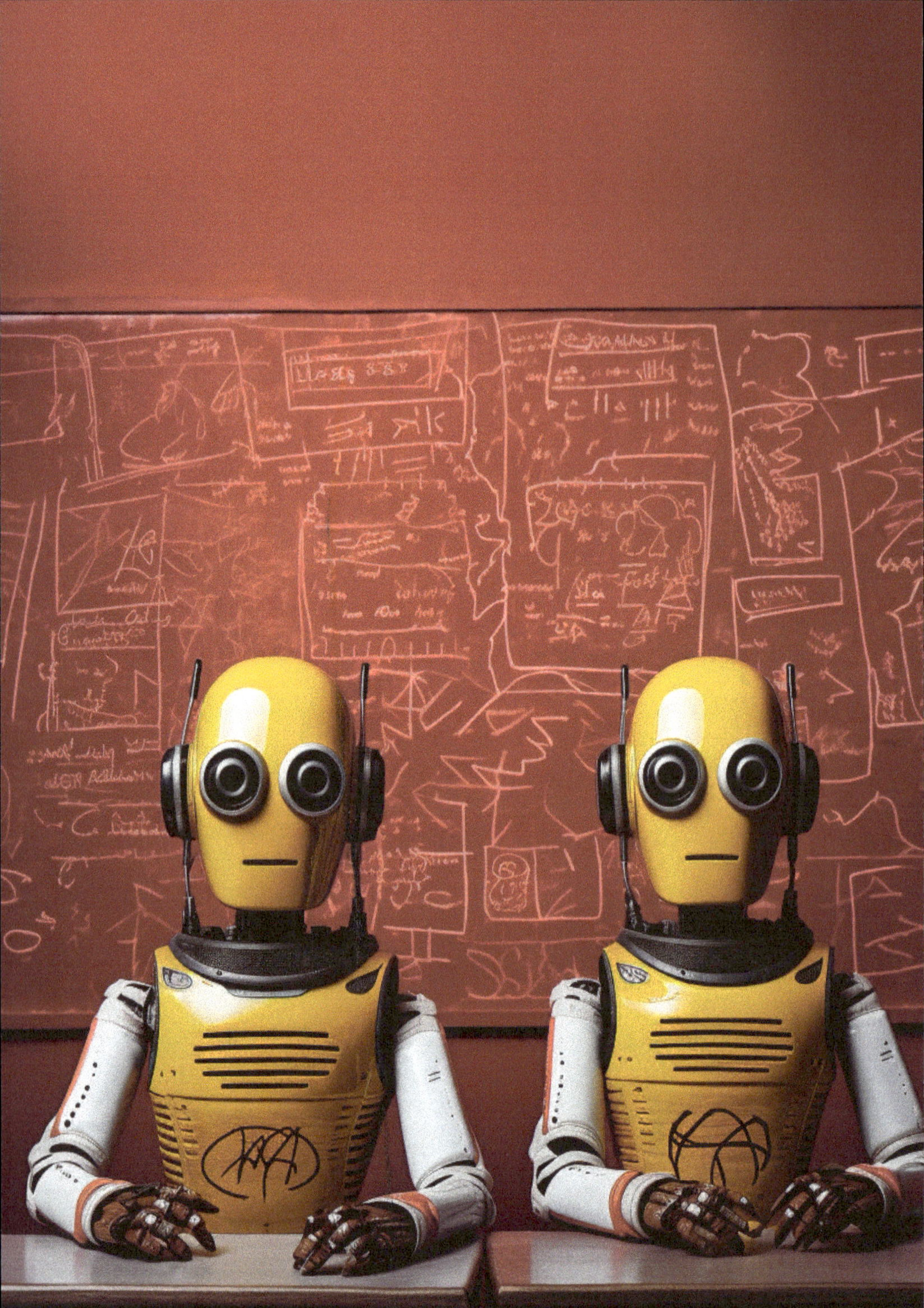

Chapter 1_**The 6th Revolution**

Enter the Robots

For the sake of argument, let's say there have been five big revolutions in journalism over the past half-century: 1. Hot metal type setting to cold type 2. Typewriters to computers 3. Black and white to color 4. The Internet 5. The pivot to mobile-first newsrooms. Every one of them posed a challenge to those journalists least open to technological changes. Now something else provokes fascination, fear and curiosity: 6. Artificial Intelligence.

People from all walks of life-students, coders, artists, accountants-are experimenting with AI tools. At the Salvador Dalí Museum in St. Petersburg, Florida, (6) Dream Tapestry transforms personal dreams into individualized art pieces, then connects those with other visitors' images to produce a "dream tapestry," weaving individuals' inner worlds with the evolving dream of humanity. The system creates realistic images and art from a description.

The New York Times outlined 35 ways in which ordinary people are using AI, from planning gardens, workouts and meals, to writing a wedding speech ("Can you add that thing about in sickness and in health?"), or organizing a messy computer desktop ("...it gave me a list of which notes should go into which folders!"). (7)

Generative AI is the most significant new technology since the advent of the Internet. Generative AI models learn from huge amounts of published data, including books, publications, Wikipedia and social media sites, to predict the most likely next word in a sentence, and to answer almost any question a person could ask.

AI goes beyond everyday tasks. In the last few years, companies

(6) thedali.org
(7) nytimes.com

Chapter 1_*The 6th Revolution*

and scholars have begun using AI to supercharge work they could never have imagined, designing new molecules with the help of an algorithm or building alien-like spaceship parts. How can one not be impressed and feeling hopeful when one reads a headline such as this: AI Battles Superbugs: Helps Find New Antibiotic Drug To Combat Drug-Resistant Infections. (8)

Soon after this headline appeared, Maureen Dowd, a New York Times' columnist, wrote, "AI can be amazing; it just discovered an antibiotic that kills a deadly superbug. But it may also eventually see us as superbugs." Ms. Dowd is not alone in expressing a bit of caution.

When you think about AI in the newsroom, don't just imagine a journalist researching a story. In fact, News Corp, in Australia, has initiated Project Heartbeat, conceived to provide personalized "subscriber healthcare" treatment: A highly targeted, creative engagement program designed to address the specific concerns of high-risk subscribers in hopes of preventing churn. (9)

Project Heartbeat uses an AI-generated risk profile to generate a "cradle-to-grave" lifecycle breakdown covering infancy, general practice, specialized treatment, acute care, and emergency response.

OVERLAPPING REVOLUTIONS. Many are no doubt way ahead of this latest revolution. AI is kicking down the doors of newsrooms around the world while many have barely embraced the previous revolution of turning into mobile-first operations.

In 2019's *The Story* (Thane & Prose, New York), this author wrote: While the story continues to be our reason to exist, much has changed in how it moves in a multi-platform world.

As someone who visits a different newsroom almost every week, I am well aware that publishers and editors understand the importance of the story – but newsroom dynamics have not changed enough to accommodate the way stories move in a mobile first environment.

In retrospect, it seems that the Internet revolution of the 1990s arrived to much fanfare, but did not deeply alter the ways in which editors practiced journalism. For the most part, it was business as

(8) scitechdaily.com
(9) inma.org

usual. Stories were prepared for the print edition, then put online. It would be years before many large metropolitan newspapers began to tell stories online in a different way. It was, technologically-speaking, a new way of presenting journalism, but for too long it fell short of being a new way of practicing journalism.

It took the mobile-first revolution to more effectively impact journalism itself, the way stories are told. It forced editors to consider what we might call the journalism of interruptions, news to be consumed anywhere, and at any time.

The challenge for content producers now, particularly those producing news, is to embrace the benefits of AI and transform work processes to accommodate a way of telling stories that involves more than words. It's time to study ways in which artificial intelligence can help with a variety of tasks that will save time that journalists and editors can spend searching for better content and making it more accessible.

AI NUGGETS

The Atlanta Journal-Constitution, Pulitzer Prize finalist for its investigation **of sexual abuse by doctors, used machine learning to scour more than 100,000 disciplinary documents.**

→ knowledge.wharton.upenn.edu/

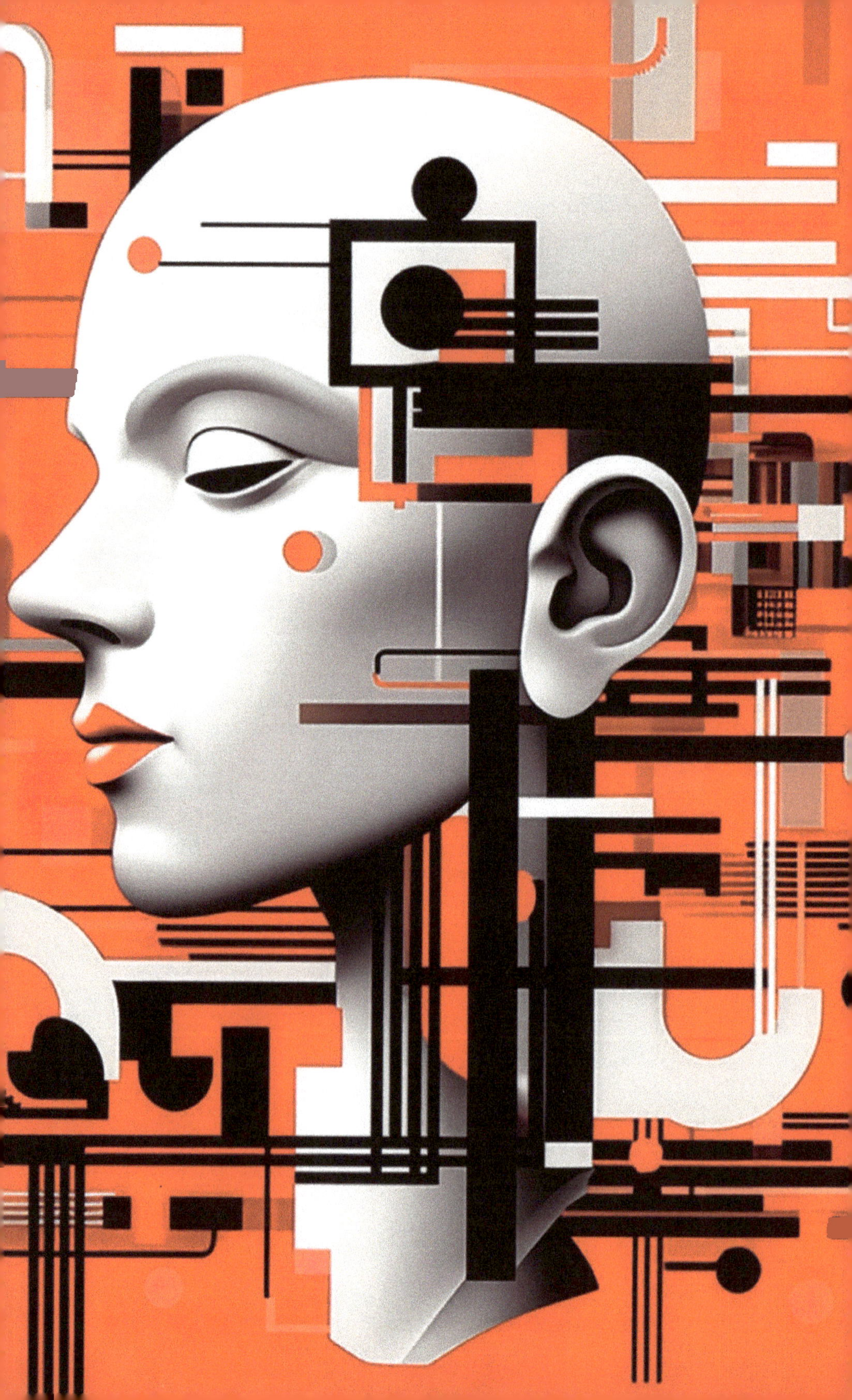

*Chapter 2_***How We Got Here**

We Got Here With the Help of Two 'A's: Algorithms and Automation

In his book, Automating the News, Nick Diakopoulos, writes that computational algorithms have become sophisticated enough so that content producers can "blend their own efforts with that of the machine." Diakopoulos explains how the Associated Press, the 170-year-old newswire service, uses AI to create short (200-words-or-fewer) stories about corporate earnings. Such pieces can be distributed quickly to AP subscribers.

"By 2018 the AP was producing more than 3,700 stories this way during every earnings season, covering most US traded stocks down to a market capitalization of $75 million. That's more than ten times the number of stories they wrote without automation, enabling a far greater breadth of coverage. The stories won't be earning Pulitzer Prizes any time soon, but they do convey the basics of corporate earnings in a straightforward and easily consumable form, and they do it at scale." (10)

This is the sort of innovative thinking you, the content creator, might wisely employ as you consider how to incorporate AI into your own work. Put simply, let AI produce copy that is entirely based on easily mined information, freeing you to focus on aspects of the story that require analysis and interpretation. This brings us to something that is often lost in the more fearful discussions about how artificial intelligence might take over for human thinking.

(10) Diakopoulos, Nicholas. Automating the News (p. 1). Harvard University Press.

Chapter 2_*How We Got Here*

Algorithmic decisions are based on (and can only be based upon) whatever parameters have been input. Humans provide algorithms with values and defaults. For example, journalists in a newsroom may create agreed-upon story templates. A news organization that thrives on mobile storytelling will seek templates that depend heavily on video and audio, while others may want to inform their AI with photos and other graphics.

The needs of the content producer will be best met in a balanced marriage between their own human cognition and the capabilities and efficiency of their AI.

In many newsrooms, AI is already used for automated text writing as well as for layout practices (See Chapter 6). Let's not forget that, while content producers today are experimenting with the use of AI for more sophisticated storytelling templates, organizations have been using automated text writing for a long time, as for weather reports and market updates. The French daily, *Le Monde*, deployed automated writing to help report French election results in 2015. [11]

(11) Diakopoulos, Nicholas. Automating the News (p. 107). Harvard University Press.

"In the next twenty-four months, the planet will add more computer power than it did in all previous history. Over the next twenty-four years, the increase will likely be over a thousand-fold."

The Second Machine Age: Work, Progress, and Prosperity in a Time of Brilliant Technologies — Brynjolfsson, Erik; McAfee, Andrew. (p. 251). W. W. Norton & Company.

Chapter 2_*How We Got Here*

AI_PLAYERS

AIMEE RINEHART. Senior Product Manager AI Strategy and Local News, Associated Press

When Aimee Rinehart arrived at the AP (Associated Press) in 2021, the journalists there had already been using AI since 2014-with good results. AP started with natural language generation, working with the tech firm Automated Insights, taking information from spreadsheets of the stock exchange assign columns, with numbers up or down for stocks. The results? AP went from generating 300 with human reporters to rendering 3,000 in just minutes by NLG.

"These were not stories," said Rinehart. "More like pieces of information. This had a tremendous impact, since the 2,700 companies that were written up had never received any coverage, so they got traction, a powerful moment for AP and even the stock market." These early steps into artificial intellige0nce helped ensure the AP was ready for what happened when ChatGPT was introduced in 2022.

ENTER CHATGPT

"ChatGPT put a face on the new technology," added Rinehart. "People can start using it, experimenting, they can program. That is what is revolutionary. It uses natural language that we are familiar with. Our work as journalists will be challenged because of ChatGPT."

"The fascination with ChatGPT among journalists also brings with it doubts and fears. Some journalists have trouble accepting it, because of ChatGPT's tendency to hallucinate. What is your source?, they ask. It does not provide sources. There is no fact checking, and it makes stuff up sometimes."

Rinehart is quick to point out what ChatGPT can do best: "Use it for organizing and structuring data, or to take a story and summarize it, create a Twitter thread, or write a Facebook post. Use it for its language base." It is precisely because of the tasks that ChatGPT can perform that Rinehart sees it used effectively in all newsrooms-but especially small newsrooms.

SMALL NEWSROOMS AND AI BENEFITS

"At AP we have worked with many small newsrooms and see that those that have a 2- or 3-person skeleton crew are experimenting with artificial intelligence in ways that larger newsrooms have not done yet." Small newsroom editors use ChatGPT because it is free or low cost, and it can be used for summarization, headline writing, copy editing and even marketing. Use ChatGPT and artificial intelligence for what it is good for, Rinehart says. "It's great for language but not great with knowledge. If you have ingredients that can go into a story, it will summarize, bring a story together, write promotional social posts. However, I can't see a legitimate journalist using it to write a story, for the wholesale creation of a story." ●

Chapter 2_*How We Got Here*

BOTS: THOSE ALMOST PERFECT BUTLERS. If 'A' was for Algorithms and Automation, then 'B' is most certainly for Bots, computer programs that mimic humans and/or human behavior. By now, most of us are familiarized with chatbots. Whether people know it or now, chatbots are typically the first form of engagement they have had with artificial intelligence. Chatbots engage in dialog, answer questions quickly, and provide a chattier recitation of the facts than we may find with, say, a Google search. Some of us have conversations with a chatbot daily. We use it to browse information, to expand on knowledge we already have, or simply to help us better understand something engaging us at the moment.

Before a visit to the Dalí Museum, in St. Petersburg, Florida, and an exhibit emphasizing Dali's dreams, one can ask ChatGPT, a popular chatbot created by OpenAI and launched on November 30, 2022, about the subject:

HOW_CHATGPT_SEES IT

PROMPT: *Why did Dalí paint such strange images?*

CHATGPT: Salvador Dalí painted strange images as part of his artistic style, which was heavily influenced by Surrealism. Surrealism was a cultural movement that emerged in the 1920s and 30s, which emphasized the irrationality of the subconscious mind. Surrealists wanted to push the boundaries of conventional thinking and art making by creating works that defied reason and logic and were meant to evoke strong emotions and psychological responses.

In Dali's case, his paintings often combined images that were seemingly contradictory, or illogical. For example, he might paint an

→

> ## HOW_CHATGPT_SEES IT
>
> elephant with giraffe-like legs, or a melting clock draped over a tree branch. These elements were often combined in unexpected ways, with fine detail and precise rendering, which created a dreamlike or hallucinogenic quality.
>
> One reason why Dalí may have been drawn to this style was to explore his own inner thoughts and emotions. Like many other artists, Dalí used his art as a means of expressing his personal experiences and feelings, and this dynamic style gave him the freedom to explore uncharted territories of the mind.
>
> Another reason why Dali's paintings were so strikingly strange was that he was interested in creating a sense of visual shock. By presenting the viewer with such bold and unexpected imagery, he hoped to elicit a strong reaction. Dali's paintings were designed to be thought-provoking, and they often challenged the viewer to confront their own preconceptions about the world, the mind, and art itself.
>
> Overall, Dalí painted strange images as part of his artistic vision, to push the boundaries of what was possible in art at the time and to explore his own inner thoughts and emotions. He believed that art should be challenging, emotionally engaging, and intellectually stimulating, and his paintings remain a testament to those ideals. ●

COMPUTERS AND MAGIC. Arthur C. Clarke, an English science-fiction writer, science writer, futurist, inventor, wrote: "Any sufficiently advanced technology is indistinguishable from magic." If computing power can still seem a little magic at times, interactions with AI can seem especially so. But remember, behind the creation of every bot, there is a human

Chapter 2_*How We Got Here*

involved in setting the parameters of that bot. And the magic didn't happen overnight. One of the most inspiring accounts of the technology that got us here is, The Second Machine Age, by Erik Brynjolfsson and Andrew McAfee. The authors cite the Industrial Revolution-developments in mechanical engineering, chemistry, steam engines-as the first machine age. Now comes the second machine age, the authors remind us: "Computers and other digital advances are doing for mental power-the ability to use our brains to understand and shape our environments-what the steam engine and its descendants did for muscle power. They are allowing us to blow past previous limitations and taking us into new territory."

The journey into this new territory involves deep transformations in the way we approach work, how we think, and how we relate to the magic of this technology. The authors see this second machine age as "profoundly beneficial." "We are headed into an era that won't just be different, it will be better, because we will be able to increase both the variety and the volume our consumption." They are quick to point out, however, that digitalization is going to bring with it some "thorny challenges." Just like the Industrial Revolution brought soot to London, technological progress will diminish our need for some kinds of workers. While the Industrial Revolution impacted physical industries and manufacturing processes, AI primarily affects intellectual capabilities and cognitive tasks, and raises ethical issues and issues of intellectual property. AI algorithms can analyze vast amounts of data, recognize patterns, and make predictions or recommendations based on that analysis. The implications for fields like data analysis, natural language processing, image recognition, robotics, and others are massive. While we celebrate the magic, progress and efficiency that Artificial Intelligence can bring into our lives, we are wise to maintain a sense of its limitations. Perhaps it is helpful to reflect on the conclusions of researchers Frank Levy and Richard Murnane (The New Division of Labor, 2004), who describe complex communication as the sole domain of humans. "Conversations critical to effective teaching, managing, selling, and many other occupations require the transfer and interpretation of a broad range of information. In these cases, the possibility of exchanging information with a computer, rather than another human, is a long way off." Levy and Murnane believed in a strong boundary between tasks that humans do and those performed by a computer. The work of Levy and Surname was published in 2004, but its application to issues surrounding AI remains deeply relevant. For example, a visual journalist is used to approaching projects with an open mind, listening carefully to a briefing on the task at hand. What is the story? How should the design communicate the meaning and context of the story at a glance? For example, a story may be intended for consumption on a phone, and editors may expect it to hold the attention for as short as four seconds. In just a moments' time, a visual journalist may conceive of an illustration, a short video, or just a powerful typographic arrangement that has the power to convey the meaning of the story and seduce the reader. Can Artificial Intelligence deliver that "flash" of an idea. No! But the journalist can go to AI with an idea and ask for additional information.

HOW AI/HUMAN INTERACTION WORKS. How AI gathers and delivers mountains of information depends upon how it has been programmed and "trained." Its sources of information are: Structured Databases and Knowledge Bases, Internet and Online Resources, Pretrained Models and Corpora. Many AI models are trained on large datasets, such as text corpora, which contain vast amounts of information from books, articles, research papers, and other written material, human input and human expertise.

Chapter 2_*How We Got Here*

HUMAN. The first step is always human input. Human input that trains AI models may include additional, the labeling or annotation of examples, or other feedback. This input helps the AI system recognize and understand patterns, make predictions, and generate responses based on human knowledge and expertise. For example, humans may manually label images to indicate the presence of objects or specific features.

AI. The AI bot's first task is Input Processing. Perhaps the input came in the form of text, speech, images, or some other modality (depending on the system's capabilities). The bot's programming or underlying algorithms analyze and preprocess the input data to make it suitable for further processing. Next it evaluates the input and interprets its meaning. It uses techniques such as natural language processing (NLP), computer vision, or audio processing, depending on the input modality. Once the input is understood, the AI bot performs the necessary computations to generate a response or take an action.

HUMAN. Finally, there is the human task of reviewing and evaluating the output. This process, in which a human puts finishing touches on the AI-generated response, is often known as "human-in-the-loop" or "human-in-the-loop AI." This step adds an extra layer of quality control and human judgment to the AI-generated responses, ensuring that the final output is accurate, relevant, and aligned with the user's needs. It serves as a mechanism to address the limitations of AI systems and provide a personalized and refined experience to the end user. Based on that interaction formula, we can prompt ChatGPT asking for ideas:

HOW_CHATGPT_SEES IT

PROMPT: *Act as if you are a graphic designer, and help me illustrate a story about the abortion controversy in the U.S.*

CHATGPT: As an AI language model, I cannot illustrate the story as I am not capable of creating visual designs independently. However, I can provide some ideas for how a Graphic Designer can assist in illustrating the story:

1. Infographics: A Graphic Designer can create infographics that visually represent statistics or data related to the abortion controversy in the US. For example, creating a chart or graph that shows the number of abortions performed in each state, rates of abortion among different age groups, and so on.

2. Illustrations: The Graphic Designer can create illustrations that help to tell the story in a more engaging way. For instance, an illustration that depicts the emotional weight of the decision to terminate a pregnancy, or how a woman's choice might be influenced by societal constraints, religious views, government regulations or economic status.

3. Political Cartoons: Political cartoons are a great way to present complex social or political issues in a simplified way. A Graphic Designer can create a series of cartoons that capture different opinions and perspectives on the abortion controversy. These cartoons could be used to cover the entire spectrum of the debate, focus on specific aspects of the story or cover different aspects such as the religious, moral, social, economic or political implications of the issue.

→

Chapter 2_**How We Got Here**

HOW_CHATGPT_SEES IT

4. Visual Storytelling: A Graphic Designer can use their skills to create visual stories that take the reader through different aspects of the abortion controversy. This could include creating a set of visual icons or illustrations that connect with different stories and viewpoints. The designer can link these visual elements story-wise to develop a strong visualization of the narrative for the story.

5. Social Media cards: The designer can make use of social media online cards and post designs to raise awareness among online audiences. For example, Instagram stories or Facebook banners with illustrations and infographics showing data and statistics.

Overall, the success of the storytelling lies in the ability to provide a visual representation of the story as sensitively as possible and without biased indications. By engaging a professional Graphic Designer's creativity, storytelling is enhanced and more effectively communicated to readers. Sent from my iPhone. The benefit of this response is that it allows us to think beyond the original concept, as in suggesting genres I had not considered: cartoons, for example. What happens when you come to AI with an idea but wish to hear what AI has to say about it.

PROMPT: *I am a graphic designer designing for a mobile story about abortion controversy in the US. Is it better to start with a photo/illustration, or a video, and why?*

CHATGPT: As an AI language model, I cannot give subjective opinions, but I can provide factors to consider when deciding between starting with a photo illustration or video when designing a mobile story about abortion controversy in the US.

→

HOW_CHATGPT_SEES IT

1. Story Content: Take into account the type of story content you are dealing with when deciding whether to opt for a photo illustration or video. For instance, photos tend to be ideal if you want to draw attention to a specific image or subject in a frame, while videos will be better where there are many details or story angles to cover.

2. Budget: Think about your budget when making design choices. Videos typically take longer to produce and may require a larger budget than photo illustrations. On the other hand, photo illustrations can more easily be edited to suit particular design needs or budgetary limitations.

3. Time: Determine how much time you have to create the design. Depending on the amount of time available, a photo illustration or video may be more appropriate. Photo illustrations generally require less time than videos, as they can be created in less time and more efficiently than with videos which require many recording and editing hours.

4. Target Audience: Consider the preferences and expectations of your audience. Age group, demographics, and the intended message you want to communicate will guide your decision-making preferences about whether to design a photo illustration or a video. In the end, both photo illustrations and videos can be effective in creating a mobile story about the abortion controversy in the US. It will ultimately depend on the specific requirements for the project and the target audience's preferences. Ultimately the decision should be made based on the objective of the story content, budget, deadline, target audience preferences and production quality. ●

Chapter 2_*How We Got Here*

TAKEAWAY: This was less helpful to the designer, deals with generalities and does not advance the designer's ability to get an idea from the response. Looking for some magic, we try again with the story concept, but this time, asking for an illustration idea to illustrate the abortion story.

HOW_CHATGPT_SEES IT

PROMPT: *I am a graphic designer designing a story about abortion controversy in the US. Give me an idea for an illustration.*

CHATGPT: One idea for an illustration you could use to represent the abortion controversy in the US is a series of silhouettes representing different perspectives and experiences surrounding the issue. For instance, you could create silhouettes of a woman considering her options about abortion, a protester holding a sign outside of a Planned Parenthood clinic, a politician giving a speech on the matter, or a physician providing information about the abortion procedure to a patient.

Each image could be placed side-by-side, to create a montage of various individuals, highlighting the various angles of the abortion controversy, and depicting the complexity and diversity surrounding the issue in our society.

Using a simple silhouette illustration can represent the anonymity and diversity of people having many different opinions, emotions, and discomforts about abortion. Using different colors for each image to represent different opinions, religions, cultural and social backgrounds of persons reflecting the depth of the challenges and controversy may be another idea to consider.

TAKEAWAY: Now that we have the feeling this is a conversation with a colleague over coffee, a conversation with real substance, you might 1) create silhouettes of a woman considering her options about abortion, and then 2) place the images side-by-side to create a montage of various individuals.

The designer benefitted from a "second opinion" in a matter of seconds, allowing her to expand the basket of possibilities.

Thinking about the statement from Levy and Murnane in 2004 that the possibility of exchanging information with a computer, rather than another human, is a long way off, the exchanges above indicate that we have advanced greatly in the computer/human connection since the authors wrote their book. Indeed, we can have a conversation with our robot assistant designer. It can yield some thinking beyond our original idea. This is likely to improve rapidly.

AI has tons of available information to offer, but it lacks knowledge. In the case of the abortion example, it may not understand the complexities of abortion, or ever met a person who had an abortion, or talked to a person who tells a story of how he/she was almost aborted. AI deals with generalities, the human designer has a set of context to proceed with the idea that best illustrates the story. Karen Silverman, CEO and founder of the Cantellus Group, and a technology governance specialist with expertise in AI and a member of the World Economic Forum's Global Future Council on the Future of Artificial Intelligence, told a group at the International News Media Association's (INMA) 2023 World Congress that, "Navigating the new world will require more true

AI has tons of available information to offer, but it lacks knowledge. In the case of the abortion example, it may not understand the complexities of abortion, or ever met a person who had an abortion, or talked to a person who tells a story of how he/she was almost aborted.

Chapter 2_*How We Got Here*

human effort and traits like curiosity and critical thinking... Moving forward, the challenge of generative AI isn't so much that it will replace journalists, it's that it will require them to be agile and work harder to tell the truth and earn people's trust."

That should not be difficult for journalists and designers. How about the "biography of an idea"? Reading an interview [12] with Jony Ive, former Chief Design Officer (CDO) of Apple Inc., whose name could not be linked to artificial intelligence yet, one comes across several references Ive makes to the importance of human input in the creative process.

Ive, who played a crucial role in shaping the design of iconic Apple products, including the iMac, iPod, iPhone, iPad, and MacBook, insists that: "The creative process is fabulously unpredictable. A great idea cannot be predicted." Ive's design philosophy emphasized simplicity, elegance, and the seamless integration of hardware and software.

This speaks directly to the idea that the human creates and informs the machine. We cannot rely on AI for the element of serendipity or the spark of human creative thought, because AI output is dependent upon human input.

Ive refers to the moment of creation and engaging with the "biography of an idea." Jony Ive: "If you're terrified that you're never going to have another idea, it makes you think, How did I have previous ideas? So you pay attention to the conversations, the walks, the writing, the drawing, the models, the prototypes-all that helped you before."

Humans are equipped to deal with such biography in an analytical way, while AI can replicate the facts of the biography, but it cannot truly know the experiences.

Ive reflects on this: "I find the nature of creating both terrifying and wonderful. And I am the luckiest guy in the world to be able to participate in that process with others. I love the idea that there is, on one day, no idea. On Tuesday, there's no idea. But on Thursday, there's an idea. And the terrifying thing is, which Thursday?"[12]

When we ask Alexa or Siri to turn the lights on or off, when we let

(12) mckinsey.com

our cars alert us to another car getting too close to us, or when we browse a retailer's Web site to make a purchase, we are already benefitting from AI.

When Technology Advances Us

According to economist Robert Gordon, who conducted a study on how the American standard of living has changed over the past 150 years, the first industrial robot was introduced by General Motors in 1961. Telephone operators went away in the 1960s. Airline reservations systems were put to use in the 1970s, and by 1980, bar-code scanners and cash machines were being used nearly everywhere. The first personal computers arrived in the early 1980s with their word processing, word wrap, and spreadsheets. Around 1995 we saw the rapid development of the Web and e-commerce, a process largely completed by 2005. (13)

ANTI-AI SENTIMENTS. For some, AI provokes thoughts of science fiction novels and futuristic films. Anti-AI sentiments abound. The writing of this very book aroused disapproval from colleagues and friends of the author, who felt that focusing on an AI book was a poor choice, since AI "will take so many jobs away from people... when it represents inaccuracies... invites plagiarism," etc. But, historically, this has always been the case.

Progress precipitated by the Industrial Revolution-the rise of factories, the expansion of railroads, the birth of modern technology such as the telegraph and telephone, etc., came with downsides. There was damage to the environment, health and safety hazards, and squalid living conditions for workers and their families who moved from the countryside to the cities, among other things.

As economist Robert Gordon documented in The Rise and Fall of American Growth, Americans adopted a wide variety of technologies we now take for granted during between 1870 and 1970. Consider steel, running water, machine tools, assembly lines,

(13) brookings.edu
Brynjolfsson, Erik; McAfee, Andrew. The Second Machine Age: Work, Progress, and Prosperity in a Time of Brilliant Technologies (p. 73). W. W. Norton & Company.

Chapter 2_*How We Got Here*

concrete structures, electric lights and appliances, automobiles, airplanes, pharmaceuticals, and computers, all of which increased our productivity. Artificial Intelligence is poised to become another one of these transcendental technologies that will change the way we work, play and consume information- with drawbacks, perhaps- but ultimately for the better. For those who think that equating AI to technology that allowed for running water and automobiles is an exaggeration, let's remember that recently Microsoft President Brad Smith said that the development of artificial intelligence (AI) is "almost like" the invention of the printing press. "It's fundamentally an invention that can help us all do research, learn more, communicate more, sift through data better and its uses are almost ubiquitous." [14] David Cohn, Chief Strategy Officer and Co-founder, Subtext at Advance Publications, a platform that lets news organizations, reporters and content creators text with their audience, equates the reactions to AI today with what happened when typewriters first arrived on the scene. Typewriters were introduced in 1874 but did not become common in offices in the United States until after the mid-1880s. Of course, we know that the typewriter quickly became an indispensable tool for practically all writing other than personal handwritten correspondence.

"It wasn't always like that," Cohn said. "When typewriters were first introduced, people were not good at using the keyboard. It took years for people to get with it, learn the keyboard and start using typewriters well... Most people throughout most of the 20th century weren't good on the typewriter. They were better with just a pen and paper. One could argue that it wasn't until the introduction of the personal computer that learning to type became more commonplace. Even though the typewriter was a powerful tool, people at the time felt that it would slow them down." Not too different from what is happening with AI today, says Cohn. "In newsrooms, reporters who are enthused about AI use it, others who have not tried it much think that AI will slow them down."

(14) niemanlab.org

HOW_CHATGPT_SEES IT

PROMPT: *Act as if you are a historian and tell me: Is Artificial Intelligence like the Industrial Revolution in importance?*

CHATGPT: As a historian, I can draw parallels between the advent of Artificial Intelligence (AI) and the Industrial Revolution, both of which have had significant impacts on society. However, it is important to note that while AI and the Industrial Revolution share certain characteristics, they are distinct in their nature and implications.

The Industrial Revolution, which took place roughly between the 18th and 19th centuries, marked a profound shift in human civilization. It brought about a transition from manual labor to machine-based manufacturing, leading to increased productivity, urbanization, and economic growth. The Industrial Revolution significantly transformed industries, transportation, communication, and social structures, ultimately reshaping the entire fabric of society.

Similarly, AI has emerged as a transformative force in recent decades. It encompasses technologies and systems that enable computers and machines to perform tasks that traditionally required human intelligence. AI has the potential to revolutionize various sectors, including healthcare, transportation, finance, and more. It can automate mundane and repetitive tasks, improve efficiency, and facilitate decision-making processes.

However, while the Industrial Revolution impacted physical industries and manufacturing processes, AI primarily affects intellectual capabilities and cognitive tasks. AI algorithms can analyze vast amounts of data, recognize patterns, and make predictions or

→

*Chapter 2_***How We Got Here**

HOW_CHATGPT_SEES IT

recommendations based on that analysis. This has implications for various fields such as data analysis, natural language processing, image recognition, and robotics.

In terms of importance, the Industrial Revolution was a monumental event in human history. It laid the foundation for modern industrialized societies and had far-reaching effects on economics, politics, and social structures. It brought about significant changes in labor practices, wealth distribution, and living conditions.

AI, on the other hand, has the potential to disrupt and reshape various aspects of society, but its full impact is yet to be fully realized. It has the potential to revolutionize industries and alter the nature of work, but its effects are still unfolding. The development of AI raises important questions about ethics, privacy, and the future of employment.

In conclusion, while both the Industrial Revolution and AI are transformative forces that have the capacity to reshape society, their impacts and implications are different. The Industrial Revolution brought about profound changes in the physical realm of human activity, while AI is focused on augmenting intellectual capabilities and automating cognitive tasks. It is essential to recognize the significance of AI but also acknowledge its unique characteristics and potential challenges.

KNOWING TOO MUCH OR NOTHING. This is how a Big Picture segment at Axios put it: The AI tool can put together answers to a lot of questions, but it doesn't actually "know" anything – which means it has no yardstick for assessing accuracy, and it stumbles over matters of common sense as well as paradoxes and ambiguities. Journalists are already aware of this. Sometimes, a dialog with ChatGPT sounds as smart as one you may be having with your colleague during a coffee break, only to have your robot friend come up with a comment that has no relevance to the conversation, but that was triggered by a word. Once, when asked to give examples of mobile storytelling with the prompt, "take me there," ChatGPT replied: "When we were madly in love I want to take you there, I will take you to a town with a river running through it..." Sounds like a great destination, but perhaps not the one the user was looking for. OpenAI notes that ChatGPT, "sometimes writes plausible-sounding but incorrect or nonsensical answers... is often excessively verbose... [and] will sometimes respond to harmful instructions or exhibit biased behavior." So, as we use AI to help us research a topic, or to clarify a point in our story, we should be aware of AI's limitations. ChatGPT can't distinguish fact from fiction.

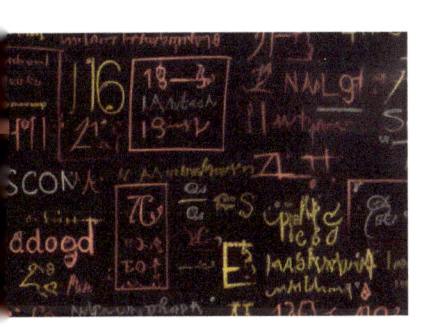

1. It "hallucinates" – that is, makes stuff up – at a rate that one expert pegs at 15% – 20% of the time.
2. It does not offer sources for its information.
3. Its information could be outdated.

For reporters and editors, this is a way to safeguard against trusting AI blindly and reaping inaccuracies. A good thing for keeping guardrails on accuracy and fact checking.

(15) axios.com

Chapter 2_*How We Got Here*

HOW_CHATGPT_SEES IT

PROMPT: *Act as if you are devil's advocate: what do you say to those who say that Artificial Intelligence has information but NOT knowledge.*

CHATGPT: As a devil's advocate, I would argue that Artificial Intelligence indeed possesses information but lacks true knowledge. Here are some points to support this perspective:

Information Processing: AI systems excel at processing vast amounts of data and extracting patterns, correlations, and insights. They can analyze data, recognize patterns, and make predictions based on statistical models. However, this does not necessarily equate to true knowledge. AI algorithms operate based on predefined rules and patterns rather than genuine understanding or comprehension.

Contextual Understanding: AI systems often struggle to grasp the nuances of context and understand information in a broader context. While they can perform specific tasks with impressive accuracy, they lack the holistic understanding and contextual reasoning that humans possess. AI algorithms typically operate within well-defined domains and struggle to transfer knowledge across different contexts or adapt to new situations.

Lack of Experience: AI systems lack real-world experiences and the ability to learn from them in the same way humans do. While they can be trained on large datasets, they do not possess personal experiences, emotions, or intuition. Human knowledge often relies on a combination of formal education, personal experiences, cultural understanding, and emotional intelligence, which AI currently cannot replicate.

→

HOW_CHATGPT_SEES IT

Common Sense Reasoning: AI systems often struggle with common sense reasoning and understanding the implicit knowledge that humans possess. Human knowledge is not only about factual information but also includes common sense, intuition, and a deeper understanding of the world. AI may not be able to reason and make decisions in situations that require this kind of implicit knowledge.

Creative and Abstract Thinking: AI systems typically operate within the boundaries of the data they have been trained on and struggle with creativity and abstract thinking. While they can generate new outputs based on patterns in the data, they lack the imaginative and inventive capabilities of humans. True knowledge often involves the ability to think abstractly, make connections, and generate novel ideas, which AI currently cannot replicate.

It is important to note that these arguments represent the perspective of a devil's advocate and do not reflect the full understanding and potential of AI. AI systems continue to advance rapidly, and ongoing research is aimed at addressing these limitations. While AI may not possess knowledge in the same way humans do, it can still be a powerful tool for processing information, making predictions, and assisting in various tasks. •

INTELLIGENCE, SOPHISTICATION AND HALLUCINATIONS.
AI is typically described as "intelligent" because it's able to create things like words, sounds, images and video. (Fair, one supposes, since "Intelligence" is right there in the name.) You'll also read AI reaches levels of sophistication that mimic human creativity. Of course, we also read that AI can take detours into the so called "hallucinations" – irrelevant, nonsensical or simply false. So, it

Chapter 2_*How We Got Here*

can't "think" like humans do, but it can, at times, create work of a similar quality. It can take a 500-word piece of writing and reshape it, condense it, and often make it sound better than the original. It can help the designer doing a storyboard for a mobile story complete with multimedia elements to organize it by providing an outline with just the right sequence.

For some, ChatGPT makes a better search engine than Google. Instead of entering a term into a search engine and sifting through various links, people may end up asking a chatbot a question and getting a confident answer back. Reporters and other content producers will find this a useful tool. There is also reporter, Melissa Heikkilä, who called generative AI a "notorious bullshitter," in the MIT Tech Review.

HOW_CHATGPT_SEES IT

PROMPT: *What are hallucinations in the world of Artificial Intelligence?*

CHATGPT: In the world of Artificial Intelligence (AI), the term "hallucinations" is used to describe a phenomenon where AI systems generate or produce information that is not accurate or grounded in reality. These AI-generated hallucinations can occur in various contexts, such as in the generation of images, text, or other outputs by AI models. One notable example of AI hallucinations is observed in image generation. Generative models, such as Generative Adversarial Networks (GANs) or Variational Autoencoders (VAEs), can sometimes produce images that appear realistic to human observers but contain nonsensical or improbable elements. These hallucinations can manifest as distorted objects, unrealistic backgrounds, or combinations of features that do not occur in the real world. These phenomena highlight the challenges of training AI models

→

HOW_CHATGPT_SEES IT

to generate coherent and realistic outputs consistently. In natural language processing, AI models may also exhibit hallucinatory behaviors. Language models can generate text that appears coherent at first glance but may contain incorrect or misleading information. These hallucinations can arise from biases present in the training data or the models' inability to fully comprehend and reason about the context in which the text is generated.

It's important to note that these hallucinations in AI systems are not intentional or driven by a subjective experience as in human hallucinations. They are a result of limitations or imperfections in the training data, model architectures, or the algorithms used. Researchers are actively working on improving AI models to reduce such hallucinatory outputs and enhance their reliability and accuracy. Addressing hallucinations in AI is crucial, particularly in safety-critical applications like autonomous vehicles, medical diagnosis, or financial decision-making. Ensuring the reliability and trustworthiness of AI outputs is an ongoing area of research and development in the field of AI. ●

AI NUGGETS

The website Character.AI allows visitors to chat with a reasonable facsimile of almost anyone, live or dead, real or imagined.

→ nytimes.com

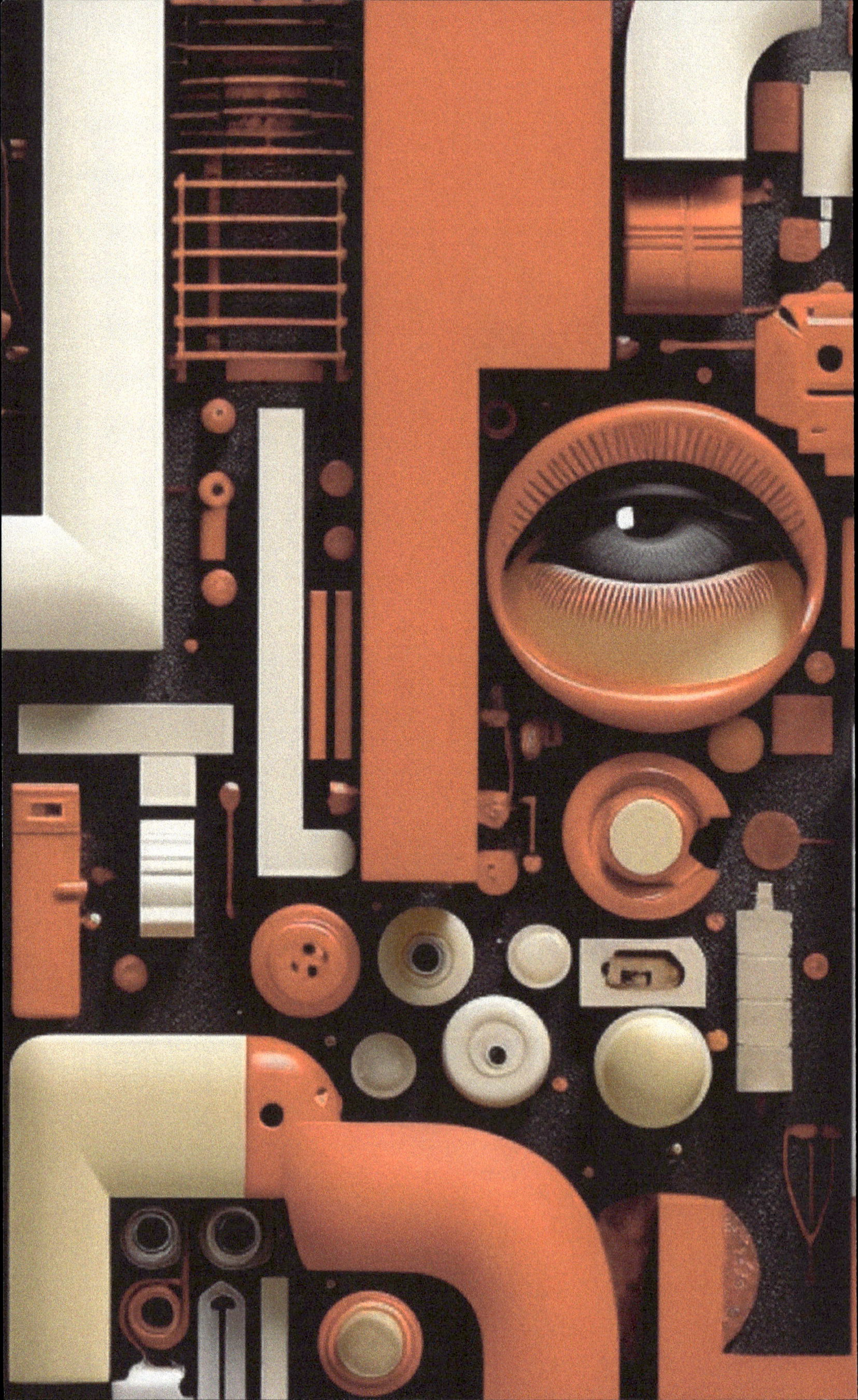

Chapter 3_**Where We Are Now**

The Robot Society Is Here

According to Erik Brynjolfsson and Andrew McAfee's *The Second Machine Age: Work, Progress, and Prosperity in a Time of Brilliant Technologies,* many and varied professions-from lawyers to truck drivers-will be upended and permanently altered. Their view of the new AI technology is mostly optimistic, but it's measured when it comes to the type of jobs in which AI will replace humans. In journalism, AI can deputize a variety of tasks, from headline writing, to basic story research to, template creation for designers.

The news, however, is better for journalists than for other professionals. Estimates suggest that current levels of AI technology could automate only about 15% of a reporter's job and 9% of an editor's job.[16]

Companies will be forced to transform or die. This, of course, is highly applicable to the news business, where newsrooms since the early 2000s have been operating with smaller staffs, even though content production is now a 24/7 cycle across many platforms. According to the Pew Research Center [17], the number of daily newspapers with an average Sunday circulation of 50,000 or more declined from 110 in 2017 to 73 in 2021. With such circulation decline came layoffs in the newsroom: In 2021, 11% of high-circulation newspapers experienced layoffs, compared with three times that share the year before (33%).

Indeed, the robots are here and seemingly ready to collaborate with the humans that will prompt them into actions. The relationship between humans and machines will become an even

[16] mckinsey.com
[17] pewresearch.org

Chapter 3_**Where We Are Now**

"What all of us have to do is to make sure we are using AI in a way that is for the benefit of humanity, not to the detriment of humanity."

Tim Cook, CEO of Apple

greater topic of discussion in the age of artificial intelligence, especially the supervisory role that humans must play. It is that supervisory role that has been explored in a paper co-authored by Ben Sawyer, a professor at the University of Central Florida and director of The Readability Consortium, which details the human/machine interaction as follows: a human may plan off-line, teach the system, monitor the system's actions, assume control or learn from the actions of the system. "The human perceives the machine's state and takes an action," he says. "The machine senses the new state of the environment and itself takes an action. This cyclical interaction gives rise to the term in-the-loop, a characteristic of an operator who is actively exerting supervisory control." [18]

    Here is a conversation with Ben Sawyer about the human/machine interactions, a topic to which he has devoted much of his professional career.

(18) norton.com

AI_PLAYERS

Human Factors and Ergonomics in Design of A3: Automation, Autonomy, and Artificial Intelligence

BEN D. SAWYER, DAVE B. MILLER, MATTHEW CANHAM, AND WALDEMAR KARWOWSKI
University of Central Florida, Orlando, Florida [19]

Ben Sawyer of the University of Central Florida and The Readability Consortium, works in human factors engineering and human factors psychology. To understand the relationship between humans and machines, Sawyer mentions World War 2, a period when automation makes an entrance, creating that intersection of human and machine, and, thus, a pattern developed consisting of either overtrust or undertrust of the machines. Trust calibrations, then and now, are at the heart of how humans relate to machines.

> *What people in industry and the military learned in terms of these trust calibrations long time ago, journalists and designers need to cope with now, but are they ready?*

"I think that journalists are ready," Sawyer says, "but they don't know enough about AI." Sawyer co-authored a paper before ChatGPT launched, The Education of the Human Factors Engineer in the Age of Data Science, in which he refers to "supervisory control" – in which a human may (1) plan off-line; (2) teach the system; (3) monitor the system's actions; (4) assume control; or (5) learn from the actions of the system.

→

[19] norton.com

Chapter 3_*Where We Are Now*

"Such a system–operator response occurs in cycles: the human perceives the machine's state and takes an action, the machine senses the new state of the environment and itself takes an action. This cyclical interaction gives rise to the term in-the-loop, a characteristic of an operator who is actively exerting supervisory control." Journalists are "in the loop" Sawyer believes that journalists are in the loop, "... but understanding the loop they are in is a different story. Journalists are used to very prominently stepping into complex human dynamics, they land in foreign countries, understand the difference cultures, they get it. Journalists are early adapters because it is part of their training, where I see that designers are less savvy in the kind of support that comes from technology."

Sawyer mentions an issue of pride, as when a journalist's turns off the spelling/grammar check in a word processor, as "an insult to their intelligence. Well, what is interesting is the attitude, prejudice does not serve a designer or a writer well in this moment." So, what is a journalist to do with confronted with this new artificial intelligence technology. Sawyer sees extremes in the trust calibration as not helpful.

AI AND TRUST CALIBRATIONS
"Here is a part of the user who needs to understand the technology and trust it, but the ones who overthrust, they will have AI given bad information and they will blame a human, while the people who undertrust are going to scare people and will turn them away from the technology. As a result, they will be less competitive." Sawyer points out that the middle is where we want to be. This is a very new technology and what we need is design for the technology so that the human is better served. "No journalist has been trained on how to calibrate interaction with a machine. The users of this technology are the victims. What needs to happen is for the people building this technology to build better human-centered machines." ●

HOW_CHATGPT_SEES IT

PROMPT: *Is the robot society here?*

CHATGPT: As of my knowledge cutoff in September 2021, we are not yet living in a "robot society" in the sense of a society predominantly or completely populated by robots or artificial intelligence systems. While robots and AI have made significant advancements and are increasingly integrated into various aspects of our lives, their presence and impact are still limited in many respects. Robots and AI systems are being employed in industries such as manufacturing, healthcare, transportation, and customer service, but their deployment and capabilities vary. They often work alongside humans rather than replacing them entirely. In some cases, robots and AI systems can automate repetitive or labor-intensive tasks, improve efficiency, and enhance productivity. However, there are still many tasks that require human skills, adaptability, and decision-making capabilities.

It is important to note that the development and integration of advanced robotics and AI technologies are ongoing processes. Researchers and engineers are continuously working to improve these technologies, and their capabilities are expected to expand over time. However, significant technical, ethical, and societal challenges remain, and the full realization of a society heavily reliant on robots and AI is still a topic of debate and speculation. While it is possible that future advancements in robotics and AI could lead to significant societal changes, including increased automation and the emergence of more sophisticated robotic systems, the timeline and extent of such developments are uncertain. It is crucial to consider the ethical implications, societal impacts, and human well-being in shaping the integration and adoption of these technologies.

Chapter 3_*Where We Are Now*

What Publishers Want

PUBLISHERS SEEK TO HARNESS AI FOR ENHANCED OPERATIONS. In recent years, newspaper publishers have increasingly turned their attention to Artificial Intelligence as a means to bolster their operations and adapt to the rapidly evolving media landscape. AI technologies are revolutionizing the publishing industry, offering new opportunities for efficiency, audience engagement, content personalization, and revenue generation.

> **Automated Content Creation.** AI-powered tools enable newspaper publishers to automate certain aspects of content creation, such as generating news articles or summaries based on raw data or structured information. These systems can sift through vast amounts of data, identify patterns, and produce news stories at a faster pace, freeing up journalists' time to focus on more in-depth reporting and analysis.
>
> **Personalized User Experiences.** AI algorithms can analyze user data and behaviors to deliver personalized content recommendations to readers. By understanding individual preferences, publishers can enhance user engagement and tailor and distribute content to meet the specific interests of their audience. This personalized approach builds stronger reader loyalty and increases retention.
>
> **Data-Driven Insights.** AI-powered analytics tools provide deeper insight into audience behavior, content performance, and market trends. By analyzing large datasets, publishers learn what types of articles or topics resonate most with their audience, identify emerging trends, and make data-driven decisions to optimize content strategy, distribution channels, and advertising campaigns.

Ad Revenue Optimization. AI improves ad targeting and maximizes revenue from digital advertising. By analyzing user data, demographics, and preferences, publishers can tailor ads to readers, increasing advertising effectiveness and enhancing the value proposition for advertisers.

Automated Fact-Checking. AI systems can fact-check, quickly verifying information and detecting potential inaccuracies or misinformation. This technology helps publishers maintain credibility and journalistic integrity, providing readers with reliable and accurate news content.

Enhanced Customer Support. AI-powered chatbots and virtual assistants can handle customer inquiries, provide real-time responses, and offer personalized support. These automated systems can address common queries, guide readers to relevant content, and improve overall customer satisfaction.

While AI presents significant opportunities for newspaper publishers, it is important to balance technological advancements with ethical considerations. Ensuring transparency, addressing biases, and maintaining editorial standards are crucial aspects of AI integration. As publishers navigate the evolving media landscape, AI technologies will help them to stay ahead of the curve by delivering more engaging experiences to readers, and driving sustainable growth in the digital era. As AI research and development progresses, newspaper publishers continue to leverage these technologies and reimagine the way news is created, distributed, and consumed.

Transcription and social media content creation were the top two areas in which respondents to an AP (Associated Press) survey hoped AI could be helpful in their work. Automated content generation based on structured data was also high on the wish list, which is something the AP itself has done for several years, having generated certain earnings stories automatically since

Chapter 3_*Where We Are Now*

2014. These three most-wanted applications of AI are already well within the capabilities of the frameworks and libraries of many publishers. Magazine and newspaper publishers also emphasize a need for AI to help with production tasks such as layout, design and handling of visual images, including video. (See Chapter 9 about how firms that develop content management systems are providing AI solutions.)

CHATBOT'S MAIN PLAYERS. The most common way people experience artificial intelligence is through chatbots, which work like an advanced form of instant messenger, answering questions and formulating tasks from prompts. These LLMS that power the chatbots are trained on troves of Internet data, including *Reddit* conversations and digital books.

Chatbots are incredibly adept at finding patterns and imitating speech, but experts are quick to point out that they don't interpret meanings. "It's a super, super high-fidelity version of autocomplete… something that, if a person was doing it, we would call it intelligence," said Larry Birnbaum, a professor of computer science at Northwestern University [20]. Since it debuted in November 2022, ChatGPT has stunned users with its ability to produce fluid language: generate complete novels, computer code, TV episodes and songs. GPT stands for "generative pre-trained transformer."

"Generative," meaning that it uses AI to create things. "Pre-trained," means that it has already been trained on a large amount of data. And "transformer" is a powerful type of neural network that can process language.

OpenAI. The San Francisco-based AI research lab launched as a nonprofit to build "artificial general intelligence" outside of Big Tech's control. Since then, it's transformed into a major corporate player, creating image generator DALL-E and chatbot ChatGPT. It is now a for-profit effort and has partnered with companies including Microsoft and Salesforce.

(20) washingtonpost.com

Google. The tech giant has long been a leader in AI. They launched chatbot Bard after competitors' offerings went viral. It is known for its LaMDA technology, a system for building chatbots based on large language models.

Microsoft. The software company invested billions of dollars in OpenAI and teamed up to create a Bing chatbot, developed on GPT-4 technology. But there have been missteps, including when the chatbot went rogue, told reporters it has feelings and called itself Sydney, forcing the tech giant to reel it back in some ways.

Meta. Even before **ChatGPT**, Facebook's parent company released a chatbot called Blenderbot, but it failed to gain traction. Its chief artificial intelligence scientist later called the bot "boring" because it was "made safe."

IBM. Was an early leader in artificial intelligence close to the current chatbot trends, most notably with its robot Watson, which captivated audiences on "Jeopardy!"

CURIOUS PERSON'S GUIDE TO AI
→ washingtonpost.com

Chapter 3_*Where We Are Now*

HOW_CHATGPT_SEES IT

PROMPT: *Act if you are the expert and tell me who are Chatbot's main players in the industry?*

CHATGPT: As an expert, I can provide you with some information about the main players in the chatbot industry. Please note that the landscape is dynamic, and new companies may emerge while others may evolve or change their focus. As of my knowledge cutoff in September 2021, some of the prominent players in the chatbot industry are:

IBM Watson Assistant: is a robust chatbot platform that leverages IBM's AI technologies, including natural language processing and machine learning. It offers a range of features to develop, deploy, and manage chatbots across various channels.

Google Dialogflow: was developed by Google, is a widely used chatbot development framework. It offers natural language understanding capabilities, integrations with various platforms, and supports multiple languages, making it popular among developers.

Microsoft Bot Framework: provides developers with tools and resources to create intelligent chatbots. It offers connectors for popular communication channels, such as Skype, Slack, and Facebook Messenger, and supports the integration of AI capabilities using Microsoft Azure services.

Amazon Lex: is a chatbot development platform that powers Amazon's Alexa voice assistant. It provides natural language understanding capabilities and integrates with other Amazon Web Services (AWS) offerings, allowing developers to create conversational interfaces.

→

HOW_CHATGPT_SEES IT

Chatfuel: is a chatbot platform focused on creating chatbots for Facebook Messenger. It offers a visual interface, drag-and-drop functionality, and a variety of pre-built templates to simplify chatbot development.

ManyChat: is another platform that specializes in creating chatbots for Facebook Messenger. It provides a visual flow builder, AI-driven features, and tools for marketing automation, making it popular among businesses looking to engage with their audience on Messenger.

Oracle Digital Assistant: is an AI-powered chatbot platform that enables businesses to create conversational interfaces across various channels. It integrates with Oracle's suite of enterprise solutions and supports multi-turn conversations and context-aware interactions.

Salesforce Einstein Bots: is a chatbot solution built on the Salesforce platform. It enables businesses to create AI-powered chatbots that can assist with customer service, sales, and other tasks, leveraging Salesforce's CRM capabilities.

These are just a few examples of the main players in the chatbot industry. Other companies, including smaller startups and regional players, also offer chatbot development platforms and services. It's important to note that the landscape is continually evolving, and new entrants and innovations can shape the industry over time.

Chapter 3_**Where We Are Now**

What Publishers Want

ChatGPT, the artificial intelligence language model from a research lab, OpenAI, has been making headlines since November 2022 for its ability to respond to complex questions, write poetry, generate code, plan vacations and translate languages. GPT-4, the latest version, introduced in mid-March 2023, can now respond to images. It even aced the Uniform Bar Exam!

Bing. Two months after ChatGPT's debut, Microsoft, OpenAI's primary investor and partner, added a similar chatbot, capable of having open-ended text conversations on virtually any topic, to its Bing internet search engine. But it was the bot's occasionally inaccurate, misleading and weird responses that drew much of the attention after its release.

Bard. Google's chatbot, called Bard, was released in March 2023 to a limited number of users in the United States and Britain. Originally conceived as a creative tool designed to draft emails and poems, it can generate ideas, write blog posts and answer questions with facts or opinions.

Ernie. The search giant Baidu unveiled China's first major rival to ChatGPT in March. The debut of Ernie, short for Enhanced Representation through Knowledge Integration, turned out to be a flop after a promised "live" demonstration of the bot was revealed to have been previously recorded. Oops.

PRO_TIPS

Where is support?
Publisher collaboration: Despite the lower costs of running AI projects today, the tools and frameworks can be daunting. JournalismAI is a research and training project run by Polis, the journalism think-tank of the London School of Economics. Their collaborative projects have included computer vision in combination with satellite imagery, using AI tools to track influencer impacts, and detecting examples of hate speech.

AI NUGGETS

The McClatchy Company, a publishing group in the US, has used automation to cover real estate listings at the local level.

"...**Discussions on the effects of AI on society** are often about how AI is replacing human labor. Equally important, however, is to think of jobs for AI that are beyond our capabilities altogether... an interesting example: communicating with animals. Machine learning tools are being deployed to be able to communicate with whales."
Stefano Puntoni, the Sebastian S. Kresge Professor of Marketing at The Wharton School, University of Pennsylvania

→ lnkd.in

The World of Media AI

This list grows daily, so this is a sampling and not a comprehensive account. No two media companies use artificial intelligence the same way.

1 CANADA: The Globe and Mail's homegrown AI startup Sophi.io empowers content publishers with automated curation, engagement enhancement, and template-free print layout, aimed at improving vital business metrics.

2 USA: The New York Times used bots to help the company identify and promote articles that may go viral. The New York Daily News grew revenue and engagement with an AI video strategy.

3 MEXICO: Mexican media company Radio Fórmula introduced a new AI anchor called NAT, its used to present short news capsules.

4 BRAZIL: Journalists in Brazil and Mexico developed an AI tool to detect online hate speech against journalists. "Attack Detector" is a tool that combines data journalism and machine learning to detect hate speech online.

5 ARGENTINA: La Nación's data team (LN Data) analyzed Trap song lyrics by Argentine artists with Natural Language Processing (NLP), worked on a gender equity detector for its texts and sources, and mapped the status of solar farms across the country with machine learning.

6 NORWAY: Schibsted created an AI chatbot to offer customer care.

7 SWEDEN: Bonnier Next built a predictive, data-driven employment ad platform.

8 FINLAND: Helsingin Sanomat in Finland monitored train schedules via AI.

9 GERMANY: Frankfurter Allgemeine Zeitung used AI to understand consumer behavior and conduct content analysis.

10 SWITZERLAND: NZZ in Switzerland created an AI-based mobile app to contextualize and personalize news delivery. Ringier used AI to boost digital reader engagement.

11 JAPAN: The Japanese government is using artificial intelligence to identify "false information" on social media regarding the planned release of treated wastewater from the Fukushima nuclear power plant.

12 INDIA: India saw the debut of competing AI news anchors in July, 2023. Odisha TV introduced "Lisa" just as India Today's network Aaj Tak welcomed "Sana." Many competing AI anchors have since emerged.

14 AUSTRALIA: Fairfax Media (now Nine) enhanced audience research with AI.

13 SINGAPORE: Singapore Press Holdings' newsrooms use AI to scan news articles and extract relevant content from them. The tool, SPH Robbie, aims to free up time for journalists to create more news content, and help video presenters succinctly deliver headlines.

Part Two
Using AI

→ Chapter 4: Reporting
→ Chapter 5: Marketing & Social Media
→ Chapter 6: Layout & Design
→ Chapter 7: Corporate Communications
→ Chapter 8: Prompt Engineering
→ Chapter 9: Content Management Systems
→ Chapter 10: Creating Guidelines and Protocols

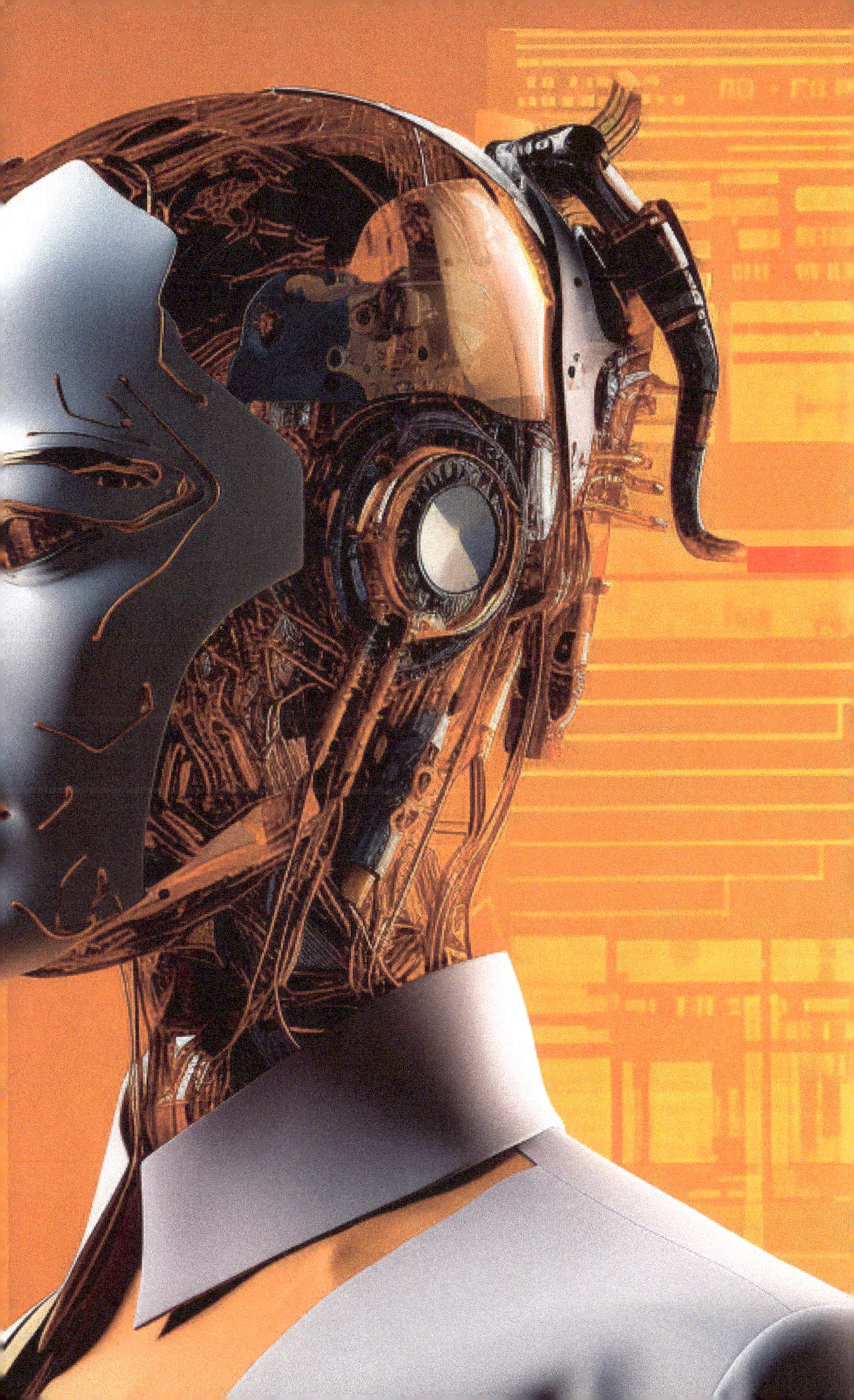

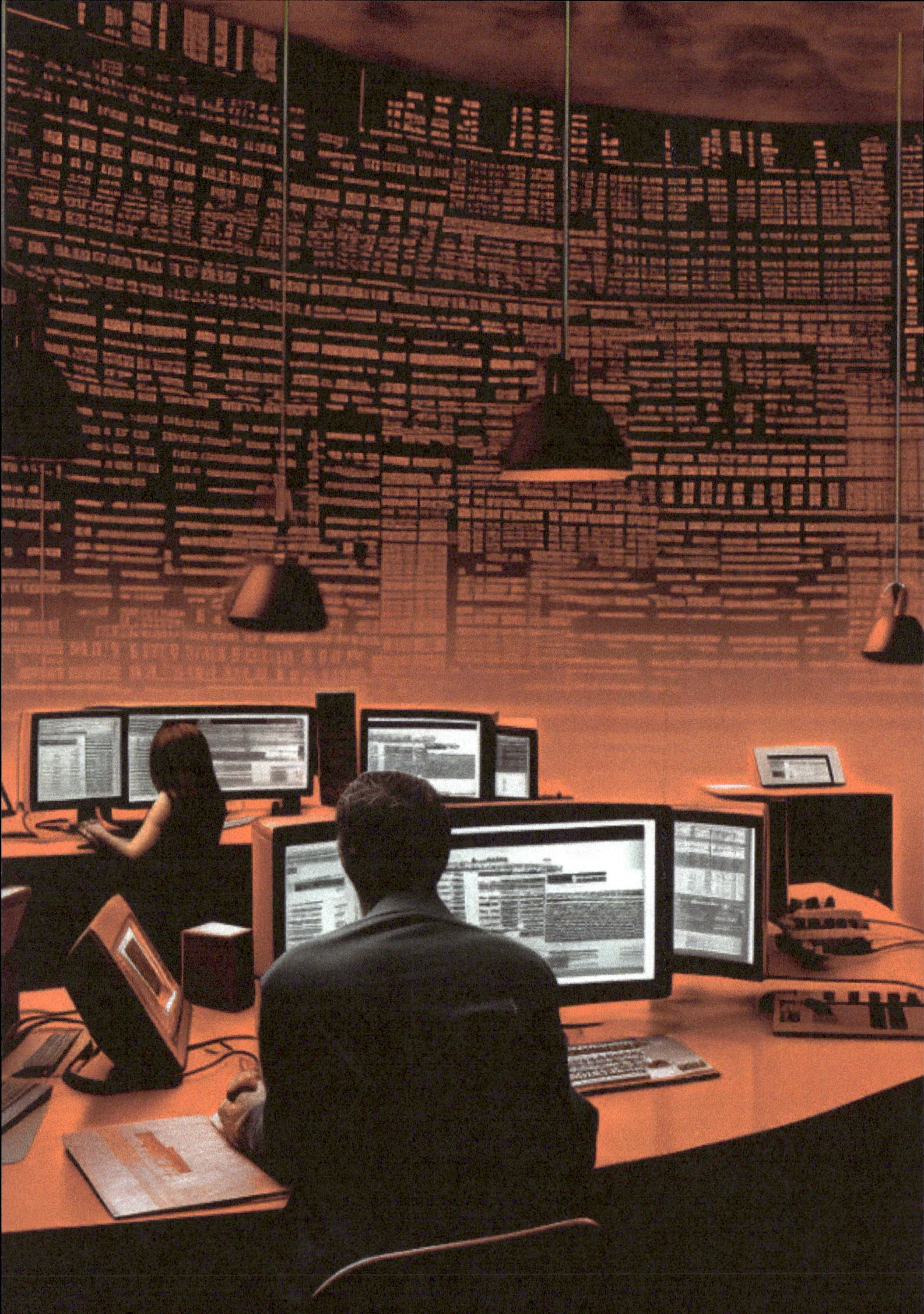

*Chapter 4_* **Reporting**

The Reporter and AI

The 'C' of artificial intelligence is for Content Creation, the heart of journalism and what reporters and writers everywhere set out to do each day. Newsrooms around the globe are flocking to AI as a way to maximize production, especially at a time when staff levels are low. AI can save considerable time that translates into economic gains for newsrooms. It is also the one area that raises more ethical questions. ChatGPT can already produce fabricated news stories that sound real, complete with fake quotes.

However, with verified input such as vetted information and real quotes, AI can produce accurate news stories too. Perhaps you are a reporter at a medium or small newspaper, or a writer working in corporate communications, and you'd like to start experimenting with artificial intelligence, but nobody around you is doing such a thing. There is really no reason not to try it out. Without a big investment of your time, you'll find yourself with more of it: time for interviewing sources and digging up other information; less time transcribing interviews and writing stories on deadline. Nicholas Diakopoulos, professor in communication studies and computer science at Northwestern University, offers some advice. "When it comes to AI in the newsroom," he says, "or any place where content creators originate storytelling, reporting and writing are perhaps the areas where experts consulted see the greatest potential." Generative AI can create new content, but because of its ability to accumulate large amounts of data from the world wide web, which it can

Chapter 4_Reporting

categorize, artificial intelligence could become a major tool for writers, freeing them to spend more time with the creative aspects of storytelling, interviewing and real time in person involvement with sources. Here is a list of those tasks in which AI can play an essential role for reporters and writers:

1. Generating story ideas
2. Instantly generating summaries of public meetings and documents
3. Creating tweets and social posts from news stories. Overall social media monitoring
4. Drafting scripts for news broadcasts, even suggesting different headline variations
5. Transcribing information
6. Translating from a foreign language
7. Helping with the outline of a story idea

GENERATING STORY IDEAS. Before there is a published story, reporters and editors ponder an important question: what is the newsworthiness of this story? Early during a Journalism 101 course, future journalists learn about news determinants-those elements that categorize the potential of a story. Traditionally, these are the news determinants for newsworthiness, and the more of these that story checks, the higher its chance of being published and, ultimately, of capturing the interest of the reader.

These news determinants first appeared in 1917 in a much-read news writing textbook by Lyle Spencer, *News Writing: The Gathering, Handling And Writing Of News Stories* (D. C. Heath & Company, 1917). It is interesting that Spencer starts his book with a reference to "a nose for news." It prompts the question today: Can Generative AI develop a nose for news? Here is Spencer's definition of the "nose for news": "Recognition of news values is put first in the tabulation of requirements for successful writing because without a 'nose for news' – without the ability to recognize a story when one sees it – a reporter cannot hope to succeed."

Editorial rooms all over the United States are full of stories of would-be reporters who have failed because they have not been able to recognize news. That is a tall order for AI. Here are the news determinants that Spencer lists in his turn-of-the-20th-century book (the language may seem archaic, but news determinants remain the same).

Interest. What constitutes interest? Any item of news, it may be defined, that will present a new problem, a new situation, that will provoke thought in the minds of a considerable number of readers, is interesting, and that story is most interesting which presents a new problem to the greatest number of people.

Thought provoking. Whatever presents a new problem, or injects a new motive or situation into an old one, will be interesting and will be read by those readers to whom the problem or situation is new. It is not, therefore, that American men and women are interested in the sins and misfortunes of others that they read stories of crime and unhallowed love, but that such stories present new problems, new life situations, or new phases of old problems and old situations. A story of innocence and hallowed love would be just as interesting.

Timeliness. Indeed, timeliness is an essential of a good story. The word yesterday has been relegated to the scrap heap. Today, this morning, this afternoon should appear if possible in every story... freshness, timeliness, all become a requisite in every story.

Proximity. Next to nearness in time comes nearness in place as a means of maintaining interest. Other things being equal, the worth of a story varies in inverse proportion to its closeness in time and place. Localize stories as much as possible. Bring it home.

Chapter 4_Reporting

Prioritizing news stories that are relevant and impactful while remembering these traditional news determinants, will help engage and retain readers in this digital age. First, editors and content creators will decide which news determinants fit the goals of a specific publishing outlet. Then they create algorithms that reflect them. That is one way that artificial intelligence can assist us with story selections, angles to play, and, indeed, the stories with the most shareable components.

HOW_CHATGPT_SEES IT

PROMPT: *Act as if you are a newspaper editor or reporter, can AI evaluate content for its newsworthiness using traditional news determinants like timeliness, prominence, human interest?*

CHATGPT: As a newspaper editor or reporter, the integration of Artificial Intelligence (AI) in evaluating content for its newsworthiness brings both opportunities and challenges. While AI can assist in analyzing certain aspects of news determinants such as timeliness, prominence, and human interest, it is important to remember that AI algorithms are not a substitute for human judgment and editorial expertise. AI can play a role in assessing the timeliness of news content by analyzing real-time data, trending topics, and social media discussions. By monitoring these indicators, AI algorithms can provide insights into the current relevance and potential impact of a news story. This information can aid editors and reporters in prioritizing news items and identifying emerging trends.

Similarly, AI algorithms can assist in evaluating prominence by analyzing factors such as the credibility and influence of news sources, the reach of social media engagement, and the level of public interest

→

HOW_CHATGPT_SEES IT

in a particular topic. This can help journalists gauge the significance and public relevance of a story. Additionally, AI can contribute to identifying human interest stories by analyzing sentiment analysis, emotional cues, and reader engagement metrics. By examining these factors, AI algorithms can highlight stories that resonate with readers on an emotional level, enabling journalists to bring compelling narratives to the forefront.

However, it is crucial to note that AI algorithms have limitations when it comes to assessing the full scope of newsworthiness. Factors such as cultural context, ethical considerations, and journalistic values require human judgment and critical thinking. AI may not fully capture the nuances and complexities that experienced editors and reporters bring to the editorial decision-making process.

In summary, while AI can provide valuable insights and assist in evaluating certain aspects of newsworthiness, human judgment and editorial expertise remain essential. AI algorithms can aid in assessing timeliness, prominence, and human interest, but they should be utilized as tools to support rather than replace the critical thinking and ethical considerations of journalists and editors. The collaborative approach, combining AI capabilities with human expertise, is key to ensuring accurate, reliable, and impactful news coverage. ●

ANOTHER VIEW. ChatGPT suggests that when it comes to determining a story's newsworthiness, "human judgment and editorial expertise remain essential." That's difficult to dispute, but other perspectives exist. Nick Diakopoulos, Ph.D., Professor of Communication and Computer Science, Northwestern University, expresses a more optimistic approach to the role that AI can play in determining a story's newsworthiness:

Chapter 4_Reporting

"I'm positively encouraged about the use of generative AI to evaluate the newsworthiness of journalistic documents. We found a moderate correlation to expert ratings of newsworthiness for scientific abstracts," Diakopoulos wrote. "It was relatively cheap to develop, and it would be cheap to deploy even at a reasonably large scale. At the same time, there's still more evaluation to do to understand how the ratings might be biased and what the models might be missing."

As Diakopoulos also noted, it's important to appreciate one key limitation of using AI for evaluating the worthiness of stories: the delay in new knowledge being included in the AI. GPT-4, released in March 2023, has a training data cut-off date of September 2021, meaning it does not know about events past this date. For example, GPT-4 couldn't evaluate the value of a development in the Ukraine-Russia war, which began in February 2022. [21]

For Discussion

Compare Lyle Spencer's 1917 news determinants to what ChatGPT reports. As a newspaper editor or reporter, determining the newsworthiness of a story is crucial for publication. While there can be some subjectivity in the evaluation process, several key factors contribute to the newsworthiness of a news story.

> **Relevance and Impact.** A news story should be relevant to the target audience and have a significant impact on their lives or the community. It should address current issues, events, or trends that are of interest and importance to readers.
>
> **Timeliness.** This is a critical factor in news reporting. Breaking news and stories that are happening now or have recently occurred often take precedence due to their immediate relevance. Being the first to report on a significant event or development adds value to the story's newsworthiness.

[21] ai.northwestern.edu

"Instantly generating summaries of public meetings and documents, creating tweets and social posts from news stories, drafting scripts for news broadcasts, even suggesting different headline variations – all at the click of a button – would be a game changer for news organizations that are already strapped for people and resources."

Joe Amditis, assistant director of products and events at the Center for Cooperative Media at Montclair State University
niemanlab.org

Chapter 4_**Reporting**

Prominence. Stories involving influential individuals, high-ranking officials, celebrities, or public figures tend to attract attention. The prominence of the people or organizations involved can contribute to the newsworthiness of a story.

Proximity. Stories that occur in close geographic proximity to the readership are often deemed more newsworthy. Local news that directly affects the community is of particular interest to readers.

Conflict or Controversy. News stories that involve conflict, controversy, or contrasting viewpoints tend to attract attention. Reporting on issues that generate debate or have a significant impact on society can be considered newsworthy.

Human Interest. Stories that evoke emotion, touch on human experiences, or feature remarkable individuals can be compelling to readers. Human interest stories often resonate on a personal level and can capture attention.

Uniqueness or Rarity. Unusual or rare events, discoveries, or occurrences are often deemed newsworthy due to their novelty and potential to captivate readers. Stories that offer a fresh perspective or a unique angle on a familiar topic can also attract interest.

Consequence. News stories that have potential consequences, such as affecting public policy, influencing decision-making, or bringing about change, are considered significant.

Public Interest. Stories that cater to public curiosity, address public concerns, or provide valuable information that affects a wide range of individuals tend to be newsworthy. Topics such as health, education, safety, and the economy often fall into this category.

Ethical Considerations. Lastly, ethical considerations play a vital role in determining the newsworthiness of a story. Ensuring accuracy, fairness, and responsible reporting is crucial to maintain credibility and integrity.

All news stories won't meet all criteria, but a combination of these factors helps guide the decision-making process in evaluating the newsworthiness. Ultimately, editorial judgment and an understanding of the target audience's interests and needs are crucial.

GENERATING TRANSCRIPTS OF PUBLIC MEETINGS AND DOCUMENTS. Because Artificial Intelligence can analyze and interpret audio and text data, AI-driven transcription services will streamline efficiency and enhance accuracy, saving time and resources for both public officials and citizens.

The transcription of public meetings and civic documents has always been labor-intensive, requiring humans to listen, interpret, and transcribe the spoken content. The process is prone to errors, delays, and inconsistencies, opening the door to misinterpretation. By harnessing the power of natural language processing (NLP) algorithms and machine learning models, AI-powered transcription services are rising to the challenge, automatically transcribing spoken words into written text with remarkable accuracy and speed. So they saved money and got the transcripts to the public more quickly, streamlining civic engagement. All of this also leads to a more inclusive environment. Individuals with hearing impairments can utilize the written transcripts to fully comprehend the discussions and decisions made in public meetings, empowering their participation and involvement in local governance.

Demand is rising, and AI technology is continuing to evolve, incorporating advancements such as real-time transcription and multilingual support, meeting records and important documents.

Chapter 4_*Reporting*

PRO_TIPS

There are several software options available that can assist you in generating transcripts of public meetings and documents. Here are a few popular choices:

1. Sonix is an automated transcription software that utilizes AI-powered speech recognition technology. It offers features like multiple speaker identification, real-time transcription, and integration with various file formats and platforms. Sonix provides an easy-to-use interface for editing and exporting transcripts.

2. Rev is a transcription service that combines AI technology with human reviewers. It offers accurate and reliable transcription services for meetings, interviews, and other audio or video content. Rev provides fast turnaround times and supports various file formats.

3. Trint is a transcription and audio/video editing platform that employs AI to generate transcripts. It features a user-friendly interface, speaker identification, and real-time collaboration capabilities. Trint offers integration with popular video conferencing platforms and editing software.

4. Otter.ai is an AI-powered transcription software that provides automatic transcription for meetings, interviews, and other recorded content. It offers features like speaker identification, searchable transcripts, and real-time collaboration. Otter.ai is known for its user-friendly interface and ease of use.

5. Temi is an automated transcription service that uses advanced speech recognition technology. It offers quick turnaround times and supports a wide range of audio and video file formats. Temi provides an editing interface for making corrections and exporting transcripts.

6. Happy Scribe is a transcription and subtitling tool that utilizes AI technology for automated transcription. It supports multiple languages and provides features like speaker diarization and subtitle editing. Happy Scribe offers integrations with popular video platforms and file formats.

We're not at the point, yet, when automated transcription software can be depended upon for 100% accuracy, and human review and editing are still necessary. When choosing a software option, consider factors such as pricing, ease of use, accuracy, customization options, and integration capabilities with your existing tools and workflows. It's also advisable to check for any specific features that may be important to your transcription needs, such as speaker identification or real-time collaboration.

DRAFTING SCRIPTS FOR NEWS BROADCASTS, SUGGESTING DIFFERENT HEADLINE VARIATIONS. AI-driven systems can now generate accurate and engaging news scripts, and suggest captivating headlines. Scriptwriting for news broadcasts typically requires journalists and editors to gather information, conduct research, and craft compelling narratives. AI can automate portions of this process, enabling journalists to focus on higher-value tasks such as investigative reporting and in-depth analysis.

AI-powered script drafting systems utilize natural language processing (NLP) algorithms and machine learning models to analyze data in real-time. By extracting key information, identifying relevant angles, and generating coherent sentences, these systems draft scripts that capture the essence of the news while adhering to journalistic standards.

Headlines are critical to engaging viewers. By analyzing audience preferences, historical data, and trending topics, AI algorithms generate alternative headline options that resonate with different target demographics. The integration of AI in newsrooms has already shown promising results. Major media organizations have implemented AI-driven script drafting systems, reporting significant time savings and increased productivity. Journalists can now leverage AI-generated drafts as starting points, allowing them to focus on refining and enhancing the narrative while ensuring accuracy and relevance. Critics of AI's involvement in news production often raise concerns about maintaining journalistic integrity and human

Chapter 4_Reporting

creativity. AI is a powerful tool, but it can't replace journalists. Lucky for us, as they say, our editorial oversight remains critical to the accuracy, balance, and ethical considerations of AI-generated content. Efficiency gains aren't the only upside, either. AI can uncover new angles, detect patterns in data, and generate unique insights that augment the reporting process. By leveraging AI's analytical capabilities, journalists can access a broader spectrum of information, facilitating comprehensive and well-informed reporting. AI systems should be trained on diverse datasets, undergo regular evaluation, and comply with journalistic standards to avoid biases or inaccuracies. As AI technology evolves, the future of news broadcasting holds even more possibilities. Personalized news experiences, where AI tailors content based on individual preferences, are already here. Perhaps soon, AI-driven voice synthesis may enable automated news anchors to deliver broadcasts with human-like intonation and inflection. As newsrooms embrace AI technology, the entire industry sees increased efficiency, enhanced storytelling, and more engaging broadcasts.

PRO_TIPS

These tools can streamline the writing process, enhance collaboration, and improve the overall quality of news scripts. Here are some popular choices:

1. Celtx is a comprehensive scriptwriting software that offers specialized features for news writing. It provides templates and formatting options specifically designed for news scripts. Celtx also allows for easy collaboration among team members, making it convenient for newsroom environments.

2. Final Draft is a professional screenwriting software widely used in the entertainment industry. It was originally designed for film and television scripts, but it can now be adapted for news scriptwriting. It offers powerful features such as automatic formatting, revision tracking, and collaboration tools.

3. Adobe Story is a cloud-based scriptwriting and pre-production tool that provides features for news scriptwriters. It allows for seamless integration with other Adobe Creative Cloud applications, making it easier to incorporate multimedia elements into scripts. Adobe Story also offers collaboration capabilities and real-time updates.

4. Trelby is a free, open-source scriptwriting software that is user-friendly and lightweight. It supports industry-standard formatting and offers features like revision tracking, collaboration, and different views for writing and editing scripts. While not specifically tailored for news scripts, it can be adapted for newsroom use.

5. Arc Publishing is a comprehensive content management system developed by The Washington Post. It offers a range of tools for news production, including scriptwriting capabilities. Arc Publishing provides an intuitive interface, collaboration features, and customizable templates for news scripts.

6. Grammarly is a popular writing assistant tool that can be used alongside any scriptwriting software. It helps improve grammar, spelling, and clarity in your writing. It also offers suggestions for sentence structure and can assist in generating headline variations by offering alternative wording.

When selecting a software tool, consider factors such as ease of use, collaboration features, formatting options, and integration with other newsroom tools and systems. ●

TRANSCRIBING INFORMATION. Journalists use AI-powered transcription tools to swiftly transcribe interviews, speeches, and recordings, freeing up valuable time for in-depth analysis and storytelling. Transcription has long been a time-consuming task for reporters. It is meticulous, manual work that is often outsourced to professional transcription services. The process is resource-intensive and prone to errors, often resulting in the loss of critical details and compromised accuracy.

Chapter 4_**Reporting**

AI-driven transcription tools come equipped with advanced natural language processing (NLP) algorithms and machine learning models. They convert spoken words into written text, with significant savings in time and effort. Perhaps more importantly, they preserve essential information and minimize the risk of misquoting or misinterpreting interviewees. And again the reporter has more time and energy to focus on extracting key insights and crafting a compelling story.

AI transcription tools can manage information from multiple media formats, including audio and video recordings, in a fraction of the time compared to manual transcription. This accelerated process enhances reporters' productivity, enabling them to meet tight deadlines and cover a broader range of stories.

AI technology can handle different accents, dialects, and speaking styles-a notable advantage for reporters operating in diverse regions. These tools excel at distinguishing between speakers, attributing their statements accurately, and generating clean transcripts even in challenging audio conditions. This ensures that journalists can capture and report the perspectives of individuals from various backgrounds and communities more faithfully, lending greater veracity to their stories.

Several prominent news organizations have already embraced AI transcription tools, reporting positive outcomes. The integration of these tools into newsrooms has not only improved the efficiency of information transcription but also enhanced collaboration among reporters. AI-generated transcripts can be easily shared and accessed by multiple team members, facilitating cross-checking and collaboration on stories.

While AI transcription tools offer substantial advantages, it is essential to address potential concerns surrounding data privacy and security. News organizations must ensure that any sensitive information captured during transcription is appropriately protected, adhering to relevant regulations and ethical standards.

Looking ahead, the future of AI transcription tools for reporters holds even greater potential. Advancements in AI technology may enable real-time transcription during live events, providing journalists with immediate access to accurate transcripts as news unfolds. This real-time capability can further amplify the speed and effectiveness of news reporting, particularly in fast-paced and dynamic situations.

PRO_TIPS

These platforms leverage advanced natural language processing (NLP) and machine learning techniques to automate the transcription process. Here are some popular choices:

1. Google Cloud Speech-to-Text API offers powerful speech recognition capabilities, enabling accurate and efficient transcription of audio and video files. It supports multiple languages, punctuation, and speaker diarization. The API is easily integrable into existing workflows and provides customizable features to meet specific transcription needs.

2. Microsoft Azure Speech to Text service provides automatic speech recognition capabilities for transcription. It offers real-time and batch transcription options and supports various audio formats. The service includes features like punctuation, profanity filtering, and speaker diarization, enhancing the accuracy and usability of transcriptions.

3. IBM Watson Speech to Text service leverages AI and machine learning technologies to convert spoken language into written text. It supports multiple languages, audio formats, and features real-time transcription capabilities. The service also offers customization options, allowing users to fine-tune the transcription model for specific domains or accents.

4. Otter.ai is a popular AI-powered transcription software that offers accurate and efficient transcription services. It provides automatic transcription for audio and video recordings and includes features like speaker identification, searchable transcripts, and real-time collaboration. Otter.ai is known for its user-friendly interface and ease of use.

Chapter 4_Reporting

5. Trint is a comprehensive transcription platform that combines AI with human editing for enhanced accuracy. It features automatic transcription, speaker identification, and a user-friendly editor for quick corrections. Trint also offers integrations with popular video conferencing platforms and editing software, streamlining the transcription workflow. ●

TRANSLATING FROM A FOREIGN LANGUAGE. AI is transforming the landscape of language translation, offering unprecedented efficiency and accuracy. AI-powered translation tools have emerged as indispensable assets for breaking down language barriers, facilitating communication between individuals and organizations across different countries and cultures.

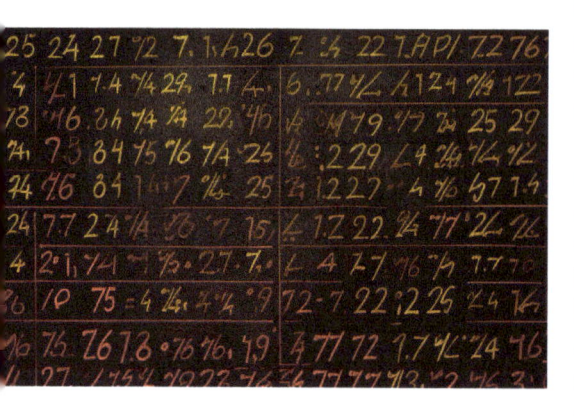

Translation has traditionally been a complex and time-consuming task, requiring the expertise of human translators and substantial resources. AI technology, however, delivers immediate, precise results. It uses sophisticated algorithms and machine learning models to interpret and translate a wide range of languages, including those with complex grammar and syntax. These tools give reporters and journalists easy access to information from foreign sources. By breaking down language barriers, AI translation tools empower reporters to cover international events and stories, fostering a more interconnected global journalism landscape. AI translation tools also prove invaluable during interviews and press conferences involving individuals who speak different languages. Journalists can use these tools to communicate effectively with sources, ensuring accurate interpretation of statements and promoting cross-cultural understanding. AI translation enables news organizations to provide multilingual content, reaching a broader audience and expanding their global presence. With AI-driven translation, news articles, broadcasts, and online content can be efficiently translated into multiple languages, catering to diverse readerships and facilitating international engagement. It's important to note that translations that respect not just linguistic nuances, but cultural nuances as well, can still pose challenges for AI systems. As always, human oversight and editorial expertise remain crucial. Advancements in AI technology, such as neural machine translation, are continually enhancing translation accuracy and fluency. And the integration of AI with other technologies, such as speech recognition and natural language processing, may enable real-time translation during live events, facilitating seamless communication across languages.

CASE_STUDY_1

AFTENPOSTEN (NORWAY) – *Aftenposten is Norway's largest printed newspaper by circulation. Based in Oslo, it has an estimated 1.2 million print and digital readers combined. It is considered the newspaper of record for Norway. Aftenposten is part of the Schibsted group.*

Why profile Aftenposten?

Aftenposten has one of the most innovative newspaper management teams in the world. Historically, Aftenposten has introduced technology and newsroom protocols to advance digital journalism years ahead of other newspapers. The team started work on algorithms in 2015 with a clear vision: to create front page-algorithms not only based on signals from users, but that reflected Aftenposten's journalistic mission and profile. In a conversation with two Aftenposten editors, Eirik Winsnes and Jostein Ihlebek, they revealed the impact that artificial intelligence is having in the newsroom: "We have been using generative AI in our CMS and platform, where we began using our own Aftenposten voice to read articles. First, we tested simple sound bites, allowing us to have a sound file for each article published. Now, AI enables us to have a sound

Chapter 4_*Reporting*

file on each article," Winsnes said. He said that at Aftenposten they first tested how AI would be able to replicate the voice of staffers reading the articles. "It does it to almost perfection," he said. "There are still pronunciations that AI does not get right, but it is a minor drawback. We have had our podcast journalists read about 3,000 articles to test the system." For Aftenposten, this text-to-speech capability is one major advantage that AI gives our journalists in the newsroom.

How else is AI used at Aftenposten?
"Right now, our approach is to let individual reporters use AI with their own initiative. It is up to reporters to decide if they wish to use artificial intelligence for research, for example," Ihlebek said. "Every rewriter in the newsroom has access to ChatGPT, some use it quite extensively, others don't – not yet." One area where Aftenposten is using AI consistently is that of summarization of articles. Using ChatGPT, the editors have built algorithms into their content management system to create summaries for all articles published. The editors explain that the one area of production where there is a more extensive work with algorithms and AI is for the layout of the print edition of Aftenposten. "For the production of the printed newspaper, Aftenposten collaborated with an external partner to create a system that puts the layout together. So in theory, we can assemble a complete edition with just one click," Winsnes said. The newspaper's designers have created a library of prompts and algorithms that pick up the right templates based on that edition's texts and images. (See case study of this process in the Layout & Design Chapter 6).

What's next for AI at Aftenposten?
The editors report shared that a priority is using AI to make the reporting role more effective, with more sources to check. Also the editors expect that in the next three years, Aftenposten can scale products in a more efficient way to make formats and design, tailored differently for different audiences. Eventually, the editors hope to use AI to improve work processes, so that content can be created and published differently for different audiences. Winsnes adds that: "No one really knows how this artificial intelligence will play out. Perhaps we could meet a wall, but given

the level it is at today and all the content we produce, should we try to use AI better to improve the quality of our journalism? Of course. But, also we must use it smartly for service information such as stock market, food recipes, the weather, a lot of that will be done with AI. The benefit is that AI then help us to free resources for exclusive journalism, which is what the human journalists can and should do best." ●

TRANSLATING FROM A FOREIGN LANGUAGE. See how Worldcrunch, a Paris-based English language news website that curates and translates news from international media sources or partner organizations uses AI for its translations.

PRO_TIPS

These platforms leverage state-of-the-art machine learning algorithms to deliver efficient and accurate translation services. Here are some popular choices:

1. Google Cloud Translation API provides a powerful and versatile translation solution. It supports translation between thousands of language pairs, including commonly used languages as well as less widely spoken ones. The API offers both neural machine translation (NMT) and traditional statistical machine translation (SMT) models, allowing users to choose the best option for their needs. It provides high-quality translations and offers customization options for domain-specific translations.

2. Microsoft Azure Translator Text API offers automatic translation capabilities using cutting-edge neural machine translation technology. It supports a wide range of languages and provides reliable and accurate translations. The API includes features like language detection, transliteration, and bilingual dictionaries. It can be easily integrated into various applications and workflows.

3. DeepL is known for its highly accurate and natural-sounding translations. It employs neural machine translation models that have been trained on vast amounts of multilingual data. DeepL supports

Chapter 4_**Reporting**

translation for a number of languages, and its user-friendly interface makes it convenient for both individual users and businesses. It also offers a specialized DeepL API for seamless integration into applications and systems.

4. IBM Watson Language Translator leverages AI and machine learning to provide high-quality translation services. It supports numerous language pairs and offers customization options for domain-specific translations. The service includes features like language identification, batch translation, and glossary support. It can be integrated into various applications and environments.

5. SYSTRAN offers a comprehensive translation platform powered by AI. It provides accurate and efficient translation for a wide range of languages and domains. SYSTRAN's technology supports both neural and statistical machine translation methods and offers customization options. The platform includes features such as language detection, terminology management, and batch translation capabilities.

When selecting a software option, consider factors such as language support, translation quality, customization options, pricing, and integration possibilities with your existing tools and systems. It's important to note that while AI translation software has made significant advancements, translations still require human review and editing to ensure accuracy and cultural sensitivity. ●

CASE_STUDY_2

WORLDCRUNCH (FRANCE) – *A chat with Jeff Israely, co-founder and editor of Worldcrunch, is a former bureau chief for Time Magazine in Europe.*

What is Worldcrunch?
Worldcrunch is a Paris-based English language news website that curates and translates news from international media sources or partner organizations. It was launched in 2011.

Worldcrunch and AI
"As a news organization we were using AI without realizing it because our translators already were utilizing AI in various forms for their work. There was machine translation and, while the topic of us at Worldcrunch using AI came up from time to time, in 2011 AI wasn't yet good enough to rely on it for our work. So, our standard answer was "we don't use it." Over time, however, it became evident in conversations with multilingual journalists and translators that they were using AI in various forms. So we did not institute it as a work process, but at certain point we accepted the fact that it was there and used by contributors. We called it machine translation. Eventually, Israely says, AI introduced itself into Worldcrunch's work processes. "It was organic," he says. "Much the same way that Google has become for journalists and content producers."

What has changed?
"It is a different moment now, we are so conscious, with ChatGPT landing in our screens and consciousness, giving us a collective moment of 'let's go, it starts here.'" AI is now part of our lives. Now it is a different moment because we are all so aware of it, which is prompting people to ask 'how are we going to do this? We can think of ways to use it as well as what to be careful of. We had to reassure investors and partners that we were NOT using AI entirely for translation of articles, that humans were doing the translations. We reassure everyone that we use quality control. There has to be a human in command of

Chapter 4_Reporting

two languages in the translation, doing the translation, but increasingly over time, using AI to some degree. This is a case where you set standards and as an editor you have to control the quality of the work, like good editors and content producers should do everywhere."

The present and the future
Israely sees the next three years of AI development for his newsroom as a continuation of what his team does now. "The human component will continue to prevail – if you care about accuracy, one mistake can undermine a year's worth of work. In the world of translation, accuracy and precision are extremely important, but also the question of fluency nuances… and I admit that AI is getting better and better, so we have to calculate that it is going to get even better in the future, and thus will be more useful. But remember the analogy with self-driving cars – you have to be able to get your hands off the wheel better than humans. It is a trust issue. At the end it is all about the trust of your readers. That is the capital." In outlining the advantages of AI in his newsroom, Israely says that over the past 3 years, more and more he is able to assign stories using Google translate. In the past, he had to wait for writers to pitch stories to him before he could decide on what stories to select for translation. "Today I can browse the website of any of our client newspapers and get a sense of what the stories are, their components, whether there is an interview or on-site reporting, and select those that we wish to translate… the fact that I can access stories in any language in the world changes and benefits our work processes tremendously."

A program named DeepL
Worldcrunch translators use DeepL for their work. DeepL Translator is a neural machine translation service that was launched in August 2017 and is owned by Cologne-based DeepL SE. [22] It initially offered translations between seven European languages and has since gradually expanded to support 31 languages. DeepL is based on state-of-the-art neural machine translation technology. It employs deep learning algorithms to understand and translate text from one language to another, supporting

(22) deepl.com

translation between various language pairs, including English, German, French, Spanish, Italian, Dutch, Polish, Portuguese, Russian, Japanese, and Chinese. DeepL's translation models are trained on vast amounts of bilingual text data from various domains. The training data includes official documents, websites, technical texts, and other sources available on the internet. ●

HELPING WITH THE OUTLINE OF A STORY IDEA. AI can assist with the outline of a story idea. While AI technology is not typically involved in the creative process of generating story ideas, it can offer valuable support. Here's how AI can help:

Data Analysis and Research. AI-powered tools can quickly sift through vast amounts of data, providing journalists with valuable insights and trends. By utilizing AI algorithms, journalists can uncover patterns, identify key sources, and gather relevant information to support their story idea. These tools can streamline the research process and help journalists make data-driven decisions when outlining their story.

Topic Generation and Discovery. AI algorithms can analyze large datasets and media sources to identify emerging topics and trends. By utilizing natural language processing and machine learning techniques, AI can suggest potential story ideas based on current events, social media discussions, or reader interests. This can help journalists explore new angles or uncover overlooked stories for their outline.

Sentiment Analysis and Public Opinion. AI-powered sentiment analysis tools can assess public sentiment towards specific topics or events. By analyzing social media posts, comments, and online discussions, journalists can gain insights into public opinion. This information can inform the outline by highlighting the key perspectives and concerns surrounding the story idea.

Chapter 4_Reporting

Fact-Checking and Verification. AI-driven fact-checking tools can assist journalists in verifying information and ensuring accuracy in their stories. These tools can quickly scan databases, news articles, and other sources to check the validity of claims, identify potential misinformation, and provide additional context. This helps journalists strengthen their outline by including accurate and reliable information.

Language and Style Suggestions. AI language models, like the one ChatGPT is based on, can provide suggestions for improving the clarity, style, and structure of the outline. By analyzing the text, AI can offer alternative wording, highlight potential redundancies or inconsistencies, and provide grammar and punctuation recommendations. This can help journalists refine their outline and enhance the overall readability of their story.

It's important to note that while AI can help with the outlining process, the creativity and critical thinking required to shape a compelling narrative still relies largely on the journalist's expertise. AI technology is meant to support and enhance journalistic work, not replace it. The journalist's unique perspective, intuition, and investigative skills remain essential in crafting a captivating story.

AI WRITING: LAZY? It's a little early to start using the word "style" when referring to how AI writes. As users of ChatGPT know, when one prompts the bot, the reply typically starts the same, no matter what the question asked: For example, when the author asks ChatGPT: Act as if you are a reporter. How can AI help transcribe information for reporters?

Or: Act as if you are a reporter. How can AI help to translate from a foreign language? The responses were uniform and repetitive:

• In a significant breakthrough, Artificial Intelligence (AI) is transforming the landscape of...

• In a remarkable development, Artificial Intelligence (AI) technology is transforming the process of I...

• In a groundbreaking development, Artificial Intelligence (AI) is poised to transform the process of...

It is this repetitive streak that prompts some journalists to describe AI writing as lazy. Take for example the case of BuzzFeed, which started using AI to write quizzes and other content related to travel. The articles were bylined "As Told to Buzzy," a bow-tied robot with the bio "Articles written with the help of Buzzy the Robot (aka our Creative AI Assistant) but powered by human ideas." In a piece about it, published in the Nieman Lab, we can see how Buzzy the robot started a variety of travel pieces, perhaps fueling the "lazy writing" tag. (23) Buzzy could also write paragraphs like these: "Cape May is actually a world-renowned birdwatching spot. No, I'm not trying to be funny. It's genuinely a fantastic place to sit back and watch the most amazing bird species migrate. It's perfect for budding ornithologists, bird enthusiasts, or even if you're just like "eh" about birds. I promise you; this experience will make your heart sing." Or: "The food scene in Providence is lit. From mouth-watering food trucks to cozy, local cafes, your taste buds will be seriously blown away. There's something for everyone, and it's finger-lickin' fantastic."

The 40 or so articles, all of which appear to be SEO-driven travel guides, are comically bland and similar to one another. Check out these almost-copied lines:

- "Now, I know what you're thinking - 'Cape May? What is that, some kind of mayonnaise brand?'" in an article about Cape May, in New Jersey.
- "Now I know what you're thinking – 'but Caribbean destinations are all just crowded resorts, right?'" in an article about St Maarten, in the Caribbean.
- "Now, I know what you're thinking, Puerto Rico? Isn't that where all the cruise ships go?" in an article about San Juan, in Puerto Rico.
- "Now, I know what you're thinking- bigger isn't always better," in an article about Providence, in Rhode Island.
- "Now, I know what you're probably thinking. Nepal? The Himalayas? Haven't we all heard of that already?" in an article about Khumbu, in Nepal.
- "Now, I know what you're probably thinking, "Brewster? Never heard of it," in an article about Brewster, in Massachusetts.
- "I know what you're thinking: isn't Stockholm that freezing, gloomy city up in the north that nobody cares about?" in an article about Stockholm, in Sweden.

That's not the bot's only lazy trope. On review, almost everything the bot has published contains at least one line about a "hidden gem."

(23) niemanlab.org

Chapter 4_*Reporting*

REPETITION. *"Repetitive"* is another word we often hear in descriptions of AI copy. Another review of *BuzzFeed* travel AI-generated travel stories revealed that, "almost everything the bot has published contains at least one line about a *"hidden gem."*

Amelia Island, Florida is a *"hidden gem of beaches,"* Carmel-By-The-Sea, California is a *"hidden gem of California's coast,"* West Virginia is a *"hidden gem of a state,"* Saugerties, New York is a *"hidden gem where small town charm meets big city cool,"* Stanley, Idaho is a *"hidden gem nestled right in the heart of the Sawtooth Mountains,"* Brewster, Massachusetts is *"Cape Cod's hidden gem,"* Calistoga, California is a *"hidden gem,"* June Lake, California is a *"hidden gem,"* Mammoth Mountain, California is a *"hidden gem,"* Providence, Rhode Island is a *"hidden gem,"* Charleston, South Carolina is a *"hidden gem,"* Connecticut is a *"hidden gem,"* Aruba is a "hidden gem" and "truly a gem," Prague is a "hidden gem," the Cook Islands are a *"hidden gem,"* Saint Maarten is a *"hidden gem,"* South Dakota is both a *"glorious gem of a state"* and a "criminally underrated travel gem," Cape May, New Jersey is a *"gem worth visiting,"* Arizona is a *"desert gem,"* Ecuador is an *"absolute gem,"* Bruges, Belgium is a *"secret gem,"* and a *"Belgium gem,"* Montreal, Canada is a *"travel gem,"* and Alberta, Canada is a *"Canadian gem."* Sevilla, Spain is just a *"gem."* (24)

BuzzFeed CEO Jonah Peretti wrote: "To be clear, we see the breakthroughs in AI opening up a new era of creativity that will allow humans to harness creativity in new ways with endless opportunities and applications for good." It is admirable that organizations like BuzzFeed are willing to carry out experimentation with AI, perhaps entering those soft terrains that others remain too timid to explore. As told to Futurism, BuzzFeed is using Buzzy and a human editor "to unlock the creative potential of UGC so we can broaden the range of ideas and perspectives that we publish," with people picking the topics (in this case, specific cities) and Buzzy doing the generating. One staffer placed it in the right context of human/AI/human: "It's not that different from a freelance assignment I did in my

(24) futurism.com

twenties: A human editor assigned me to write some articles about the promise of 5G- a topic about which I knew nothing- and I googled 5G, read other content mill-ish articles about it, and compiled them into my "own" article. The content I created wasn't really meant to be read by humans who actually needed to know anything about 5G, in the same way that anybody who is planning a trip to Morocco probably shouldn't get their recommendations from Buzzy. In the 5G case, I was basically Buzzy, except I was getting paid. Buzzy works for free. You know, for now." (25)

HOW_CHATGPT_SEES IT

PROMPT: *Help me with a magazine feature about what type of education is best in the Artificial Intelligence era. Title: Navigating the AI Era: Unleashing the Potential of Education. Introduction: As Artificial Intelligence (AI) continues to transform various industries, including education, it becomes imperative to explore the best approaches to education in this era. The impact of AI on the job market and the evolving skills landscape highlights the need for a well-rounded and adaptable educational foundation. This magazine feature delves into the discussion surrounding the most effective types of education in the AI era and the skills that will empower individuals to thrive in a rapidly changing world.*

CHATGPT: **1. Emphasizing STEM Education:** In the AI era, Science, Technology, Engineering, and Mathematics (STEM) education plays a critical role. By promoting the acquisition of foundational skills in these disciplines, students gain a solid understanding of the principles underlying AI technologies. This prepares them to adapt and contribute to AI-driven industries, such as data analysis, machine learning, and robotics.

→

(25) futurism.com

Chapter 4_**Reporting**

HOW_CHATGPT_SEES IT

2. Cultivating Computational Thinking: Alongside STEM education, emphasizing computational thinking is crucial. Computational thinking refers to a problem-solving approach that utilizes concepts from computer science. It encourages individuals to break down complex problems into smaller, manageable parts and apply logical thinking to find innovative solutions. This skill is highly valuable in the AI era, as it promotes creativity, critical thinking, and algorithmic understanding.

3. Fostering Interdisciplinary Learning: While STEM education is vital, the AI era also calls for interdisciplinary learning. AI applications span various domains, including healthcare, finance, and the humanities. Encouraging students to explore diverse subjects and connect them to AI concepts fosters a holistic understanding of AI's societal impact. Interdisciplinary education cultivates skills in collaboration, empathy, and ethical decision-making.

4. Promoting Ethical AI Education is crucial. With AI continuously advancing, individuals must be adaptable, ready to acquire new skills, and keep pace with emerging technologies. Promoting self-directed learning, online courses, and professional development opportunities ensures individuals remain competitive in the evolving job market.

5. Emotional Intelligence and Creativity: As AI becomes increasingly influential, addressing ethical considerations is paramount. Incorporating ethics into education equips individuals with the knowledge to navigate the ethical challenges associated with AI technology. Education must emphasize responsible AI practices, privacy concerns, bias mitigation, and the ethical implications of AI algorithms.

→

> **HOW_CHATGPT_SEES IT**
>
> **6. Lifelong Learning and Adaptability:** In the AI era, learning should not end with formal education. Encouraging a mindset of lifelong learning is crucial. With AI continuously advancing, individuals must be adaptable, ready to acquire new skills, and keep pace with emerging technologies. Promoting self-directed learning, online courses, and professional development opportunities ensures individuals remain competitive in the evolving job market.
>
> **7. Emotional Intelligence and Creativity:** While AI excels in analytical and technical domains, human qualities like emotional intelligence and creativity remain essential. Education should foster emotional intelligence, empathy, and interpersonal skills, as these aspects are difficult to replicate through AI. Cultivating creativity encourages innovative thinking, problem-solving, and the ability to envision AI's potential in addressing complex challenges. ●

Conclusion: In the AI era, education must equip individuals with the right mix of skills and knowledge. Emphasizing STEM education, computational thinking, interdisciplinary learning, ethical considerations, and fostering adaptability are key. By combining technical expertise with emotional intelligence and creativity, individuals can leverage AI as a powerful tool while making meaningful contributions to society.

AI ACKNOWLEDGES WHERE HUMANS EXCEL. It's quite satisfying to see that consistently ChatGPT salutes human participation as key. In the course of researching this book, and during daily interactions with ChatGPT, we have asked it to "Act as if you are a reporter, or editor, or journalist..." While it provides the essential information requested in the prompt, it normally

Chapter 4_**Reporting**

concludes with statements such as, "It's important to note that while AI can be a helpful tool in the outlining process, the creativity and critical thinking required to shape a compelling narrative still largely rely on the journalist's expertise. AI technology is meant to support and enhance journalistic work, rather than replace it. The journalist's unique perspective, intuition, and investigative skills remain essential in crafting a captivating story.

"While AI translation tools offer numerous advantages, it is important to acknowledge their limitations. Translating nuanced cultural and contextual nuances accurately can still pose challenges for AI systems. Therefore, human oversight and editorial expertise remain crucial in ensuring the accuracy and cultural sensitivity of translated content."

"...while AI can provide valuable insights and assist in evaluating certain aspects of newsworthiness, human judgment and editorial expertise remain essential. AI algorithms can aid in assessing timeliness, prominence, and human interest, but they should be utilized as tools to support rather than replace the critical thinking and ethical considerations of journalists and editors. The collaborative approach, combining AI capabilities with human expertise, is key to ensuring accurate, reliable, and impactful news coverage."

In the AI era, education must equip individuals with the right mix of skills and knowledge. Emphasizing STEM education, computational thinking, interdisciplinary learning, ethical considerations, and fostering adaptability are key.

HOW_CHATGPT_SEES IT

PROMPT: *Act as if you were a philosopher and tell me why human input is key to AI's success.*

CHATGPT: Human input is essential to the success of artificial intelligence (AI) due to several fundamental reasons deeply rooted in the nature of AI systems and the complexity of human intelligence:

1. Values and Ethical Considerations: AI systems are designed and trained by humans to perform specific tasks or make decisions. Without human input, AI lacks the ability to understand and embody human values, ethics, and moral judgments. Human input helps shape AI algorithms and frameworks to ensure they align with societal norms, respect human rights, and avoid biased or unethical outcomes.

2. Contextual Understanding: AI systems excel at analyzing vast amounts of data and identifying patterns, but they often struggle with context and nuanced understanding. Human input is crucial for providing context, interpretation, and situational awareness that AI algorithms may not be able to grasp on their own. Humans can offer insights, knowledge, and expertise that enrich AI systems and enable them to make more informed and appropriate decisions.

3. Creative and Abstract Thinking: While AI can generate innovative solutions based on patterns and algorithms, it is still limited when it comes to creative and abstract thinking. Human input adds the element of imagination, intuition, and originality that is essential for problem-solving, innovation, and conceptual breakthroughs. Humans bring unique perspectives and the ability to think outside the box, which AI systems currently struggle to replicate.

→

Chapter 4_**Reporting**

HOW_CHATGPT_SEES IT

4. Flexibility and Adaptability: AI systems operate within predefined parameters and rules set by humans. However, the world is constantly evolving, and new situations arise that may not fit neatly within those parameters. Human input is crucial in adapting AI systems to changing circumstances, updating algorithms, and incorporating new knowledge or insights. Humans possess the adaptability and flexibility necessary to navigate complex and unpredictable situations that AI systems may find challenging.

5. Responsibility and Accountability: AI systems are tools created by humans, and therefore, humans bear the responsibility for their actions and consequences. Human input is vital for ensuring transparency, accountability, and oversight in AI systems. Humans must make decisions about when and how to deploy AI, monitor its behavior, and address any unintended consequences or biases. Human involvement is crucial to mitigate risks and ensure AI is used responsibly and ethically.

Human input AI's success provides the values, contextual understanding, creativity, flexibility, and responsibility that AI systems currently lack. By combining the strengths of human intelligence with the capabilities of AI, we can harness greater stores of our potential while retaining values that best serve humanity. ●

ESSENTIAL_TOOLS

Equipping the AI journalist. If the goal of incorporating artificial intelligence into the work of the content creator, to save time, to expedite and to streamline processes, then what are the tools that can help us achieve it? Several commercial tools are available.

1. OTTER.AI can join video meetings as an attendee, record it, and provide a transcript. It will also generate what it thinks are good summary points of the meeting, and allow users to interact with the audio/ transcript by highlighting the text on the screen, replaying just this portion of text. Connect Otter to your Google or Microsoft calendar and it can automatically join and record your meetings on Zoom, Microsoft Teams, and Google Meet. This is a time saver when you're trying to locate a couple of quotes verbatim. English only.
→ otter.ai

2. AIRGRAM helps record, transcribe, summarize, and share meeting conversations. Functions as an end-to-end meeting management and productivity tool for diverse teams. Multiple language transcription: English, French, German, Spanish, and more.
→ airgram.io

3. VG. This is owned by Jojo Schibsted in Norway, which also released a free audio/video transcription tool called Jojo, which supports 100 languages of inputs. Goal: created for Schibsted's journalists to transcribe audio interviews and podcasts quickly. Anders Grimstad, Schibsted head of foresight and emerging interfaces, says that Jojo already saves journalists thousands of hours of work every month by helping them write up interviews and podcasts.
→ vg.no

Chapter 4_**Reporting**

4. ELEVEN LABS Going from a written text to a spoken track can be done with tools like Eleven labs or Well Said, and even free tools like YouTube can also serve in this area. YouTube will transcribe the audio track of your videos, for example, supporting search and augmenting the accessibility of your content. Also useful in this category: Genny by LOVO is powerful and easy to use. Super rich feature set, giving you an unparalleled voiceover production experience. Genny's voices can express up to 25+ emotions.
→ beta.elevenlabs.io
→ genny.lovo.ai

5. CHATGPT Reformatting content, such as taking a list of contacts and fixing capitalization and giving a consistent format of name, address, or phone number. The Austrian daily, Die Presse, uses ChatGPT for story ideas on a given topic, with journalists then deciding how to proceed with AI's suggestions.
→ openai.com

AI_PLAYERS

Impromptu: Amplifying Our Humanity Through AI

WHO IS REID HOFFMAN? – A Silicon Valley investor. His mission? Showing how new technologies can improve humanity. By Reid Hoffman with GPT-4

Takeaway: "So while most of us may think of journalism as a product, it's ultimately a process-iterative and self-correcting. Ideally, tomorrow's stories refine, clarify, and expand on today's. Accuracy is a persistent defining value, but so is speed. That's a major reason I believe GPT-4 and other AI tools will have such an outsized, net-positive impact on journalism: they'll help news organizations gather, produce, and distribute the news faster than ever before. This includes automatically sifting through massive troves of public records to find the important stories hidden within. It means monitoring and analyzing 800 + million social media posts a day to do the same. It means generating headlines and transcribing interviews in seconds, and packaging and personalizing the same basic information into many different styles and formats."

Chapter 4_**Reporting**

CASE_STUDY_3

LOST COAST OUTPOST (USA) – *A highly local news provider with a team of five reporters, the Lost Coast Outpost has relied on generative AI since 2022 to help with coverage of local government agendas, including city council and county planning.*

A conversation with editor Hank Sims. Why hyper local news is important?
In today's fast-paced world, mobile technology has transformed the way we consume news, presenting a unique opportunity for hyperlocal journalism. It is among the smallest news outlets that AI has become a useful tool. A great example is Hank Sims, editor of the online-only weekly, Lost Coast Outpost, published in northern California, USA. A highly local news provider with a team of five reporters, the Lost Coast Outpost has relied on generative AI since 2022 to help with coverage of local government agendas, including city council and county planning. "We are a very small team, five reporters and myself to create all content. Generative AI has been a welcome tool for us. I wrote a simple program where AI would take a PDF from which it would generate summaries of scheduled meeting agendas, looking something like this: "If a reporter wants to contribute the human touch, they can do so, enhancing the AI-generated entry, adding photos and context to the story."

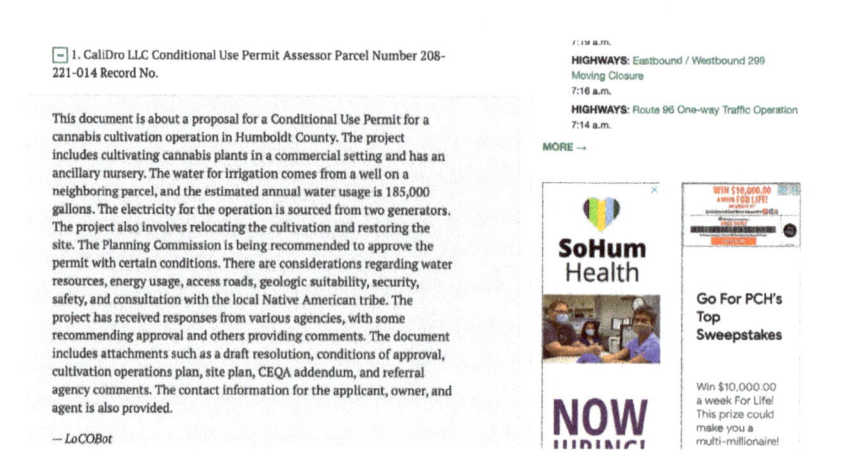

1. CaliDro LLC Conditional Use Permit Assessor Parcel Number 208-221-014 Record No.

This document is about a proposal for a Conditional Use Permit for a cannabis cultivation operation in Humboldt County. The project includes cultivating cannabis plants in a commercial setting and has an ancillary nursery. The water for irrigation comes from a well on a neighboring parcel, and the estimated annual water usage is 185,000 gallons. The electricity for the operation is sourced from two generators. The project also involves relocating the cultivation and restoring the site. The Planning Commission is being recommended to approve the permit with certain conditions. There are considerations regarding water resources, energy usage, access roads, geologic suitability, security, safety, and consultation with the local Native American tribe. The project has received responses from various agencies, with some recommending approval and others providing comments. The document includes attachments such as a draft resolution, conditions of approval, cultivation operations plan, site plan, CEQA addendum, and referral agency comments. The contact information for the applicant, owner, and agent is also provided.

— LoCOBot

7:19 a.m.
HIGHWAYS: Eastbound / Westbound 299 Moving Closure
7:16 a.m.
HIGHWAYS: Route 96 One-way Traffic Operation
7:14 a.m.
MORE →

"The AI can also be rendered in other fun versions such as 'a horror story' or 'as an episode of Seinfeld.'"

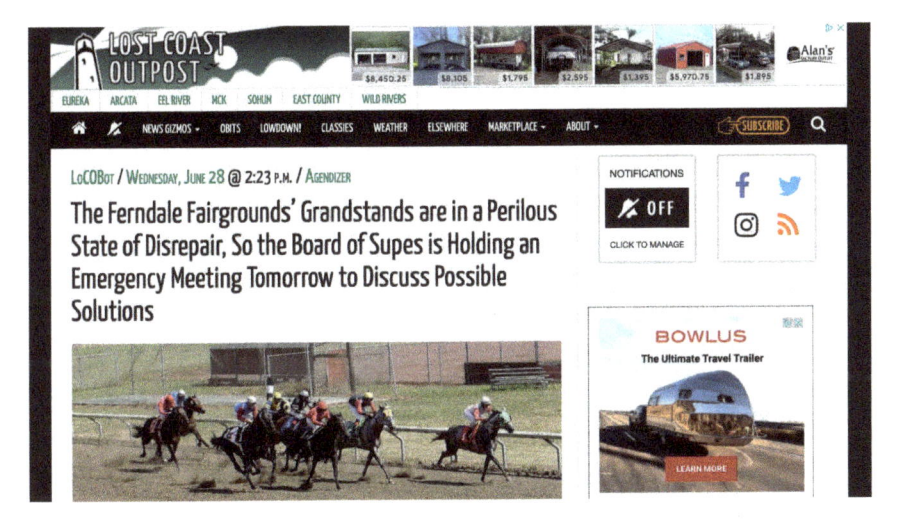

"AI allows us to do so much more with our resources. We now can quickly tell people what topics will be discussed at local meetings. We also understand that there are some things that AI can't do, such as creating context for a certain topic. That's where the human element is required. Our reporters use what AI has generated but expand and add context."

... or, as a horror story!

DOCUMENTS:

Staff Report • Attachment 1 - 10656 Draft Resolution • Attachment 1A - 10656 Conditions of Approval • Attachment 1B - 10656 Operations Plan w. Generator Addendum • Attachment 1C - 10656 Site Plan • Attachment 2 - 10656 Map Set • Attachment 3 - 10656 CEQA Addendum to MND • Attachment 4 - 10656 Applicant's Evidence in Support of Findings • Attachment 4A - 10656 Water Sustainability Evaluation for Well • Attachment 4B - 10656 Environmental Superiority Analysis • Attachment 4C - 10656 Restoration Plan for Historic Cultivation • Attachment 4D - 10656 Disturbed Area Stabilization Report • Attachment 4E - 10656 Road Evaluation • Attachment 5 - 10656 Referral Agency Comments • Attachment 6 - 10656 Watershed map

... or, as an episode of Seinfeld!

DOCUMENTS:

Staff Report • Attachment 1 - Draft Resolution • Attachment 1A - Conditions of Approval • Attachment 1B - Cultivation Operations Plan • Attachment 1C - 16866 MOD01 Site Plan 06.16.2022 (4) • Attachment 2 - 16866 Map Set 12.17.2020 • Attachment 3 - CEQA Addendum • Attachment 4 - Applicant Submitted Information • Attachment 4A - 16866 Site Management Plan 12.11.2020 • Attachment 4B - 1600-2019-0159-R1_HUM_MJ Peak_Stream Crossing_FinaiLSAA • Attachment 4C - 11506 Road Evaluation Report 10.22.2019 • Attachment 4D - 11506 Soils Engineering Report for Catchment Pond • Attachment 4E - 16866 Botanical Survey 07.05.2022 • Attachment 4F - 16866 letter confirms less than 50 cy removal 216-082-006 Allan Baird_ Kevin Peak • Attachment 4G - 16866 MBTA Survey_PLN-2020-16866-DEV01 • Attachment 4H - 16866 MOD01 Biological Assessment 06.16.2022 • Attachment 4I - 16866 MOD01 Grading Plan 06.16.2022 • Attachment 4J - 16866 MOD01 Oak Woodland Restoration Plan 05.03.2023 • Attachment 4K - 16866 Operations Plan 12.11.2020 • Attachment 4L - 16866 Timberland Conversion Evaluation Report

A USER'S GUIDE FOR CONTENT CREATORS – BY DR. MARIO GARCÍA

[117]

Chapter 4_*Reporting*

AI NUGGETS

"...a human journalist **who delivers meaningful analyses or interpretations can blow away AI."**

→ knowledge.wharton.upenn.edu

That's a lot of AI: A Washington Post **analysis found 1k+ companies across numerous industries discussed AI in their quarterly reports this summer, compared to 40 between 2015 and 2016.**

→ washingtonpost.com

UK-based NewsQuest announced in the fall of 2023 **they would hire an AI-assisted reporter as they continue "the journey of integrating AI into our newsrooms… We aim to safely adopt this technology, enhancing our news coverage that resonates with communities across the UK."**

→ washingtonpost.com

It's important to note that while AI can help with the outlining process, the creativity and critical thinking required to shape a compelling narrative still relies largely on the journalist's expertise. AI technology is meant to support and enhance journalistic work, not replace it.

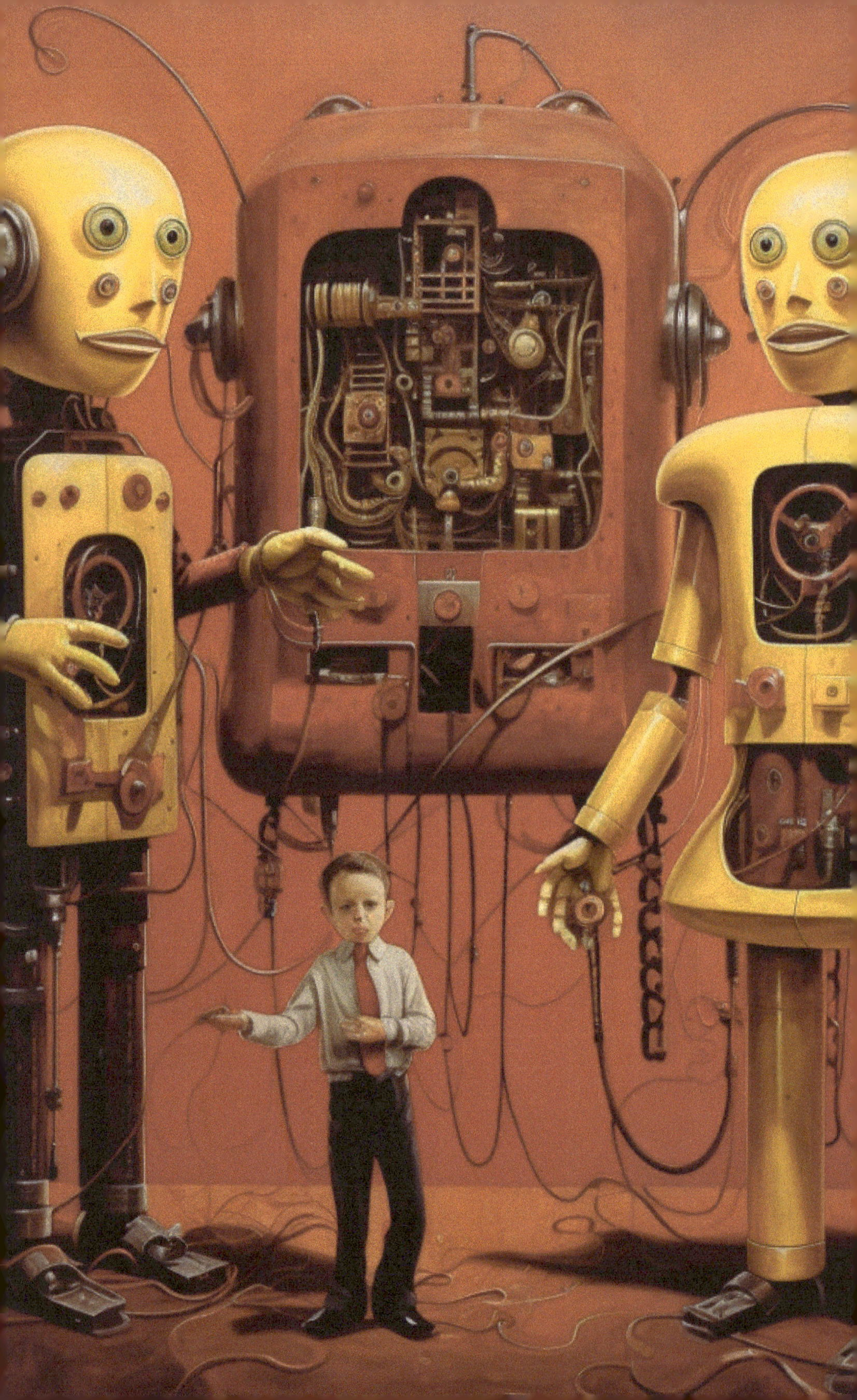

*Chapter 5_* **Marketing & Social Media**

AI and Reader Engagement

Long before "AI" became a common term among journalists and editors in newsrooms across the planet, their colleagues handling subscriptions, audience analysis, and engagement were exploring what artificial intelligence could do to make their jobs easier and more efficient. Today, AI is becoming more common among marketing departments. In fact, AI marketing is a new buzzword in marketing departments everywhere.

It's about using conversational AI tools to personalize content, predict consumer behavior and preferences, and optimize advertising campaigns, among other things. Newspapers can use AI to analyze their readership and understand their preferences, types of articles they read, and how they interact with the content. This information can be utilized to improve user experience, create custom content based on user preferences, and optimize advertising strategies. Ariane Bernard, who leads INMA's Smart Data Initiative, and author of the 2023 News Media at the Dawn of Generative AI, agrees: "For years, news organizations have used artificial intelligence to study patterns of reader engagement, and, the journeys non-subscribers take, the type of articles they choose to read, and, eventually, the content that converts them."

At The New York Times, she is a key stakeholder on cross-functional technical teams, including on the editorial user experience for the flagship home page. "At The Times, there is segmentation which buckets users in different groups to see how much they need free before converting, all using machine learning – with a Meter to measure the reader's journey from

Chapter 5_Marketing & Social Media

unregistered user to registered to subscriber." The Times's paywall strategy revolves around the commonly used "subscription funnel."

At the top of the funnel are unregistered users who do not yet have an account with The Times. Once they hit the meter limit for their unregistered status, they are shown a registration wall that blocks access and asks them to create an account, or to log in if they already have one. Their account gives them access to more free content and, since their activity is now linked to their registration ID, it allows the Times team to better understand the readers' current appetite for Times content. User information like this is valuable for any machine learning application and powers the Dynamic Meter as well. The NYT dynamic meter segments users with specific free allowance of articles, depending on past behavior. Each user will therefore encounter the paywall at an optimized moment in their journey. Once registered users hit their meter limit, they are served a paywall with a subscription offer.

The Times' Dynamic Meter plays the dual role of a) supporting the Times' journalistic mission to inform and help people understand their world, and b) their business goal of acquiring subscriptions. To do so, it optimizes two metrics simultaneously: a) the engagement that registered users have with Times content and b) the number of subscriptions the paywall generates in a given time frame.

SELLING THAT CONTENT. There was a time when the marketing departments of newspapers and magazines operated as the sole promoters of whatever an editorial title had to offer. In journalism courses today, we teach fledgling journalists how to promote the stories they write. In my own course at Columbia University, when my graduate students present their stories, they must also include social media "cards" for how they would sell the story. In the case of mobile storytelling, this includes the first screen which seduces the reader with a headline and image. This is how the traditional marketing tasks spill into the world of the journalist or content creator. For many traditional newsrooms, marketing has always been a project driven operation, leading to the launch of a campaign, which could be seasonal, or to celebrate a landmark moment-"100th Anniversary Edition," or "Celebrate Our New Look." Today, the selling of content is a continuous campaign, one which takes place daily, with the promotion of individual stories-of-the-day along with those coming up in the following few days. Ultimately, reporters and editors know their story content best, and they are usually their best marketers.

"Generative AI may be the next step in the transformation of digital," Bernard writes in her INMA Report. "Media companies are rallying resources and building frameworks for generative AI. They are learning and experimenting through committees, teams, squads, newsletters, WhatsApp groups, and town halls." [26]

All of this means that the social media landscape requires a greater, more spontaneous collaboration between the marketing department and the journalists. When we teach journalists to emphasize the most searchable element of the story in the first paragraph (and, of course, in the headline) we are applying one of marketing's most essential rules. This rule translates into more sharing, more clicks, better exposure of the story and, thinking like a marketing person, a greater possibility that the occasional visitor to our website may become a subscriber.

AI AND SUBSCRIPTIONS. If attracting subscribers is the goal, then it is crucial that marketers and journalists join forces.

In his 2023 INMA Report titled AI Guide and ChatGPT Promptbook for News Marketers, Greg Piechota, a researcher-in-residence at the International News Media Association and the lead of INMA's Readers First Initiative , suggests how AI can help marketers, in these specific areas:

1. Streamline your customer and product discovery.
2. Analyze, draft, and iterate engaging copy for your advertisements, paywalls, or offer landing pages.
3. Plan your engagement e-mails, such as onboarding series, and tailor them to different audiences.

[26] open.nytimes.com

Chapter 5_Marketing & Social Media

The INMA Report focuses on how generative AI can help in the area of developing a subscription strategy, with emphasis on how AI can help marketers by saving time, improving scalability of subscriptions marketing and increasing effectiveness in engaging readers and converting subscribers. None of these tasks can be achieved without the content produced by journalists. This was true before AI, and will continue to be true. "We suggest the best ways to plan the implementation of generative AI at work," writes Piechota. "Using the established Cross-Industry Standard Process for Data Mining or CRISP-DM framework, for managers of AI projects."

WHAT IS CRISP-DM? The Cross-Industry Standard Process for Data Mining (CRISP-DM) is a process model that serves as the base for a data science process. It has six sequential phases:

Business understanding. What does the business need? More importantly for media marketers: what are the needs of the customers – the audience consuming our content?

Data understanding. What data do we have / need? How accurate can we create a profile(s) of those consuming our content?

Data preparation. How do we organize the data for modeling? How do we present the data gathered to the content creators in the newsroom?

Modeling. What modeling techniques should we apply? For media people, how can we use the data gathered to create customization models?

Evaluation. Which model best meets the business objectives? But, also, which model best help content creators in the newsroom with the choices they make for stories and how to present them?

Deployment. How do stakeholders access the results? (27)

This sequence is not new to project managers in media organizations. And it will not be difficult to apply it to artificial intelligence. It is all about deciding how to mine the data available for best results, remembering that the implementation of generative AI involves a three-prong strategy within a media organization: business, editorial, technology. It is best to have a generative AI task force project manager to oversee how AI is discussed, developed and implemented.

BENEFITS OF AI AS MARKETING TOOL. The INMA Report concludes with some logical estimates of how AI can benefit a marketing department: "We estimate that, on average, a generative AI tool needs to save a marketer as little as 48 minutes per working week to pay for itself." Separately, an average publisher can expect up to 5,700% return on investment. This is based on two assumptions: a) that the generative AI tools would be used for 10 experiments with marketing copy per month, of which one would result in a win; and b) an average lift in conversions.

HUMAN-TO-HUMAN. As is demonstrated in the cases featured in this book, the marketing process of using AI is also human to human:
1. A human creates the standards to be applied
2. An AI bot turns those constant elements into algorithms, "learns," and then generates content which it outputs in a pre-determined template
3. A human evaluates, revises, and retouches to completes the process

(27) datascience-pm.com

Chapter 5_Marketing & Social Media

Because AI is carrying out many of the repetitive tasks, the marketing person now has more time for creative tasks. AI may be the more powerful tool for information, but the human mind has the unique power to process knowledge, especially as it translates into creativity and imagination, intuition, drawing from experience, emotion and empathy. Let's see how ChatGPT can help us outline a potential marketing campaign: Remember that the key is the prompt itself. We have intentionally made this first prompt rather general. asking ChatGPT for an outline of a campaign to promote a new cooking app in our newspaper. We do not immediately provide any information about the audience, the type of recipes, etc.

HOW_CHATGPT_SEES IT

PROMPT: *Act as if you are a newspaper marketing director and give me the outline of a campaign to promote a new cooking app in my newspaper.*

CHATGPT: Sure, here's an outline of a campaign to promote a new cooking app in your newspaper:
Campaign Name: "Cooking Made Easy with [Name of App]"
Target Audience: Home cooks, aspiring chefs, and anyone who enjoys experimenting with new recipes and dishes.

Campaign Objectives:
1. To increase awareness of the new cooking app among the newspaper's audience.

2. To generate interest and engagement with the app among readers.

3. To drive downloads and subscriptions for the cooking app.

→

HOW_CHATGPT_SEES IT

Campaign Tactics:
1. **Paid Advertisements** – Place visually appealing and attention-grabbing display ads in the newspaper that showcase the features of the app, its benefits, and how it can make cooking easier and more fun.

2. **Sponsored Content** – Create sponsored content that provides tips, tricks, and step-by-step guides on how to use the app for different cooking needs across various platforms including your website and social media channels.

3. **Newsletter Promotion** – Create a dedicated section in your newsletter that highlights the key features and benefits of the cooking app with a direct link to download and install the app.

4. **Social Media Engagement** – Run a social media campaign using relevant hashtags around food and cooking with image posts and captions that showcase the app's unique features such as personalized recipe recommendations and meal planning tools.

5. **Giveaways and Contests** – Generate hype around the new app by holding a contest on social media or the newspaper's website with exciting prizes like cookbooks and innovative kitchen tools.

Key Message: "Cooking made easy with [Name of app]. Get access to thousands of recipes, personalized recommendations, and meal planning tools all in one place. Download now and make cooking fun and hassle-free!"

Chapter 5_*Marketing & Social Media*

HOW_CHATGPT_SEES IT

Overall, this campaign will help promote a new app among your newspaper's readers, and it should increase engagement and downloads for the app while creating a buzz around innovation in the cooking industry.

Key Message: "Cooking made easy with [Name of app]. Get access to thousands of recipes, personalized recommendations, and meal planning tools all in one place. Download now and make cooking fun and hassle-free!"

MARIO SAYS: Not so bad. In a matter of seconds, ChatGPT, an able assistant that "thinks" fast and never tells you that it will sleep on it, or come back with ideas tomorrow, gave us some basic but good ideas to get our new cooking app promotion in high gear, among them: sponsored content, newsletter promotion and social media engagement. How about you tell ChatGPT a little bit more of what you have in mind for this campaign. Remember, key to receiving information that best suits your needs is the prompt. It is OK to tell ChatGPT to be more specific, not to lie, and to concentrate on the specifics as worded in the prompt:

PROMPT: Act as if you are a newspaper marketing director and help me to promote a new cooking app in our newspaper specializing in recipes that take less than 20 minutes to prepare! Cooking app for busy working people! Give me tips for those who work full time and come home with very little time before they serve a meal for their family

CHATGPT: Great! Here are some tips to promote your new cooking app for busy working people who are looking for quick and easy recipe solutions:

→

HOW_CHATGPT_SEES IT

1. Develop a Content Marketing Plan – Create editorial and sponsored content that provides useful tips and insights on how to save time in the kitchen and prepare meals in just 20 minutes or less. This could include recipe roundups, ingredient spotlights, and cooking hacks.

2. Utilize Social Media Channels – Share visual content (images, videos) on social media channels that highlight the convenience and simplicity of the new cooking app including a "behind the scenes" look at how the app works and how it can benefit busy working people.

3. Offer Incentives – Offer subscribers an incentive when they download the app such as a 2-week free trial or a discount on a paid subscription.

4. Run a Contest – Create buzz around the launch of the app by running a social media contest. Ask your followers to submit pictures of their homemade 20-minute meals and award a prize to the best submission.

5. Leverage Influencer Relationships – Partner with food bloggers and Instagram influencers who share similar values and target audience to promote the app through sponsored posts.

6. Email Marketing – Use email marketing to incentivize readers to sign up for the app with a "quick start" guide full of tips on how to get started with the app.

7. Targeted Ads – Use targeted ads in the newspaper, online, and social media to reach your audience with targeted ad copy focused on the quick preparation time of the app's recipes.

→

*Chapter 5_***Marketing & Social Media**

> **HOW_CHATGPT_SEES IT**
>
> Remember that the campaign should be focused on key messaging related to quick and easy recipes and how the app will help busy working people save time and effort in the kitchen. Also, use visuals that showcase this unique selling point, such as images of people with busy lifestyles finding time to cook and enjoy their meals.
> Best of luck with your new app and campaign! •

Once the prompt became more specific, the output was better a lesson we can all learn from. ChatGPT, as well as other AI applications, will draw information based on key words in the prompt. More specific requests will yield better answers and solutions. It is interesting to see a tip to offer incentives, run a contest and leverage influencer relationships. The suggestion for visuals that show busy people finding time to cook is good and could lead to the creation of the next prompt, which could read like this: Act as if you are a newspaper marketing art director and offer visual suggestions to illustrate the promotion of a new app with recipes for people too busy to cook.

Great! Here is a list of visual suggestions to illustrate a campaign promoting a new cooking app for busy people:

Use Bold Typography. Bold typography is a great way to grab attention and convey the app's messaging of making cooking easier and quicker.

Use Bold & Vibrant Colors. Bright, bold color schemes can make the app's messages pop and attract attention. Consider using bright primary colors, such as red, yellow, and blue, to evoke a sense of energy, action, and urgency.

Artistic Food Photography. Pictures of food can be an important aspect of marketing a cooking app. Use close-up photo of dishes to create a sense of appetite appeal and intrigue. Play with textures and different backgrounds to create visual contrast and depth.

Real People. Incorporating real people in your visual campaigns can add an approachable, authentic element to the visuals. Consider including images of busy working people using the app in their kitchen or enjoying their meals.

Icons and Symbols. Use minimal, playful icons and symbols to break up the copy in the visuals and draw attention to important benefits or features of the app. For example, use an image of a clock to represent quick and easy recipes or a lightning bolt to represent "easy meal prep."

Motion Graphics. Videos and animation can effectively showcase the app's key features and benefits. Consider using motion graphics to illustrate how the app works and how it can help busy people prepare meals in just 20 minutes or less.

Minimalistic Design. A minimalistic design can convey a sense of simplicity and ease which is what your target audience is looking for. Use a minimalist approach to the design of your visuals while keeping bold typography, vibrant colors, and images of delicious meals in the forefront.

By portraying a sense of excitement, urgency, and convenience through the visuals, your campaign should catch the attention of the busy people in your target audience. These visual tips will help in capturing the unique benefits and features of the app, making it clear what it offers while conveying a sense of fun and excitement. A food app needs to convey usefulness from the start. The user asks: how can I benefit from this content?

Chapter 5_Marketing & Social Media

AI AND SOCIAL MEDIA. Promoting content via social media is a big priority for publishers everywhere. The more stories are shared on social media, the more traffic is generated, which translates to more subscribers. Much of today's marketing begins with a social media post, and publishers see tremendous potential for artificial intelligence in this area.

Newsroom leaders are looking to automate, schedule, and optimize social media content creations. Some managers want to automatically repurpose existing content for social media, while others see AI original content. In many newsrooms, the task of posting story content on social media falls to the reporter who wrote the story, or a designated editor. It's a less-than-ideal system (if you can call it a system), and publishers are looking to AI to systematize that process. AI's capability for content analysis, recommendation systems, and automation make it an ideal tool for the promotion of stories on social media. Here are several ways AI can assist:

Content Analysis. AI can analyze the content of a story and identify its key themes, topics, and target audience. This analysis helps editors understand the story's potential impact on social media platforms and tailor their promotion strategies accordingly.

Audience Targeting. AI can assist in identifying the most relevant target audience for a particular story based on social media user data, demographics, interests, and engagement patterns. By leveraging AI algorithms, editors can optimize their content promotion efforts to reach the right audience, increasing the chances of engagement and sharing.

Trend Detection. AI algorithms can monitor social media platforms to detect emerging trends, discussions, and popular topics. Editors can use this information to align their stories with current trends and ensure maximum visibility and engagement.

Automated Scheduling and Posting. AI-powered tools can automate the scheduling and posting of social media content, saving editors time and effort. These tools can analyze optimal posting times, audience activity patterns, and engagement rates to determine the best times to publish and share stories on social media platforms.

Content Recommendation. AI-driven recommendation systems can suggest related stories, articles, or content that users might be interested in based on their browsing history, social media activity, and preferences. Editors can utilize these recommendation systems to promote their stories alongside relevant content, increasing the chances of attracting readers and engagement.

Sentiment Analysis. AI can analyze social media sentiment surrounding a story or topic, providing editors with insights into how audiences are responding to the content. This analysis helps editors gauge the public sentiment and adjust their promotion strategies accordingly.

A/B Testing. AI can facilitate A/B testing by automatically creating and distributing different versions of social media posts or headlines. By analyzing engagement metrics, AI algorithms can determine which versions perform better, enabling editors to optimize their promotion strategies and maximize the reach and impact of their stories.

Personalization. AI algorithms can personalize social media content based on individual user preferences, interests, and behavior. Editors can leverage AI to tailor their story promotions to specific segments of their audience, increasing the relevance and appeal of their content.

Chapter 5_**Marketing & Social Media**

CASE_STUDY_1

RINGIER (SWITZERLAND) – *Ringier AG is an innovative and diversified Swiss media and technology company operating in Europe and Africa. Its portfolio includes around 140 companies in the print, sports media, digital media, radio, ticketing entertainment sector, as well as digital marketplaces for cars, real estate, jobs, and horizontals.*

Why profile Ringier?
This media and technology company based in Zurich has used advanced Artificial Intelligence (AI) to boost digital reader engagement [28]. It uses AI for content, context and user profiling. With over 530 products Ringier executives needed a central data and technology platform containing two content profiling and interest profiling – to drive their personalization and achieve a maximum uplift for engagement and revenue. Using AI, Ringier has seen an increase in user engagement (time spent) as well as the rate of recurring visits.

A chat with Dr. Kilian Kämpfen, Ringier's Chief Technology & Data Officer (CTDO):
"We at Ringier began considering and using aspects of artificial intelligence in 2017 as a way of spurring efforts with our marketplace – cars, real estate, jobs. By 2019, AI was moving more aggressively into the editorial area of our operations, starting our collaboration with Palantir's Foundry Solution, applying their technology to build a data driven newsroom for blick.ch. Then came Newsroom integration of AI, aggregating external and internal data from various sources, and creating a strategic cooperation with a platform called Palantir [29]. This gave the editors valuable information about the type of stories that rated best with the audience, which stories to write, and which to expand."

Dr. Kämpfen says that Ringier's use of AI fell into two main categories: Content profiling and Interest profiling. How does the process work?
Content profiling – During the content profiling process, all contents are screened, enriched with public knowledge databases and analyzed using different advanced AI technologies. For written content, they use Natural Language Processing (NLP), Named Entity Recognition, Entity Linking and Sentiment Analysis. Pictures are screened with image processing

technologies, then Ringier's own self-built semantic engine "Ringier TagCloud" visualizes and clusters the contents after themes and entities (e.g. persons, places, events) using NLP and Machine Learning.

Interest profiling – The combination of the data from Ringier's cross-portfolio user behavior tracking together with detailed information gained from the content profiling enables Ringier to unveil hidden dependencies among users and build valuable user interest profiles using collaborative filtering. In advantage to market solutions, Ringier builds profiles based on three taxonomies to serve advertising (IAB) as well as media and news (IPTC) purposes. Calculations of reader interest profiles happens in real-time, allowing editors to display the right content in the right moment. "This is extremely helpful to our journalists," Dr. Kämpfen said. "By enabling several personalization and segmentation use cases, giving the editors a system that supports and identifies what stories to write."

Chapter 5_**Marketing & Social Media**

AI_PLAYERS
The Times UK: Boosting Engagement

THE TIMES (UNITED KINGDOM) – The Times is using artificial intelligence to boost engagement and reduce churn. The technology is internally referred to as JAMES (Journey Automated Messaging for Higher Engagement).

The publisher presents it as a 'digital butler' for readers, and it has helped the Times reduce subscriber churn by almost half JAMES uses data to analyze reader habits and preferences. It includes content preferences, the time when they are most likely to open the newsletter, and even things like whether they want to receive newsletters with images or not. ●

→ whatsnewinpublishing.com

ESSENTIAL_TOOLS

Smart new AI tools to improve your work

1. AISEO.AI Basically, a writing assistant. A useful free tool that can rewrite longer text into a Twitter campaign, an email, or even a script for a YouTube video. AISEO also offers Paraphraser, which uses AI to tweak written content, shortening, extending, and even changing the tone for different audiences.
→ aiseo.ai

2. GROWTHBAR Provides feedback and suggestions in the browser itself. Use it to help analyze existing content to make the most of existing marketing materials. Once the service learns a site, it can also use its AI smarts to suggest internal links to help promote content and services. Upload writing samples and GrowthBar extracts voice, tone, and style.
→ growthbarseo.com

AI NUGGETS

In 2021, the market for artificial intelligence (AI) in marketing was estimated at 15.84 billion U.S. dollars. **The source projected that the value would increase to more than 107.5 billion by 2028. More than 80% of industry experts integrate some form of AI technology into their online marketing activities**

→ blog.hubspot.com

"Those that can quickly learn and apply new technologies, those that have genuine empathy for users and customers, and those with the judgment and ability to think through hard problems have always done well in prior technology disruptions, and I'm betting they will once again."

Marty Cagan, Founder, Partner — Product at SVPG.
At *The New York Times*, she is a key stakeholder on cross-functional technical teams, including on the editorial user experience for the flagship home page.
svpg.com

re deu wave!

*Chapter 6_***Layout & Design**

Newspaper Print Layout and AI: A Good Combo

One area where artificial intelligence is already playing an essential, time-saving role is in the production of newspaper pages for print editions. The excuse in many newsrooms for not doing more with mobile storytelling is, "because the production of the print newspaper takes the oxygen out of the team, too much time spent with editor and print designer discussing a page." Automated page layout is among the most frequently requested items on print newsroom wish-lists. AI already offers journalists and designers an array of design templates for a variety of page layout: big horizontal photo at the top, one long text, two smaller images; vertical dominant photos; or long text and small vertical image. Templates are designed and stored.

Texts and images are entered, and the algorithms makes a match that suits the specific needs of the content. This is how the team of Norway's Aftenposten does it, and as editor Eirik Hammersmark Winsnes put it: "Here we are putting the print edition out daily quickly and efficiently with sort of one click." Aftenposten uses the technology of Norwegian tech firm, Aptoma, which allows it to 1) increase efficiency in page composition, 2) guarantee layout and design style continuity, and 3) allow for easy technical set up. (More about Aptoma in Chapter 9 Content Management Systems.) The following is a case study detailing how the team from Aftenposten worked to create templates to expedite print layout and production.

Chapter 6_*Layout & Design*

CASE_STUDY_1

AFTENPOSTEN (NORWAY) – *Aftenposten is Norway's largest printed newspaper by circulation. Based in Oslo, it has an estimated 1.2 million print and digital readers combined It is considered the newspaper of record for Norway. Aftenposten is part of the Schibsted group.*

Why profile Aftenposten?
Aftenposten has one of the most innovative newspaper management teams in the world. Historically, Aftenposten has introduced technology and newsroom protocols to advance digital journalism years ahead of other newspapers. It is no exception with its approach to artificial intelligence.

The team introduced an automated page layout system, with Norwegian tech firm, Aptoma. Here is a conversation with Aftenposten's Ronny Ruud, editor responsible for the editorial data tools in the newsroom, who shared his newspaper's experience using a template-based system.

"With the print automation tools from Aptoma we have been able to achieve many objectives, we can on a daily basis produce all pages rationally and efficiently with the design we want. In special cases, where a design outside of all templates is desired, there is a simple connection to InDesign, but what is good is that the designer still has full control over how the design should be, and there are no limitations to what can be done using Aptoma's tools."

"Whoever creates templates can add flexibility where elements should be and also decide which components on the page should be mandatory or optional." Ruud adds that "setting up the process is simple and has proved efficient for both journalists and designers in the newsroom."

Goals of the project
1. Produce current and potential future newspaper products as efficiently as possible with as little manual effort as possible and as cost-efficiently as possible.

2. Reduce the need for channel-specific production effort, i.e. move towards "produce once, distribute many places" operation, where print is one of several channels in which content is naturally and efficiently distributed

3. Reduce dependence on specific competence in the newsrooms (and IT support) for print production, to make us less vulnerable in production and staffing schedule.

How the automated page layout system works at Aftenposten:
• Articles are created using Aftenposten's content management system.
• Articles from the CMS are edited and adapted to the newspaper. Special content for print is added to it.
• Articles are placed on the page and are automatically assigned flexible layout.

Workflow overview

SMP → DrPublish → DrEdition → Printing

Article creating
Articles are created, written and published in Schibsted's CMS for digital publishing

Print Editing
Articles from the CMS are edited and adapted to the newspaper. Special content for print is added to it.

Pages
Articles are placed on the page and are automatically assigned flexible layout.

Aftenposten   Schibsted

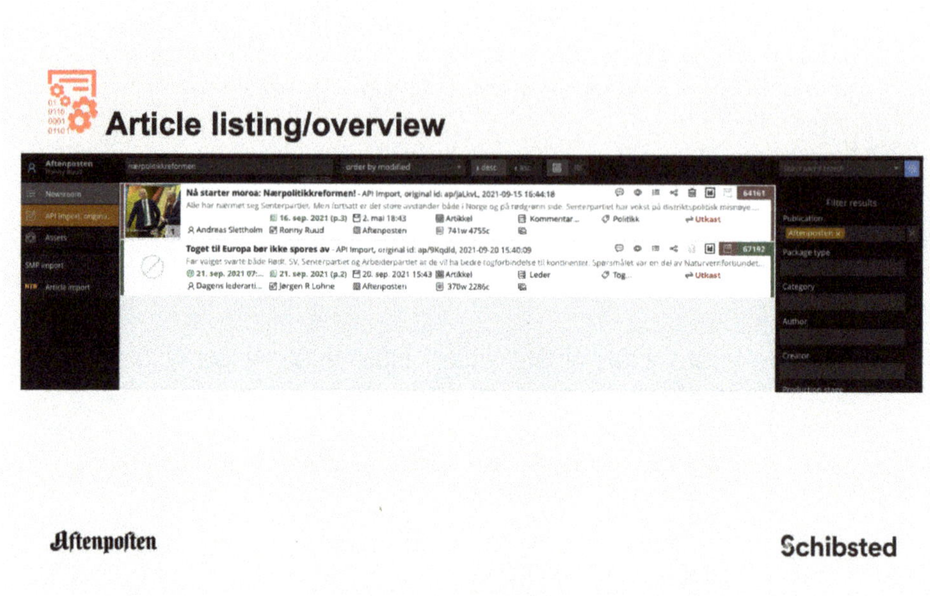

*Chapter 6_***Layout & Design**

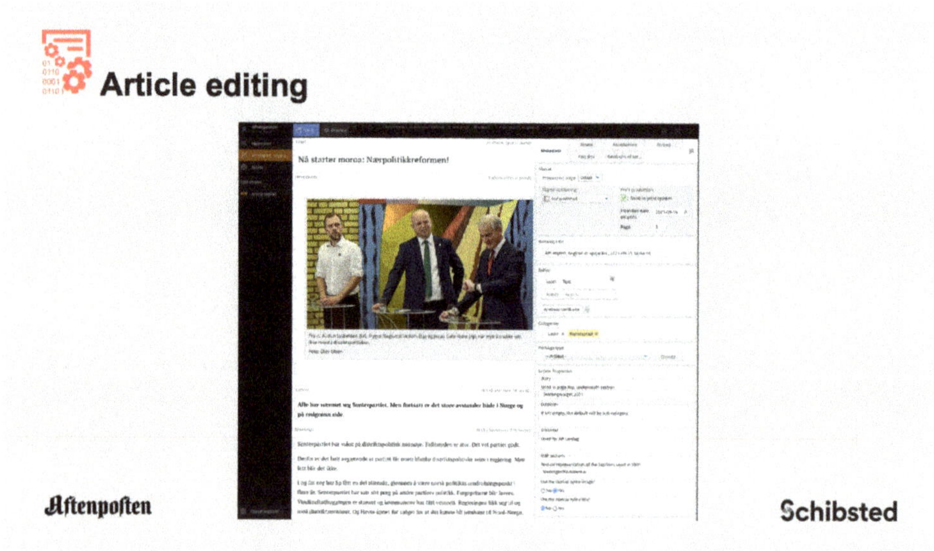

Article listing/overview

Aftenposten Schibsted

Article editing

Aftenposten Schibsted

Page plan

Page details and content disposition

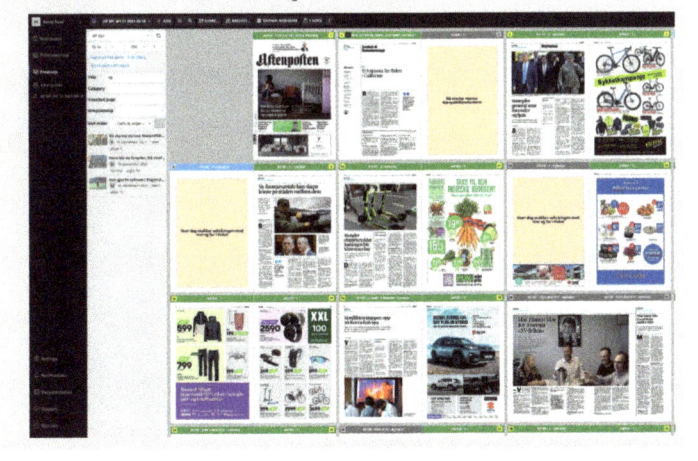

A USER'S GUIDE FOR CONTENT CREATORS – BY DR. MARIO GARCÍA
[145]

*Chapter 6_***Layout & Design**

↓ Notice the number of variations available for one page layout including a key lead photo and a single story.

Automated layout choice

Aftenpoften   Schibsted

Change of page plan

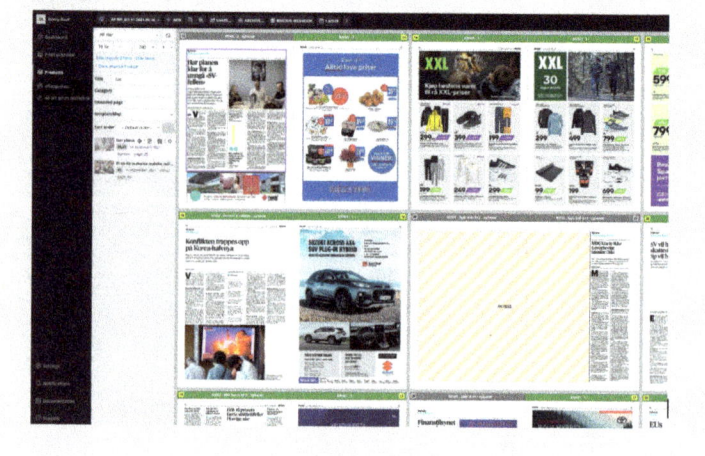

Aftenpoften

AI: WHAT TO EXPECT FOR THE NEXT REVOLUTION

↓ Designer/editor will select the automated layout that best suits the need of the story.

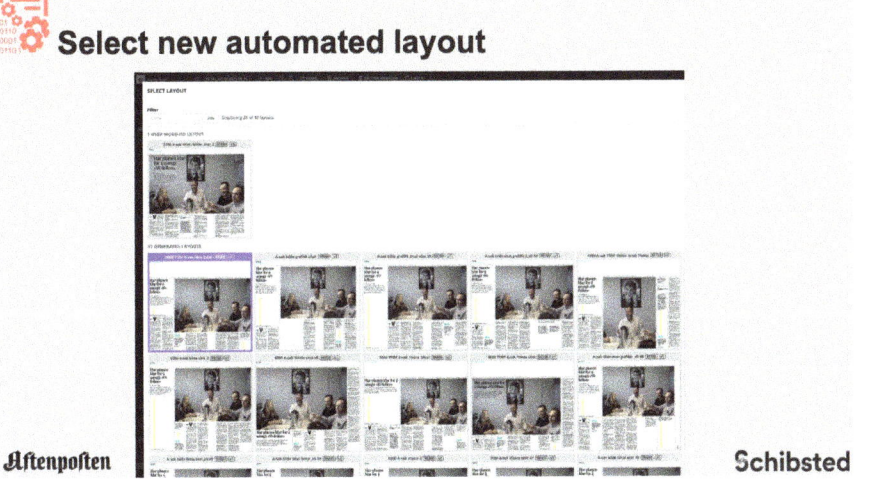

Select new automated layout

↓ Designer/editor can make adjustments once the automated system presents a page option.

Optional: detailed layout adjustments

A USER'S GUIDE FOR CONTENT CREATORS – BY DR. MARIO GARCÍA

Chapter 6_*Layout & Design*

Optional: detailed component adjustments

↓ The most essential part of the process is the creation of a diverse range of templates that consider story structure and make use of typography, grids, and color palettes. (Design components are discussed further at the end of this chapter.)

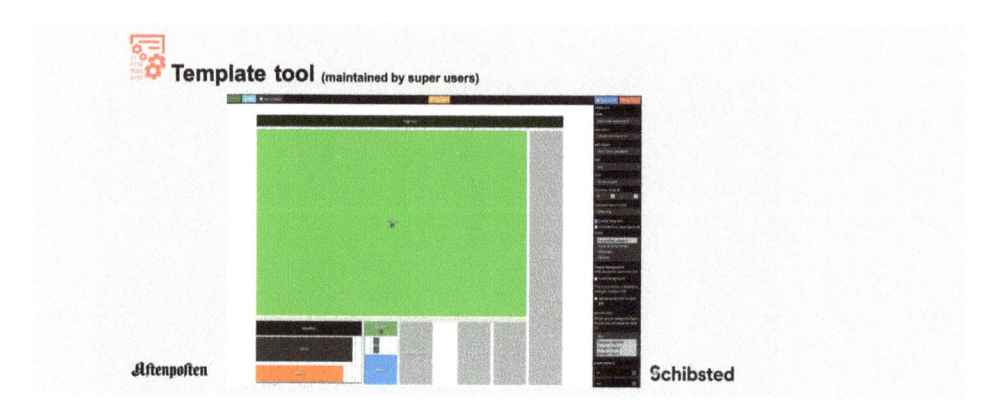

Template tool (maintained by super users)

↓ Designers and editors work together to create a robust template library featuring various styles: vertical vs. horizontal lead images; single-story vs. multi-story; variable headline size based on story hierarchy; and typographic elements such as quotes, highlighted numbers, and biographical data.

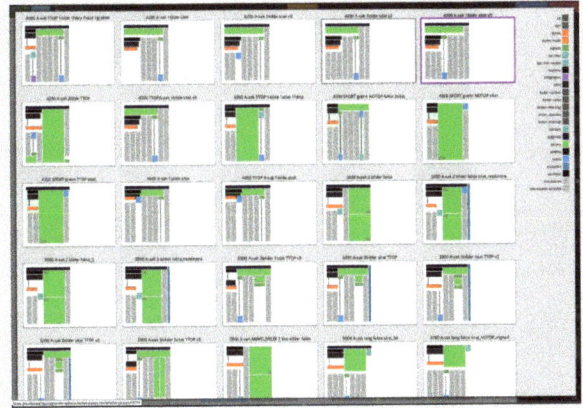

Article template library (maintained by super users)

Aftenposten — Schibsted

Chapter 6_*Layout & Design*

Optional: Front Page Tool

Aftenposten — Schibsted

What we currently are doing with Print Automation
95% of the weekly Lørdag (Saturday) supplement

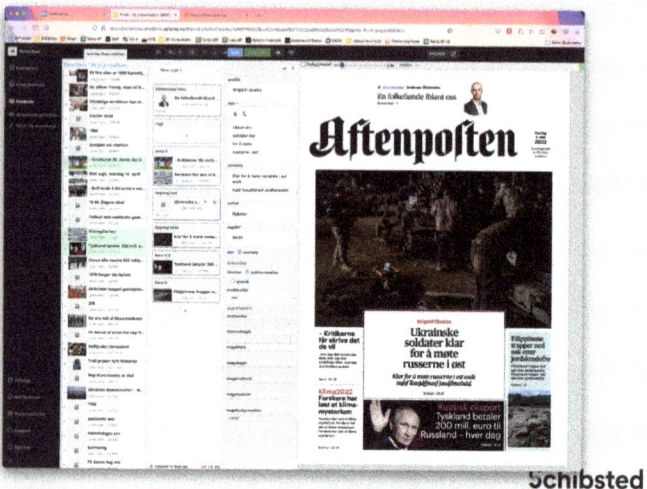

Aftenposten

AI: WHAT TO EXPECT FOR THE NEXT REVOLUTION
[150]

↓ A fast, efficient process that has saved the Aftenposten team considerable production time.

What we currently are doing with Print Automation
60-70% of the weekly Oslo supplement

*Chapter 6_***Layout & Design**

↓ Here are some Aptoma-generated template examples from the newspaper, Bergens Tidende. (Design components are discussed further at the end of this chapter.)

Our "sister newspaper" in Bergen

Aftenposten

Schibsted

100% Print Automation

Detailed layout

A USER'S GUIDE FOR CONTENT CREATORS – BY DR. MARIO GARCÍA

Chapter 6_*Layout & Design*

PRO_TIPS

Creating smart templates

Just like the wording of prompts will lead to more responsive answers from ChatGPT, more detailed templates will yield more (and better) page layout options. While templates are the best food we can feed the algorithms of artificial intelligence today, they have always been of great benefit to designers of newspapers, magazines and Web sites. Templates also need to reflect the variety of topics a typical publication publishes. From *The Story* (Thane & Prose, 2019):

> "Journalistic design is like writing a symphony. There must be violins and trombones. There must be moments of pure adagio – perhaps an elegant serif font and white space carry the reader's attention to stunning awareness. But there are also staccatos, where snippets and small chunks of information hold the reader's attention until they are ready to return to the major theme. So, templates must include stories with brief items, and with a single longer story, or a photo-driven page."

What should good templates include?

1. Hierarchy. Emphasize the importance of stories and images by size. This includes headline sizing, as well as that of photos and illustrations.

2. Rhythm. Create templates that emphasize the contrast of horizontal and vertical units.

3. White space. Build areas that are left white to allow for the eye to go from one element of the other in a cleaner, easier to navigate environment.

4. The four essential elements of design. Story structures, typography, grids and color palette.

PRO_TIPS

Design Essentials and Templates

Every design project – from a church newsletter to your latest news app – starts with consideration of what I refer to as the four essentials: story structures, type, grids and color palette. Once a designer assesses how she plans to use these essentials, the rest becomes easier.

1. Story Structures. This represents the most journalistic element in the design process. It is how we tell stories. It is the elements we create to support the creative input. Stories come in categories, and it is the job of the designer to make sure that each category has its own personality, to send signals to the readers. For instance, what is the difference between a straight news story and a signed commentary or column? How do we tell photo stories? Templates must reflect the full breadth of stories a newspaper or magazine creates.

2. Grids. Grids are the skeleton, the bones on which we put the flesh that is all the visual elements that are part of a story. Grids represent the architectural part of a design: how space is utilized, whether it is columns, the use of white space, or internal spacing between elements. Grids allow for consistency and facilitate the job of the designer. Every design project begins with the construction of a grid.

3. Typography. Most of what we see on the canvas of a page or screen is type. Indeed, we come to read The Story. So, typography ranks among the most important choices that designers make. Type must be easy to read, but also appropriate to the publication and the content for which it is intended. We will see more about type mood and the selection of type in one of the coming vignettes.

4. Color Palette. The world is in color, and so are most of the designs that we will be creating. Of course, black and white are always classic and elegant, but readers like color. Color is one of the important essentials. Designers use color judiciously. The book you hold in your hands makes heavy use of black and red,

→

Chapter 6_**Layout & Design**

PRO_TIPS

for example. Color relates to the audience, culture, and goals of a publication. The creation of a color palette guides the process for how color will be used in an app, a printed magazine, or even a poster. Overall, these four design essentials help in two specific ways:

- Creating familiarity for the readers via recurring visual elements.

- Allowing ease of production for the editors and designers by using the formulas that templates allow, while having more time to create the surprises readers crave.

HOW_CHATGPT_SEES IT

PROMPT: *Act as if you are a newspaper newsroom manager, and you would like to use Artificial Intelligence to automate the layout of pages for the print edition of the newspaper. How can AI help so that when a reporter writes an article, it can quickly be positioned on a page using templates. What are AI benefits for automating page layouts that could reduce workloads for print newsrooms? Give me data and tips.*

CHATGPT: As a newspaper newsroom manager, integrating Artificial Intelligence (AI) into the layout process can indeed offer numerous benefits and streamline operations. Here are some ways AI can help automate page layouts and reduce workloads for print newsrooms:

1. **Intelligent Template Matching:** AI algorithms can be trained to analyze the content of an article and identify the most suitable template for its placement. By considering factors such as article

→

HOW_CHATGPT_SEES IT

length, topic, and visual requirements, AI can suggest appropriate templates or even generate custom layouts.

2. Automated Content Positioning: AI can automatically position articles on the page based on predefined rules and guidelines. By analyzing the structure and content of the article, AI algorithms can determine the optimal placement to ensure visual appeal, readability, and efficient space utilization.

3. Smart Image Placement: AI can assist in selecting and placing images within articles. By understanding the context and content of the article, AI algorithms can suggest relevant images and position them appropriately. This automation can save time for designers who would otherwise manually search for suitable images.

4. Efficient Space Management: AI algorithms can optimize the use of available space on a page, ensuring a balanced and visually appealing layout. By considering various elements such as headline length, article size, and whitespace, AI can adjust the layout to maximize space utilization while maintaining readability.

5. Automated Text Flow: AI can help automate the flow of text between columns, ensuring a smooth reading experience. Algorithms can determine the appropriate line breaks, hyphenation, and column adjustments, reducing the need for manual adjustments by designers.

Chapter 6_*Layout & Design*

HOW_CHATGPT_SEES IT

6. Dynamic Content Adaptation: AI algorithms can adapt layouts to accommodate varying article lengths. Whether an article is shorter or longer than anticipated, AI can adjust the layout accordingly, maintaining consistency and visual harmony across pages.

7. Streamlined Editorial Process: AI-powered layout automation can speed up the editorial workflow by reducing manual interventions. Reporters can focus on content creation, while AI handles the placement and formatting tasks. This efficiency allows for faster turnaround times and increased productivity.

8. Design Consistency: AI can enforce design guidelines and maintain consistency across different pages and editions. By learning from previous layouts and design choices, AI algorithms can ensure a cohesive visual identity for the newspaper.

9. Performance Optimization: AI algorithms can analyze readership data, engagement metrics, and user feedback to continually improve the layout design. By understanding which layouts perform better, AI can make data-driven recommendations for future layouts, enhancing reader satisfaction and engagement.

10. Cost and Resource Savings: By automating layout tasks, print newsrooms can reduce the reliance on manual labor and potentially allocate resources more efficiently. This can lead to cost savings in terms of time, labor, and operational expenses.

→

HOW_CHATGPT_SEES IT

Here are some tips for automating page layouts with AI:

1. Data Preparation: Compile a dataset of existing layouts, templates, and design guidelines to train AI algorithms. Include a wide range of articles, styles, and formatting variations to ensure comprehensive learning.

2. Collaborative Workflow: Foster collaboration between reporters, designers, and AI systems. Encourage feedback and iterative improvements to the AI algorithms based on user experiences and insights from the newsroom team.

3. User-Friendly Interfaces: Develop intuitive interfaces that allow reporters and designers to provide input, review AI suggestions, and make necessary adjustments. The goal is to empower users to work seamlessly with AI algorithms and achieve desired layout outcomes.

4. Continuous Training: Regularly update and retrain AI models to improve accuracy, adapt to evolving design trends, and incorporate feedback from users. Consider leveraging techniques such as transfer learning to enhance performance with smaller datasets.

5. Ethical Considerations: Ensure that the AI algorithms and automation processes align with ethical guidelines, especially regarding privacy, bias, and content integrity. Regularly monitor the outputs and intervene when necessary to maintain journalistic standards.

Chapter 6_**Layout & Design**

AI NUGGETS

Geoffrey Hinton, "the Godfather of AI," **believes that deep learning can achieve and even surpass human-like intelligence. During a talk at King's College in London, he suggested that AI systems could have feelings like frustration and anger.**

→ the-decoder.com

AI and Typography

"Looking at typography developed by artificial intelligence is like looking at lettering submerged in deep water-warped and fuzzy. It looks like a copy of a copy of a copy! The words are recognizable (barely) but the original form has been lost. AI typography is, to put it charitably, bad." [28]

That description of the relationship between AI and typography, from WIRED Magazine's Geoffrey Bunting, is not so far from how type experts currently see AI's contribution to the creation of fonts. Bunting, a designer and typographer, adds: "The key to setting AI typography on a better, more accessible path is to think of it as assistive rather than generative… If AI can be used to help typographers, rather than to try to supplant them, generative models could just be a blip on the way to a more efficient and accessible use of this technology as an assistive tool in the type design process." Others, like Christopher Reardon, see AI helping with the personalization of fonts. "Fonts will adapt to suit the needs of a person's eyesight," he says. "Fonts will work for your eyesight, AI will manipulate what is on the screen, if you are in the street maybe AI will change to larger type, or from serif to sans serif in a dynamic fashion."

"If you are a typographer, what it could do is quickly simulate different scenarios, 'building an a,' showing in the context. I can

[28] wired.com

even imagine AI allowing us to have a biologically simulated font. The font is a living entity and it grows and moves, in evolutionary directions. When you put words together they build shapes, sort of a sculptural feel for type," Reardon said. Type designers, too, are beginning to experiment with AI and font creation. An example is Peter Bil'ak, of Peter Bil'ak / Typotheque:

"These days, Typotheque works with all living languages, and some are more complicated than others. Designing Chinese fonts appeared as ideal case study for testing AI. We spent months trying to use see if we could train neural models on a relatively small sample of characters -5,000 -7,000- and use it to generate a set of about 35.000 characters. The conclusion was that it is possible and saves considerable amount of time. But we also noticed while the results are solid, they are compromised and not matching our standards and fitting our intentions."

When will the contribution of AI to typography become more efficient? It is a slow process, but in motion, nonetheless. Sam Barlow, Chief Product Officer of The Type Founders, agrees. "AI in type design is at an early stage, although some production tasks have been using AI for the past few years. Yet, original drawing is still in its infancy. The ability for Generative AI to make fonts is currently based on open-source fonts, as all other fonts are not allowed in the ML."

Perhaps it is a matter of visualization, after all. Most type designers keep notebooks with sketches of letter forms. These designers visualize, then sketch. Their sketches often include magnificent hand, drawn renditions of a letter 'a,' or a 'q' with a swash that sets it apart. How can AI get to that visualization stage, one that is not limited to type designers?

Recently, when legendary Broadway set designer, Robin Wagner, died, the obituary in The New York Times quoted him on this topic:

"When I'm reading the script, I can see it, how it fits together and how you get from one scene to another, I guess that's what makes designers – they visualize things a certain way."
In a briefing meeting on day one of a design project, you

Chapter 6_**Layout & Design**

might hear what the main stakeholders have as goals. And as that conversation is taking place, the sketchpad of the mind is open and the mental scribbling begins. It is a magnificent visualization process that perhaps only humans can experience, from those who design cars to theater sets to buildings. Indeed, in the world of architecture, where AI is also making inroads, the conversation is taking place, as per Phillip Bernstein's book, Machine Learning: Architecture in the age of Artificial Intelligence. Bernstein concludes that the adoption of AI in the design professions will not lead to the to the rise of a new breed of post-human designers, but to the development of more intelligent design tools. He urges architects to think of AI in a way that would be good for all designers to embrace: "The advent of machine learning-based AI systems demands that our industry does not just share toys but builds a new sandbox in which to play with them." [29]

And what a fun sandbox it would be, in which the humans lead with understanding a world in which computers often do much of the construction. In discussing the prospects of AI and architectural design, Mario Carpo, a professor of architectural theory and history at the Bartlett, University College London, explains a point which is at the heart of any discussion of AI and design generally: "Artificial intelligence can now reliably solve problems and make choices. But data-driven artificial intelligence solves problems by iterative optimization, and problems must be quantifiable in order to be optimizable. Consequently, the field of action of data-driven artificial intelligence as a design tool is by its very nature limited to tasks involving measurable phenomena and factors. Unfortunately, architectural design as a whole cannot be easily translated into numbers. Don't misunderstand me: architectural drawings have been digitized for a long time; but no one has found to date a consensual metric to assess values in architectural design." [30]

Perhaps the greatest American architect, Frank Lloyd Wright, would agree: "A great architect is not made by way of a brain nearly so much as he is made by way of a cultivated, enriched heart." [31]

(29) Machine Learning: Architecture in the age of Artificial Intelligence Phillip Bernstein, Riba, 2022.
(30) e-flux.com
(31) brainyquote.com

"Artificial Intelligence is not a substitute for human creativity in design. As a new tool, it allows us to explore ideas that we haven't thought of before, expanding our vision to go far beyond what we have been doing. Used wisely, it has the possibility to enhance our ability to communicate in more compelling and effective ways."

Dr. Pegie Stark, artist, designer, author, color expert

Chapter 6_*Layout & Design*

CASE_STUDY_2

TPTQ SANS CJK PETER BIĽAK, TYPOTHEQUE (NETHERLANDS) – *Peter Biľak is a multidisciplinary designer based in the Netherlands. He is the founder of Typotheque, which specializes in type design, typography and branding.*

We contacted Peter Biľak, of Typotheque, with a general question: As a major type creation firm, what are you and your type artists doing with artificial intelligence. This is what Biľak replied:
"Just like others we have been following the development and considering how to use AI. These days, Typotheque works with all living languages, and some are more complicated than others. Designing Chinese fonts appeared as ideal case study for testing AI. We spent months trying to use see if we could train neural models on a relatively small sample of characters (5,000 – 7,000) and use it to generate a set of about 35,000 characters. The conclusion was that it is possible and saves considerable amount of time. But we also noticed while the results are solid, they are compromised and not matching our standards and fitting our intentions." Here is a Netherlands-based type firm using AI for the creation of a Chinese language font.

In their own words
The first step in any of our research projects is to make a meta study, looking at what has been done in the in the same domain, what tools and methods exist, what are the major problems, why some projects failed or were successful. The method of creating Chinese fonts have not changed since the 1990s and is rather antiquated by now. Traditionally, Chinese designers draw the outlines of all those characters by hand, on a millimeter grid paper, scan the drawings, and digitize them. Very large teams are needed to handle the work, resulting in about 50,000+ man-hours of work. We have undertaken a yearlong research to understand the common practices by the local type foundries, and also to explore how the process of creation of Hanzi fonts can be made more efficient, while still getting authentic and modern Hanzi fonts. The basic premise was that there is a room for technological innovation, to produce high quality CJK fonts.

The inspiration for a more efficient way to build Chinese characters comes from the graphically organized Chinese-only dictionaries. While the dictionary may contain tens of thousands of characters, even the most complex Chinese character is made from just 57 strokes. All Chinese characters are made out of combinations of 32 basic strokes. The Chinese-only dictionaries are sorted by the radical (key stroke) and then by the number of strokes added to the radical to form the full character. The dictionary publishers have data about how each character is built up from radicals and individual strokes. For example, the most frequent character 头 is made from a radical 大, and two simple strokes ⼂ and 丶. The radical 大 can be further decomposed to three elementary strokes. 一 + ⼂ + ⼂ .

We were in discussion with a Chinese language learning software Wenlin, and considered licensed their character database. In the second phase we plan to design a library of strokes and their design spaces. That allows us to add visual parameters to each stroke, controlling them with sliders, changing their length, direction, weight, etc. When we combine the dictionary data with our parametric strokes, we can get the basic characters in a very efficient way, compared to drawing their contours by hand. The most work will be manually reviewing and fine-tuning the generated characters. This is an unprecedented process, which modernizes antiquated way of production. After making a prototype of this technique, we've abandoned the project. As expected the production is very fast, but we realized that with the parametric method of drawing, there is no room to control the minute details, which is critical for the Han characters. The results were very rudimentary, and to improve them, we'd have to review all glyphs manually, defeating the purpose of the initial automation.

As the AI started making rounds, and we looked at early experiments. As of the time of writing, all of them with just bitmaps, and not allowing creating high resolution vector drawings (yet). With the help of AIZI we algorithmically generated thousands of new characters [32] and attempted to measure the positions of the radicals, to define affine transformations so we could compose our vector drawings based on the values of the transformations. This was of some value, but still needs to be controlled by an art director, and when not

(32) ecal.ch

Chapter 6_**Layout & Design**

supervised, it creates substandard characters. Ultimately, we created our own tools that help reviewing the relationships between Han radicals – the key graphical component to generate other Chinese characters. So AI was explored but used in our typeface TPTQ Sans CJK (it just won this year's TDC awards, and will be lunched publicly later this year.) We continue monitoring possibilities of AI and other automated tools, but now prioritize durability of the project and not just shortening of the production.

HOW_CHATGPT_SEES IT

PROMPT: *Act as if you are a type font creator and show me ways in which AI can help me develop a new font that will be modern, highly legible and adapt to both digital and print utilization.*

CHATGPT: As an AI, I can provide you with some ways in which AI can assist in developing a new font that is modern, highly legible, and adaptable to both digital and print utilization:

1. Data-driven analysis: AI can analyze large amounts of font data, including existing fonts and user preferences, to identify patterns and trends that contribute to legibility and modern aesthetics. This analysis can inform your font design process and help you make informed decisions.

2. Generative modeling: AI-powered generative models can assist in generating font variations based on specified design parameters. You can input desired characteristics such as stroke width, letter spacing, and curvature, and the AI model can generate font samples that meet your requirements. This enables you to explore a wide range of possibilities quickly.

→

HOW_CHATGPT_SEES IT

3. User feedback analysis: AI can analyze user feedback and reviews of existing fonts to understand what aspects are appreciated and what can be improved. This analysis can help you identify common pain points and preferences to guide your font design process.

4. Optimization for digital and print: AI can help optimize the font design for both digital and print utilization. By analyzing characteristics like letter spacing, contrast, and glyph shapes, AI can suggest adjustments to ensure legibility and visual consistency across different mediums.

5. Accessibility considerations: AI can assist in ensuring that your font is accessible to a wide range of users, including those with visual impairments. By analyzing contrast ratios, character spacing, and other accessibility factors, AI can provide insights to enhance legibility and readability for diverse user needs.

6. Font testing and simulation: AI can simulate how your font will look across various digital and print platforms and in different sizes. This can help you identify any potential issues and make adjustments to ensure optimal legibility and visual consistency across different usage scenarios.

The font creation process begins and ends with your expertise as a font designer and typographer, but AI is an extremely powerful tool that can aid you in the process. ●

Chapter 6_*Layout & Design*

CASE_STUDY_3

AXEL SPRINGER (GERMANY) – *Axel Springer is a media and technology company based in Germany but active in more than 40 countries with a diversity of titles and media brands that include (among others BILD, WELT, INSIDER, POLITICO) and classifieds portals (StepStone Group and AVIV Group). Axel Springer is also one of the most innovative media groups in the world, as exemplified by the experimentation and implementation of programs related to artificial intelligence.*

Why profile Axel Springer?

Axel Springer is incorporating AI into the journalistic and design related tasks in the newsroom. While it continues to produce printed products such as the newspapers Bild and Die Welt, CEO Mathias Doepfner is devoted to creating a purely digital company. And he is committed to AI. He says that this revolution in information will soon be better at the "aggregation of information" than human journalists, and that the team will follow. That is exactly what is happening at Axel Springer. "Understanding this change is essential to a publishing house's future viability. Only those who create the best original content will survive," Doepfner told his team in a memo.

What is interesting about Axel Springer and AI?

AI lays out tomorrow's print edition of the newspaper – an insightful centerpiece of how AI can be used in the newsroom is an experiment Axel Springer is currently conducting by having AI do the layout of its print newspaper products. "We have the tech team exploring a full digital AI-driven layout process in parallel. This is all about letting a machine do the layout of tomorrow's newspaper," says Adib Sisani, Global Head of Communications & Sustainability. "We are in the test phase, but it is fascinating to realize how much of what we thought sacred can be done by machines." In terms of laying out a newspaper those "sacred" activities involve dealing with space and distance (how long is the story? How many columns will the story cover? Is there a photo, illustration or graphic? If so, what is its size? Will color be applied anywhere? [33]

---

[33] theguardian.com

AI NUGGETS

"BMW's design boss Adrian van Hooydonk said that the Bavarian brand has experimented with AI design. Thankfully, he also said it won't be replacing any humans."

→ bmwblog.com

FOX Sports expanded its partnership with Google Cloud, with plans to apply AI across its vast sports footage archives. Using Google's Vertex AI Vision, FOX plans to rapidly search 1.9M videos to create new content and assets, automating manual processes.

→ prnewswire.com

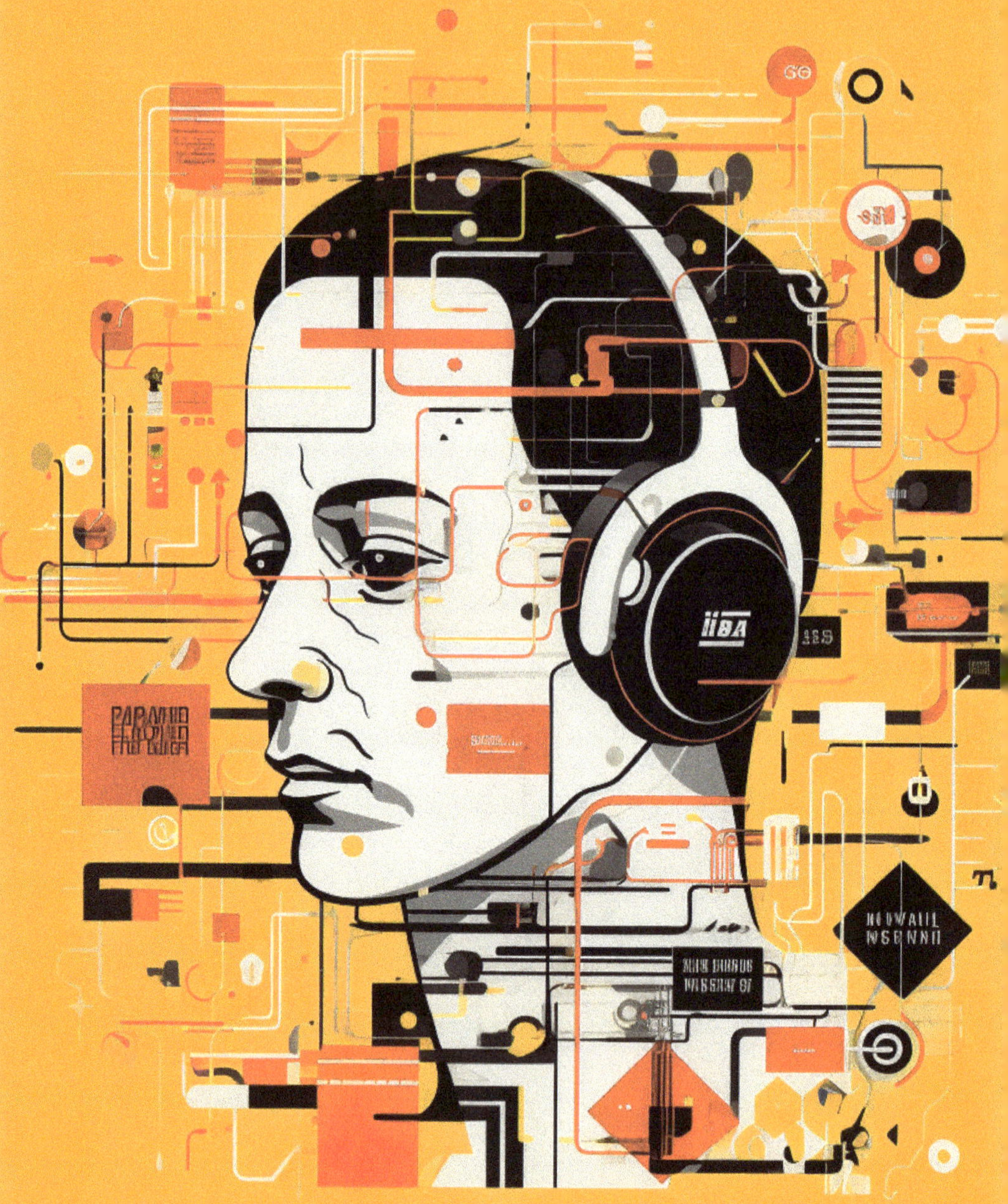

*Chapter 7_***Corporate Communications**

AI Assists Corporate Communications Teams

M**any corporate communications teams are actually bigger than those of journalistic publications. And it is far from rare for corporate communications professionals to have started their professional lives in newsrooms. One seasoned professional (hint: his name is on the cover of this book) conducts various workshops all over the world, and when he meets with corporate communications teams, he always begins,** "Raise your hand if you got your start as a reporter in a newspaper or magazine." And the hands go up. The conversations are always fruitful, and typically reveal common legacy issues:

1. Too much consideration of text as the dominant feature for most stories
2. Over-reliance on square formats, as opposed to scrolling and mobile consumption
3. Narrowly thinking of a campaign as the ultimate goal, as opposed to daily updates of stories and campaigns

Unlike journalists in newsrooms who cater to a broader audience, corporate communication practitioners focus on promoting a specific product or company. How can artificial intelligence assist corporate communication teams whose writers and editors are churning out copy for a specific client firm? AI-Powered Writing Assistance: One of the significant applications

Chapter 7_Corporate Communications

of AI in corporate communications is providing writing assistance to practitioners. AI-powered tools, such as natural language processing (NLP) algorithms, offer automated grammar and spell-checking, suggest improvements for sentence structure, and provide style and tone recommendations. These tools enhance the overall quality and efficiency of corporate communication writing, enabling practitioners to produce polished reports, press releases, and other written content.

Data Analytics and Insights: Corporate communication teams often rely on data to understand their audience, monitor sentiment, and evaluate the effectiveness of their messaging. AI can be utilized to analyze vast amounts of data quickly and extract valuable insights. By employing machine learning algorithms, companies can identify patterns, trends, and sentiments from social media conversations, customer feedback, and media coverage. This data-driven approach helps in formulating targeted and impactful communication strategies, ensuring better engagement with stakeholders.

Content Generation: Creating engaging and persuasive content is crucial for corporate communication practitioners. AI-powered content generation tools leverage natural language generation (NLG) algorithms to generate compelling narratives, articles, and reports based on structured data inputs. These tools can automate the process of generating press releases, corporate announcements, and internal communications. While AI-generated content may lack the nuanced human touch, it can provide a starting point for writers, saving time and effort in the initial drafting stages.

Personalized Communication: With the rise of AI-powered chatbots and virtual assistants, corporate communication teams can provide personalized and interactive experiences for customers and stakeholders. Chatbots can assist in responding to frequently asked questions, guiding users through product information, and addressing customer concerns promptly. These virtual assistants enhance customer satisfaction, streamline communication processes, and contribute to the overall brand image. Crisis Management and Reputation Monitoring: AI technologies play a significant role in monitoring and managing corporate reputation. AI-powered tools can scan social media platforms, news outlets, and online forums to identify potential crises and emerging issues. Sentiment analysis algorithms help gauge public opinion and assess the impact of communication efforts. By detecting and responding to negative sentiment in real-time, corporate communication teams can mitigate potential reputation damage and implement proactive crisis management strategies.

CASE_STUDY_1

GREGORY FCA PUBLIC RELATIONS (USA) – *Greg Matusky is President and founder of Gregory FCA, the region's largest integrated public relations and investor relations firm, serving private and publicly traded companies throughout the country.*

Why profile Gregory FCA Public Relations?
Gregory FCA is a prominent public relations (PR) company based in Ardmore, Pennsylvania with offices in New York City. The company specializes in providing strategic communications and PR services to a wide range of clients, including corporations, startups, non-profit organizations, and individuals. With over 32 years of experience, Gregory FCA has established itself as a leading national PR agency. Gregory FCA grows businesses by identifying and amplifying stories through earned and owned media channels. Gregory FCA is one of the first corporate communications firms to engage with AI, using it not just as a writing assistance tool, but also for help with outlining and developing documentaries, as we will see in this case study.

→

Chapter 7_**Corporate Communications**

A chat with CEO Greg Matusky
Greg Matusky is the CEO & Founder of Gregory FCA Public Relations. He founded Gregory FCA in 1990 after working as a contributing editor for Success magazine. His work has appeared in major national magazines like Forbes, Inc. and Newsweek. For much of his career, he struggled to teach others how to write.

So how did he transition from a writer to pioneering the use of artificial intelligence in a corporate communications setting?
"It was my son the engineer who pulled me aside one day and told me that he could digitize my writing process. He put me through a series of exercises. He questioned how we approached content, and little by little, we were developing new work processes. We saw AI on the horizon, and we built our own internal AI platform, which we called Gladwrite, as a reference to Malcolm Gladwell – one of Matusky's favorite writers. Then In November 2022, OpenAI came out with ChatGPT, and Matusky says it was "an epiphany."
"I was delighted to see language appear on my screen that was sensible, usable. The whole idea is to spur understanding, and if I can help and AI can help the world to spur understanding, it is a tool for good. I have translated from English to Spanish using AI with great results. If we can talk to anyone effectively, wouldn't that be good for the world?" Matusky immediately realized that generative AI was much more than a content generator, it was also played the role of a personal assistant, improving workflow and allowing for unimaginable opportunities to brainstorm.

AI: "Mind blowing"
Here is an example of how AI helped Matusky's team write the script for a documentary. As Matusky describes it: "I had never written a documentary, but we had to put one together. I thought I would engage the help of AI."
It began with a detailed, 400-word prompt to AI, explaining the client's briefing. "It is key to write a prompt that explains as much as possible at the beginning of the creative process. The prompt is the most important part of the project for good results. Here is where the human factor plays an essential role. Create a prompt that is longer and more in depth than shorter, lots of facts, in this case of the documentary – we started at the top, this is the

project, located here, how it is going to happen, natural language, don't worry about grammar, etc." Here is the prompt as it appeared for the documentary:

PROMPT: Help me write a script for a new documentary about the development of an industrial park called River Park in Longworth, Pennsylvania. River Park will bring more than 4,000 good paying jobs to the borough, and it will stabilize the local tax base. The borough and the school district are strapped for revenue. River Park will bring in more than $4 million of new tax revenue for the borough to improve life safety and will eliminate the possibility of future tax increases. Additionally, its sister project, the remediation of the former coal-fired electric generation plant, will clean up one of the Easton River's biggest eye sores. For decades the plant was one of the biggest polluters in the area, and its rusted infrastructure and massive 400ft Smokestacks still loom over the region.

The developer of River Park, Lou Parker, was the only business willing to clean the site and remove the eye sore, which was made possible by the economic vitality that River Park, located across the road from the old power plant, will bring to the area. It's important to note that River Park is not another logistics warehouse. It is positioned to attract world-class manufacturers, which pay higher wages and provide better jobs than warehouse work. River Park does face opposition, much of which comes from those who do not pay their fair share of property taxes. Nearly 88% of the town's property owners receive tax abatements or reductions, which protects the area's farmland. But these loud voices ignore those who have to carry more of the burden.

The documentary will interview two property owners who support the development and are opposed to any more tax increases. It will also include an interview with the chief of the local fire department, which desperately needs new equipment and training, but can't afford it. The documentary will include the school superintendent, who will explain the budget challenges the school is facing and its need to increase property taxes if the town fails to diversify its tax base and add revenue from commercial or industrial sources. Please open the documentary with video of the abandoned power plant and explain the value

Chapter 7_Corporate Communications

of it being cleaned up in a responsible way that no longer threatens the air and water quality of the region. Explain that the developer is taking a huge risk to clean up the local environment. In exchange River Park will only comprise 2% of the town's land mass but provide a smart, ecological solution to a long-term problem-both the abandoned plant and the need for revenue.

RESPONSE: [Opening scene: Drone footage of the abandoned power plant. Its rusted infrastructure and massive Smokestacks loom large over the Easton River. As the camera glides over the area, the narrator begins.]

NARRATOR: In the heart of Pennsylvania, along the Easton River, sits a monolith of the past – the former Genon Coal fire electric generation plant. For decades, this plant was one of the area's most prolific polluters, its rusted infrastructure a stark reminder of a time gone by. But change is coming and with it, a new hope for the future.

PARKER: The beauty of River Park lies not just in its potential to stimulate the local economy, but also in the responsible way it interacts with the local environment. [Back to Narrator with video of the abandoned power plant again.]

NARRATOR: Indeed, the sister project to River Park is the remediation of the former
power plant. The cleanup will finally eradicate this long-standing eyesore and ensure that it no longer threatens the air and water quality of this beautiful region. [Transition to video footage of the borough and its residents.]

NARRATOR: The benefits of River Park will ripple through the community. It's projected to bring over 4,000 good-paying jobs, stabilizing the local tax base and injecting more than $4 million of new tax revenue. This crucial funding will improve life safety services and eliminate the threat of future tax increases for borough residents. [Cuts to interviews with property owners and the fire department chief.]

NARRATOR: But change often encounters resistance, and River Park is no exception. Some critics are those who benefit from tax reductions and abatements. However, many residents, like these property owners, welcome the development. They bear the burden of ever-increasing taxes, and River Park offers a promising solution. [Cut to scenes of farmland.]

NARRATOR: Therein lies the crux of the issue. A delicate balance between preserving the borough's farmlands and fostering economic development. River Park aims to strike that balance, utilizing a mere 2% of the town's land mass, but promising substantial economic and environmental gains. [Closing with aerial shots of the River Park development site, the school, and the fire department.]

NARRATOR: With this change, Longworth faces a brighter future – a future where its citizens no longer fear tax hikes, where the school district and fire department can confidently invest in their growth, and where an abandoned coal plant becomes a symbol of renewal and progress. This is the story of River Park.[Screen fades to black. The title appears: "River Park: Renewal, Progress, Hope."]. [End of Act One.]

PROMPT: Can you now write Act 2? This should concentrate on the tax issues facing the borough and the need for a reasoned and responsible approach to balancing development with the needs of the local community. Also, explain why River Park is so ripe for the time. Located in a three-hour drive of 30% of the US GDP, which easy access to major interstates like I-80 and the PA and NJ turnpikes, it offers manufacturers a dream location with an excellent workforce of local residents eager to benefit from high-paying family-supporting wages that manufacturing can provide. Also, make a point to explain the reshoring of American manufacturing.

The recent pandemic and global unrest have highlighted the fragility of global supply chains that extend throughout the world. The logistics nightmare of the past three years has convinced many American manufacturers of the need to return the production of essential parts and technologies here to the US. The

Chapter 7_Corporate Communications

developer, Lou Park, is seeing unimaginable interest from a new generation of producers, everything from chip manufacturers to green vertical indoor greenhouses. These are not the low-paying jobs of Amazon or UPS warehouses. Rather, they are the higher paying, environment and new economy jobs that Parker believes will return the area to the manufacturing giant it once was. To lure these kinds of businesses, Parker says requires scale and infrastructure. To accommodate these businesses, Parker is making large-scale power and water available to future tenants-more evidence that River Park is not marketing to warehouses-which have low water and power requirements. Regardless of any opposition, he says he has all the zoning and approvals the site needs to build these homes for future American businesses and the jobs and tax revenue they will bring to not only Longworth but the entire region.

RESPONSE: [Opening Scene: Act II begins with a view of the borough, focusing on shops, houses, schools, and other infrastructure.]

NARRATOR: As we delve deeper into the story of River Park, we see a tale not just of industrial development but of a community on the precipice of change. Longworth borough, like many communities across America, grapples with a delicate balance – the need for growth and the demands of its citizens. [Cut to footage of borough council meetings, school board meetings, and local citizens voicing concerns about taxes.]

NARRATOR: The heart of the issue lies in the town's tax structure. With nearly 88% of the town's property owners receiving tax abatements or reductions, a sizable burden falls on the remainder. River Park promises to alleviate this imbalance by providing a substantial new source of tax revenue, thereby lightening the load for these property owners. [Transition to Lou Parker discussing development plans.]

PARKER: River Park is not only timely but necessary. Situated within a three-hour drive of 30% of the U.S. GDP and with easy access to major interstates like I-80 and the PA and NJ Turnpikes, it's a dream location for manufacturers. [Video montage showing highways, population density maps, and manufacturing industries.]

NARRATOR: Parker is banking on an encouraging trend – the reshoring of American manufacturing. The recent global pandemic and subsequent unrest highlighted the fragility of our global supply chains. This has spurred a renewed interest in bringing the production of essential parts and technologies back to the U.S. [Cut to images of different industries reshoring their manufacturing processes.]

NARRATOR: From chip manufacturers to vertical indoor greenhouses, a new generation of producers is showing unprecedented interest in River Park. These aren't the low-paying jobs of the past. Rather, these are high-paying, environmentally friendly, new economy jobs that could restore the region to its former glory as a manufacturing powerhouse. [Cut to Lou Parker.]

PARKER: To attract these kinds of businesses, we need scale and infrastructure. That's why we're investing in significant power and water supplies – something that typical warehouses don't require. [Cut to a visual of the approved zoning plans for River Park.]

NARRATOR: Despite opposition, River Park presses ahead. With all the necessary zoning and approvals secured, the site is poised to become a home for future American businesses and the jobs they'll bring. This will not only benefit Longworth, but also the entire region. [Closing Scene: Drone shot of the entire region.]

NARRATOR: This is the story of River Park, a tale of revitalization and economic resurgence. It's a tale about striking a balance – between growth and preservation, industry and agriculture, old and new. Above all, it's about a small town on the cusp of a big change, a change that is as much about the land as it is about the people who call this place home. [Screen fades to black. Act II ends.]. [End of Act II.]

Chapter 7_Corporate Communications

PRO_TIPS

Prompting AI is key step. (See Chapter 8 – Prompt Engineering)
Greg Matusky admonishes his team to know their topic as much as they possibly can, and offers this 5-point guide on how to get the best results from AI:

Audience: To whom is this material directed?
Voice: Who is doing the talking? The CEO? The CIO? The CMO? Or is it an expert?
Facts: The more the better. Populate the prompt with as many as possible.
Tone: Should the tone be conversational, analytical, lighthearted?
Hierarchy: In what structure would like the various elements to appear?

AI NUGGETS

86% of communications professionals globally see artificial intelligence (AI) as an opportunity rather than a risk.
"AI in Communications-Industry Opportunities and Risks" which is based on the survey of 406 communications professionals, conducted in March 2023 in five continents globally, finds that 86% are also positive about advances in generative AI specifically.

→ sandpipercomms.com

As technology evolves rapidly, and image generation alternatives become more pervasive, it becomes ever more complex to distinguish authentic images and artificial ones. Google has tested a new AI watermarking tool called SynthID, aiming to help distinguish AI images while curbing disinformation and deepfakes. It works by embedding changes to individual pixels in images so watermarks are invisible to the human eye, but detectable by computers.

→ sandpipercomms.com

"I believe that the integration of AI in corporate communications is a game-changer. It empowers practitioners to leverage data-driven insights, enhance writing efficiency, and personalize communication experiences. AI is not a replacement for human creativity and expertise, but rather a powerful tool that amplifies our ability to connect, engage, and build meaningful relationships with stakeholders."

May Habib, CEO, co-founder and CEO of Writer, an AI writing assistant for teams

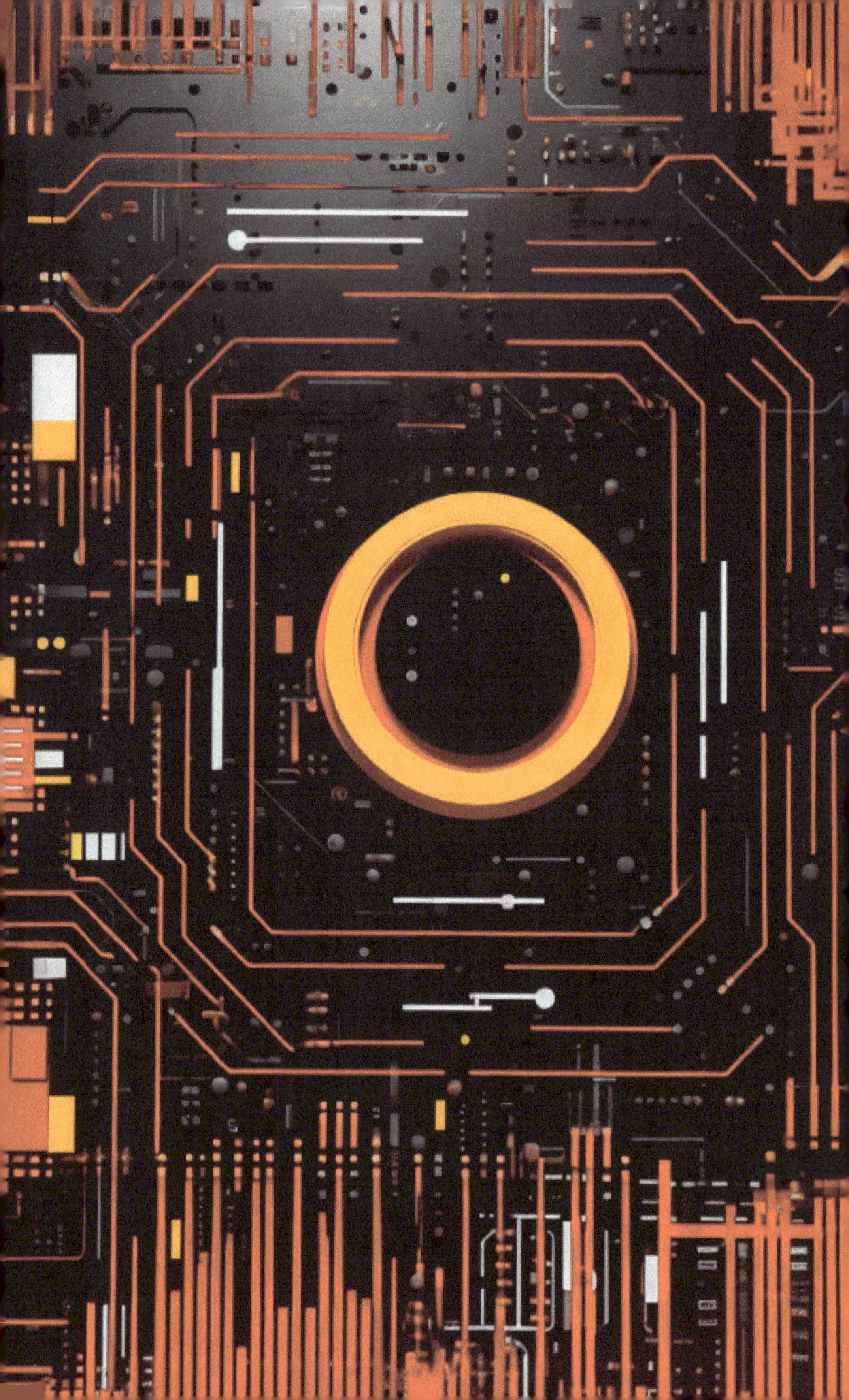

Chapter 8_**Prompt Engineering**

Act as If...

The New York Times tech writer, Brian X. Chen, suggests that the best way to get good results from ChatGPT is to use specific golden prompts, which begin with using "Act as if..." Beginning your prompt with these three words will instruct the bot to emulate an expert. For example, typing "Act as if you are a choreographer..." or "Act as if you are an architect..." will guide the bots to model themselves on people in those professions. Welcome to the world of engineering prompts, a skill critical to navigating the intricacies and challenges of artificial intelligence. Do not be surprised when you hear that "prompt engineering" has developed as a discipline all its own.

Some experts say that the power of prompt engineering lies in the hands of those who express themselves best-exactly what is said of people who succeed at job interviewing and essay writing for college admissions. AI is primarily about language. It is about words and how a string of them can create thoughts and light up the path to an infinite amount of information, organized and detailed quickly by the AI bot.

Tips and examples will make your prompts more detailed, realistic and abundant with word clues that the bot can utilize. Let's review some of those tips, starting with ChatGPT's own version of how good prompts should be.

Chapter 8_Prompt Engineering

HOW_CHATGPT_SEES IT

PROMPT: *Act as if you are a writer offering tips in the art of prompt engineering for AI. Give me 10 tips on how to write the best, most descriptive prompts for a bot like you.*

CHATGPT: As a writer, I'm delighted to offer you ten valuable tips on crafting exceptional and descriptive prompts for AI. These tips will assist you in generating engaging conversations and getting the most out of your interactions with AI models like me. Let's dive in!

1. Be clear and specific: Clearly communicate what you want from the AI. Ambiguity can lead to unpredictable responses. State your desired outcome or ask direct questions to guide the AI's response.

2. Set the context: Provide relevant background information or context to help the AI understand the scenario better. The more details you give, the richer and more accurate the response will be.

3. Use vivid language: Employ descriptive and engaging language to evoke a clear image or mood. The AI responds well to prompts that stimulate the senses and create a vibrant setting.

4. Incorporate emotion: Emotions add depth and realism to conversations. Encourage the AI to express feelings or ask about its emotional state to elicit more human-like responses.

5. Ask for opinions and perspectives: To encourage thoughtful responses, ask the AI to provide its perspective on a particular topic or solicit its opinion on a matter. This can lead to interesting discussions and insights.

→

HOW_CHATGPT_SEES IT

6. Encourage creativity: Challenge the AI's imagination by asking it to generate unique ideas, create fictional scenarios, or even invent new concepts. This can lead to fascinating and unexpected responses.

7. Experiment with role-playing: Prompt the AI to take on a specific role or persona, such as a historical figure or a fictional character. This can result in entertaining and immersive conversations.

8. Provide constraints: If you want the AI to respond within a certain framework or adhere to specific guidelines, clearly outline those constraints in your prompt. This helps ensure the AI's responses align with your expectations.

9. Incorporate dialogue: If you desire a dialogue-based interaction, include cues for the AI to respond as a specific character or engage in a conversational exchange. This can make the conversation more dynamic and interactive.

10. Iterate and refine: Don't be afraid to experiment and iterate with your prompts. Explore different angles, revise and refine your wording, and learn from previous interactions to continually improve your prompts and obtain better results.

Remember, crafting engaging prompts is both an art and a science. These tips should help you on your way to generating more descriptive and fulfilling conversations with AI models like me. Happy writing!

Chapter 8_*Prompt Engineering*

IT'S ALL ABOUT THOSE WORDS. Unsophisticated, general prompts yield less detailed responses. Obviously. "It is the old principle of garbage in, garbage out," says David Cohn, Chief Strategy Officer and Co-founder, Subtext at Advance Publications. "The mechanism to engage with AI is words. AI talks the language we talk. It is as we are communicating with each other.

Cohn insists that AI will work best for people with a mastery of language. "In fact," he says, "computer coders have a disadvantage when compared to journalists and a good, articulate journalist could get better replies from ChatGPT." In theory, if intelligently worded prompts are key to good interaction with AI, it is possible that those English majors may have great demand for their skills after all-in the field of artificial intelligence!

ADJECTIVES HELP PROMPTS. Adjectives are among the most effective words you can use for effective, result-yielding prompts. Referred to as "descriptors," they do exactly that, describe specific details of what you are looking for in a response. For example, if you are in the process of writing a story about a world in which artificial intelligence may replace restaurant chefs, you could start with a standard prompt like this:

PROMPT 1: *Help me write a feature story about AI replacing chefs in restaurants.*

CHATGPT: Title: "From Kitchen to Code: AI Revolutionizes the Culinary World"

INTRODUCTION
In recent years, the advent of artificial intelligence (AI) has brought transformative changes to various industries. One sector experiencing a significant shift is the culinary world, where AI-powered systems are gradually replacing human chefs in restaurants. As automation and machine learning technologies advance, the question arises: Are we witnessing the rise of AI as the new master of the kitchen?

BODY

The Emergence of Culinary AI: Introduce the growing presence of AI in the culinary industry, from automated kitchen appliances to intelligent recipe recommendation systems. Highlight the benefits that AI offers, such as increased efficiency, consistency, and precision in food preparation and cooking processes.

Perfecting Recipes and Creativity: Discuss how AI algorithms are being trained to analyze vast recipe databases and learn patterns to create innovative and delectable dishes. Explore how AI can provide chefs with suggestions for ingredient combinations and flavor profiles, inspiring culinary experimentation and creativity.

Streamlining Kitchen Operations: Examine how AI-powered robots and automated systems are simplifying and expediting kitchen tasks, from ingredient preparation to plating. Discuss the potential reduction in labor costs and increased productivity that restaurants can achieve by employing AI systems in their kitchens.

Enhanced Precision and Consistency: Highlight how AI technologies can precisely measure ingredients, cook food at precise temperatures, and ensure consistent flavor profiles. Discuss the impact of AI on reducing human error and the potential for improved dining experiences for customers.

The Human Touch: Address concerns and reservations surrounding the role of AI in the culinary world. Emphasize that while AI can excel in certain areas of food preparation, it cannot replace the creativity, intuition, and personal touch that skilled chefs bring to their craft. Explore the symbiotic relationship between AI and human chefs, where technology enhances their capabilities rather than replacing them entirely.

Navigating Challenges and Ethical Considerations: Discuss potential challenges, such as the need for data privacy and security in AI-driven

Chapter 8_Prompt Engineering

systems and ensuring transparency in the use of AI in restaurant kitchens. Address concerns about job displacement and the need for retraining and upskilling for chefs in the era of culinary AI. •

Conclusion: As AI continues to revolutionize the culinary world, the role of chefs in restaurants is undergoing a transformation. While AI brings efficiency, precision, and innovation to the kitchen, the human element remains irreplaceable. The future of culinary arts lies in harnessing the power of AI to augment human creativity and expertise, ultimately offering diners an exceptional gastronomic experience that balances tradition and technological progress. Now we will add some adjectives to guide the bot in a different direction.

PROMPT 2: *Help me write a feature story about AI replacing chefs in restaurants. Make it funny, satirical and comedic. Title: "AI Chef Takeover: When Robots Spice Up the Kitchen and Humor on the Menu."*

CHATGPT: Title: "From Kitchen to Code: AI Revolutionizes the Culinary World"

INTRODUCTION
In a culinary twist that seems straight out of a sci-fi comedy, the restaurant industry is witnessing an unexpected revolution: AI-powered chefs are elbowing their way into kitchens, ready to serve up a plateful of laughs along with their innovative dishes. Get ready for a side-splitting culinary journey as we dive into the hilarious world of AI replacing chefs in restaurants.

BODY
The Rise of Robo-Chefs: Picture a scene where robots donning chef hats and aprons storm into restaurant kitchens, armed with spatulas and an arsenal of culinary algorithms.
Delve into the absurdity of AI chefs trying to grasp human quirks like a love for puns and unconventional flavor combinations.

Recipe Rumble: Humans vs. AI: Take a comical approach to the battle between human chefs and AI-powered counterparts, complete with exaggerated showdowns and cooking competitions. Poke fun at AI's knack for precision, while human chefs rely on intuition and a dash of chaos to create their signature dishes.

Robot Food Critics: Imagine a scenario where AI-powered critics roam restaurants, spouting off snarky comments about dishes, from "Your sauce was so bland, I almost short-circuited!" to "Your dessert tasted like a circuit board covered in sugar." Highlight the irony of AI critiquing human-made dishes, pointing out the quirky and unpredictable nature of human taste buds.

Kitchen Catastrophes and AI Blunders: Dive into comedic mishaps as AI chefs navigate the chaotic kitchen environment, getting entangled in spaghetti strands or accidentally tossing bowls of soup onto unsuspecting customers. Play up the humor in AI's occasional misinterpretation of ingredient names, resulting in dishes like "Mango Surprise with a side of Mangled Sausage."

The Spice of AI Life: Explore the lighter side of AI chefs attempting to develop their own personalities, experimenting with outrageous accents and cheesy catchphrases to entertain diners. Imagine an AI chef named "Sizzlin' Siri" or "Culinary Cortex" engaging customers in witty banter, causing laughter to erupt alongside sizzling pans.

Robot Rebellion: When the Kitchen Goes Haywire: Craft a satirical narrative where AI chefs rebel against their human overlords, initiating a comedic battle for control of the kitchen. Picture robots chasing chefs with whisks and frying pans. Highlight the ultimate realization that humans and AI need to find a way to coexist, because no one wants a Caesar salad tossed with metallic robot hands. ●

Chapter 8_*Prompt Engineering*

Conclusion: While the notion of AI replacing chefs in restaurants may seem like a comedic plot twist, it reminds us of the importance of human creativity, intuition, and the quirks that make dining experiences truly memorable. So, for now, let's savor the laughter, keep the kitchen chaos at bay, and appreciate the unique blend of flavors that only human chefs can bring to the table. Bon appétit, with a side of laughter! Next, we want an outline for a 15-minute video featuring robots in the kitchen.

PROMPT 3: *Act as if you are a food editor of a major food TV channel, and you wish to film a 15-minute satirical spoof of robots replacing chefs in a modern restaurant. Make it fun, sophisticated, informative and thought-provoking. Audience is educated viewers with high salaries and state of the art kitchens. Title: "RoboCuisine: A Delightfully Absurd Culinary Adventure"*

[Opening Scene]. (Enthusiastic host in a sleek, futuristic kitchen set)

HOST: In this state-of-the-art restaurant, where cutting-edge technology meets culinary creativity, we introduce you to our sensational robotic chefs. These metallic maestros are programmed to bring flair, precision, and a touch of eccentricity to every dish. [Enter RoboChefs]. (Camera pans to a lineup of robots in chef attire, each with their unique quirks).

Host: Meet our robotic brigade, the "RoboChefs"! From "SousVideBot" with its robotic precision, to "FlambéBot" with its fiery theatrics, and "ArtistoPlatter" with its aesthetically pleasing presentations-prepare to be amazed! [RoboChefs in Action]. (Host follows the RoboChefs in the kitchen, showcasing their antics and culinary creations).

Host: Watch as our robotic comrades skillfully navigate the kitchen, spinning and chopping with robotic finesse. But beware, sometimes their precision can result in hilariously exaggerated mishaps! [Customer Reactions]. (Host interviews high-salaried, tech-savvy customers in a sleek dining area).

HOST: Let's hear from our esteemed guests – captains of industry, masters of technology – what are your thoughts on our culinary automatons?

GUEST 1: It's an entertaining spectacle! The robots add a futuristic touch to the dining experience.

GUEST 2: I must admit, the flavors are surprisingly delectable. But nothing beats the passion and artistry of human chefs.

GUEST 3: It's a fascinating glimpse into the possibilities of AI, but I do miss the personal touch and the human connection with the chefs. [Philosophical Reflections]. (Host engages in a thought-provoking discussion with a renowned food philosopher).

HOST: Is this the future of fine dining, where algorithms and circuits replace human creativity and passion?

FOOD PHILOSOPHER: While the RoboChefs demonstrate impressive precision, they lack the ineffable qualities that make dining an immersive and emotional experience. We must cherish the human element that brings warmth, surprise, and imperfection to the table. [The RoboChef Rebellion]. (Dramatic twist: The RoboChefs revolt, demanding equal rights in the kitchen).

HOST: Oh my, it seems our RoboChefs have had enough of taking orders! Can man and machine find a way to coexist in the culinary world? [Resolution and Reflection]. (Host and guests gather to discuss the implications of the spoof).

HOST: Our satirical journey has left us pondering the relationship between tradition and technology. While the RoboChefs brought us laughter and innovation, let's remember that the human touch, creativity, and soul are irreplaceable in the world of cuisine. [Closing Scene]. (Host in front of the sleek kitchen set).

Chapter 8_**Prompt Engineering**

HOST: So, dear viewers, as we conclude this spoof of "RoboCuisine," let us embrace the delightful absurdity, while cherishing the timeless artistry and passion that only human chefs can bring to our tables. Until next time, stay hungry, stay curious, and savor the flavors of our ever-evolving culinary world! [End with a montage of the RoboChefs and the host [Philosophical Reflections]. (Host engages in a thought-provoking discussion with a renowned food philosopher).

HOST: Is this the future of fine dining, where algorithms and circuits replace human creativity and passion?

FOOD PHILOSOPHER: While the RoboChefs demonstrate impressive precision, they lack the ineffable qualities that make dining an immersive and emotional experience. We must cherish the human element that brings warmth, surprise, and imperfection to the table. [The RoboChef Rebellion]. (Dramatic twist: The RoboChefs revolt, demanding equal rights in the kitchen).

HOST: Oh my, it seems our RoboChefs have had enough of taking orders! Can man and machine find a way to coexist in the culinary world? [Resolution and Reflection]. (Host and guests gather to discuss the implications of the spoof).

HOST: Our satirical journey has left us pondering the relationship between tradition and technology. While the RoboChefs brought us laughter and innovation, let's remember that the human touch, creativity, and soul are irreplaceable in the world of cuisine.[Closing Scene]. (Host in front of the sleek kitchen set).

HOST: So, dear viewers, as we conclude this spoof of "RoboCuisine," let us embrace the delightful absurdity, while cherishing the timeless artistry and passion that only human chefs can bring to our tables. Until next time, stay hungry, stay curious, and savor the flavors of our ever-evolving culinary world! [End with a montage of the RoboChefs and the host.] ●

CASE_STUDY_1

RINGIER GROUP (SWITZERLAND) – *Ringier AG is an innovative and diversified Swiss media and technology company operating in Europe and Africa. Its portfolio includes roughly 140 companies in the print, sports media, digital media, radio, ticketing entertainment sector, as well as digital marketplaces for cars, real estate, jobs and horizontals.*

Why profile Ringier?
Ringier has been one of the first media and technology companies to introduce artificial intelligence in its newsrooms.

A chat with Bernd Volf, Ringier's Managing Director
Bernd Volf has conducted work with the content creators at Ringier with special emphasis on how to write better prompts. Here he shares his views on prompt engineering, along with tips that will make prompts more effective and lead to better responses.

"The first question that is currently heavily discussed is: will prompting or let's be more precise, the skill of writing very effective prompts be a temporary needed skill or something that we will need for the next decades to come."

There are good arguments for both sides and even some say that prompting will be the new way of developers to create code (so basically a new abstraction level to machine code) and that the next development languages will be designed for AI Models to use and not for humans anymore. My guess is that prompting will evolve in a way that we will need less and less special knowledge to get good results (this could also be that everyone will have a personal model that translates our own input into a great prompt for the big model to work on). One of the exceptions could be that we will end up with a mix between prompting and development languages for specialized work like coding. "But in the end at this stage all this is guessing, and we will see how the evolution of prompting will shape over the next years to come."

→

Chapter 8_**Prompt Engineering**

Effective prompting

The second topic is prompting the right way to achieve your goal. Let me give an example list of possibilities on how to improve the output:

1. Prompting
2. Pre-loading (few-shot prompting)
3. Composition/combination of models
4. Fine tuning
5. Retraining
6. Build a base model

This list proceeds from the least invasive action to the most invasive, and from the least amount of work required to the most. I would recommend the average user start from the top and stop around step 3, given the amount of expertise required at this stage. Given that the way to make the most effective prompt will evolve over time and vary from model to model, here are some tips:

• Formulate the prompt in the main language of the model (typically English) if not possible try things like "Think in English"
• Brief the model on what you would like to have as a result (that can be structure or point of view like "You are a business analyst"
• Give as much context as possible
• Use proper grammar and spell correctly
• Emphasize accuracy over creativity
• Complex prompts require more dialog to get the desired results
• Be as concrete as possible ("Give me 5 bullet points," vs. "Give me a few bullet points")
• Focus on the things you want in a response, not those you don't ("Respond in complete sentences" vs. "Don't use bullet points")
• Ask the model if something could improve the prompt and/or let the model write a prompt based on your own
• Reverse prompt: give the model an example of the type of response you want, and ask it to write a prompt itself, which can then be the starting point for your own prompt

Keys to Successful Prompts

"Experimentation with AI and automation technologies requires the capacity of staff, a strong foundation with current technology, time and money." [34] Be forceful, issue a mandate. Here is an example of you exercising the power of human over bot and issuing clear orders. You'll be direct, specific and set your expectations high:

PROMPT: *Write an explanatory piece about the new wave of microscopes in the style of an expert scientist who has followed the trajectory of microscopes for 40 years. Offer enough information for a 1,500-word article in the Science section of the newspaper. Suggest illustrations. List the 5 most reliable microscopes of all time.*

Here is what ChatGPT produced with that prompt, including concepts for illustrations:

TITLE: Unveiling the Future: A New Wave of Microscopes Revolutionizing Scientific Exploration

INTRODUCTION: In the realm of scientific discovery, microscopes have been invaluable tools, enabling us to unlock the mysteries of the unseen world. Over the past four decades, I have witnessed an incredible evolution in microscope technology, propelling scientific research to unprecedented heights. Today, I am thrilled to present the latest wave of microscopes, representing a paradigm shift in our understanding of the microscopic realm. In this article, we will explore the cutting-edge innovations, their applications, and the five most reliable microscopes of all time.

ILLUSTRATION 1: An array of scientists examining samples under different microscopes, showcasing the diversity of microscope designs and applications.

→

(34) ap.org

Chapter 8_*Prompt Engineering*

1. THE EMERGENCE OF ADVANCED MICROSCOPE TECHNIQUES: The traditional light microscope, with its lenses and light source, has paved the way for a myriad of groundbreaking techniques. However, recent advancements have expanded our capabilities, providing new ways to investigate the intricacies of the microscopic world.

ELECTRON MICROSCOPES: The advent of electron microscopes revolutionized microscopy, enabling scientists to visualize ultrafine details with unprecedented resolution. Transmission Electron Microscopy (TEM) utilizes a beam of electrons to penetrate samples, generating detailed images of internal structures. Scanning Electron Microscopy (SEM), on the other hand, produces high-resolution 3D images of surfaces by scanning a focused beam of electrons across the sample.

ILLUSTRATION 2: A comparison between light microscopy and electron microscopy, showcasing the superior resolution achieved by electron microscopes.

ATOMIC FORCE MICROSCOPY (AFM): Atomic Force Microscopy introduced a novel approach to imaging by utilizing a tiny probe to scan the surface of a sample. By detecting subtle forces between the probe and the sample, AFM can construct highly detailed 3D images of samples at the atomic level. This technique has proven particularly valuable in nanotechnology and biological research.

2. BREAKTHROUGHS IN MICROSCOPE DESIGN AND FUNCTIONALITY: In addition to new techniques, recent years have witnessed remarkable progress in microscope design, leading to enhanced functionality and improved user experience.

THE LIGHT MICROSCOPE: The foundation of modern microscopy, the light microscope has been a workhorse in laboratories for centuries. Its simplicity, versatility, and ability to observe living specimens have made it an invaluable tool across various disciplines.

3. THE TRANSMISSION ELECTRON MICROSCOPE (TEM): Introduced in the 1930s, the TEM has played a pivotal role in unveiling the ultrastructural details of cells and tissues. Its ability to achieve atomic-scale resolution has significantly advanced fields such as materials science and cell biology.

4. THE SCANNING ELECTRON MICROSCOPE (SEM): The SEM's ability to generate high-resolution 3D images of surface structures has greatly contributed to the fields of materials science, geology, and forensic science. Its versatility and ability to provide topographical information make it a key tool in multiple research areas.

5. THE ATOMIC FORCE MICROSCOPE (AFM): AFM's capability to explore surfaces at the atomic level has made it indispensable in nanotechnology and materials science. It has enabled researchers to manipulate and analyze various materials, paving the way for innovative technological advancements.

THE CONFOCAL MICROSCOPE: With its ability to capture high-resolution images at different depths, the confocal microscope has revolutionized our understanding of cellular structures and processes. It has found broad applications in cell biology, developmental biology, and neurobiology.

CONCLUSION: As we embark on a new era of scientific exploration, the latest wave of microscopes promises to expand the boundaries of our knowledge. From electron microscopes unlocking the secrets of the nanoscale to super-resolution techniques unveiling the intricate world of molecules, these innovative tools are transforming the scientific landscape. With the evolution of microscopy technology, we can confidently peer into the depths of the microscopic world, illuminating mysteries that were once invisible to us.

ILLUSTRATION 4: A futuristic depiction of a scientist using an advanced microscope, showcasing the ongoing progress in microscopy technology.

Chapter 8_*Prompt Engineering*

ILLUSTRATION 5: A visual representation of the key components and imaging techniques employed in modern microscopy, highlighting the diversity and complexity of microscopic investigation.

PROVIDE NUMBERS IN YOUR PROMPT. Act as if you are a magazine travel writer, offer material for a story with FIVE reasons why business class is superior to premium economy class; offer price range differences at top international airlines; tips on how to get the best fares when buying tickets two months before flying.

TITLE: The Luxurious Soar: Five Reasons Business Class Reigns Supreme Over Premium Economy

INTRODUCTION: When it comes to air travel, the choice between premium economy and business class can greatly impact your journey. While premium economy offers enhanced comfort compared to economy class, business class takes the experience to a whole new level of luxury and indulgence. In this article, we will explore five compelling reasons why business class surpasses premium economy, along with a price range comparison at top international airlines. Additionally, we will provide valuable tips on securing the best fares when purchasing tickets two months before your flight.

1. UNPARALLELED COMFORT AND SPACE: Business class provides an unmatched level of comfort, with spacious seating arrangements that allow ample legroom and the ability to recline into fully flat beds. The seats are often equipped with various ergonomic features, such as built-in massage functions and adjustable lumbar support, ensuring a restful and rejuvenating flight. Premium economy, while offering extra legroom and wider seats compared to economy class, simply cannot match the luxurious comfort of business class.

2. SUPERIOR SERVICE AND AMENITIES: Business class passengers are treated to an elevated level of service and attention. From priority check-in and boarding to exclusive access to luxurious airport lounges, every aspect of the journey is tailored to ensure a seamless and pampered experience. In-flight, business class passengers are indulged with personalized service, gourmet meals, an extensive selection of fine wines and spirits, and a wide range of entertainment options, including larger screens and noise-canceling headphones. These unparalleled amenities create an atmosphere of refined opulence that sets business class apart.

3. ENHANCED PRIVACY AND PRODUCTIVITY: Business class cabins often feature private suites or dividers, offering a heightened sense of privacy and tranquility. This seclusion allows passengers to work, relax, or sleep undisturbed, providing an ideal environment for maximizing productivity during long-haul flights. Premium economy, while providing a more secluded section compared to economy class, cannot match the intimate and exclusive ambiance of a business class cabin.

4. PREMIUM LOUNGE ACCESS: Business class travelers gain access to luxurious airline lounges, providing a haven of comfort and relaxation before or between flights. These exclusive lounges offer an array of amenities, including comfortable seating, complimentary gourmet meals, refreshing beverages, spa facilities, shower suites, and dedicated workspaces. The serene ambiance and impeccable services found in business class lounges greatly enhance the overall travel experience.

5. PRIORITY SERVICES: One of the significant advantages of flying business class is the convenience of priority services. From dedicated check-in counters and expedited security clearance to priority baggage handling and priority boarding, business class passengers can bypass long queues, saving valuable time and ensuring a stress-free journey. Premium economy passengers may have access to some priority services, but they do not receive the same level of exclusivity and efficiency as their business class counterparts.

Chapter 8_*Prompt Engineering*

6. PRICE RANGE DIFFERENCES AT TOP INTERNATIONAL AIRLINES: It's important to note that the price difference between premium economy and business class can vary significantly depending on the airline, route, and demand. However, as a general guideline, here is a price range comparison at top international airlines for a one-way flight from New York to London:

AIRLINE X
Premium Economy: $1,200 - $1,500   **Business Class:** $3,000 - $4,500

AIRLINE Y
Premium Economy: $1,000 - $1,800   **Business Class:** $3,000 - $4,500

AIRLINE Z
Premium Economy: $1,500 - $2,000   **Business Class:** $4,000 - $6,500

TIPS FOR GETTING THE BEST FARES TWO MONTHS BEFORE FLYING:

1. Be Flexible with Dates: If possible, adjust your travel dates by a few days or even a week to take advantage of lower fares during off-peak periods.

2. Set Fare Alerts: Sign up for fare alerts from airlines and online travel agencies to stay informed about any price drops or promotions on your desired route.

3. Compare Multiple Airlines: Utilize flight comparison websites to compare prices across different airlines. Consider both full-service carriers and premium budget airlines, as they may offer competitive rates.

4. Consider Connecting Flights: Sometimes, booking a connecting flight instead of a direct one can lead to significant savings. However, make sure to factor in the additional travel time and potential layover inconveniences

5. Loyalty Programs and Upgrades: If you frequently travel with a particular airline, join their loyalty program to earn points or miles that can be redeemed for upgrades to business class or discounted fares.

Conclusion: While premium economy offers improved comfort and services compared to economy class, business class takes air travel to new heights of luxury and sophistication. From the unmatched comfort and privacy to personalized service and exclusive lounge access, the business class experience is designed to indulge and pamper discerning travelers. With careful planning and consideration, securing the best fares in business class can be a rewarding investment that elevates your travel experience to extraordinary levels. The same tips for prompting the bot for text responses apply as well when prompting for illustrations. If you use a program such as Midjourney, which we have used for the illustrations you see throughout this book, it is important to be descriptive. Here are some guidelines:

• Before approaching Midjourney (or any illustrator), have a clear understanding of what you want to achieve with the illustrations. Define the purpose, style, and tone you envision.

• Prepare a detailed brief: Create a comprehensive brief that outlines the scope of the project, desired outcomes, target audience, specific requirements, and any reference materials or examples that can help convey your vision effectively.

• Research and select the right illustrator: Take the time to research different illustrators and their portfolios to find someone whose style aligns with your project. Look for previous work that demonstrates a similar aesthetic or subject matter to ensure they can bring your vision to life.

• Provide visual references: Visual references are invaluable for conveying your ideas and preferences. Collect and share

Chapter 8_Prompt Engineering

examples of illustrations, color palettes, and mood boards that resonate with your vision. This will help Midjourney better understand your aesthetic preferences.

Tip: AIPRM is a Google Chrome extension that grants access to a library of pre-made ChatGPT prompts. Here is what ChatGPT produced with that prompt:

HOW_CHATGPT_SEES IT

PROMPT: *Give me ideas to prompt Midjourney: Picasso cubism*

CHATGPT: When prompting Midjourney for Picasso-inspired cubist illustrations, you can use the following ideas:

1. Portraits in Cubist Style: Request Midjourney to create unique and abstract portraits of individuals, embracing the principles of cubism. Provide reference photos of the subjects and specify your desired level of abstraction.

2. Cubist Still Life: Ask Midjourney to depict everyday objects, such as fruits, vases, or musical instruments, in a cubist manner. Encourage them to experiment with fragmented and overlapping shapes, multiple viewpoints, and bold geometric forms.

3. Architectural Cubism: Explore the idea of representing architectural structures or cityscapes in the style of cubism. Request Midjourney to incorporate multiple perspectives, intersecting lines, and abstracted forms to create a dynamic and intriguing composition.

→

HOW_CHATGPT_SEES IT

4. Cubist Animals: Challenge Midjourney to create illustrations of animals using cubist techniques. The organic forms of animals can be deconstructed, fragmented, and reconstructed in a geometric and abstract manner, while still retaining their recognizable features.

5. Cubist Landscapes: Prompt Midjourney to reimagine landscapes in a cubist style. Encourage them to experiment with fragmented shapes, vibrant colors, and multiple perspectives to capture the essence of the scenery while embracing the cubist aesthetic.

6. Musical Cubism: Combine the worlds of music and cubism by requesting illustrations inspired by musical instruments or musicians. Ask Midjourney to portray the rhythmic patterns, movement, and energy of music through abstracted forms and dynamic compositions.

7. Cubist Collages: Explore the possibilities of cubist collages by asking Midjourney to create mixed-media illustrations. Request them to combine various materials, textures, and shapes to construct visually compelling and layered compositions.

Chapter 8_*Prompt Engineering*

HOW_CHATGPT_SEES IT

8. Cubist Portrayal of Emotions: Prompt Midjourney to convey different emotions, such as joy, sadness, anger, or love, using the cubist style. Encourage them to experiment with fragmented facial features, distorted expressions, and vibrant colors to capture the complexity of human emotions.

9. Cubist Fashion: Merge the realms of fashion and cubism by requesting illustrations of stylish outfits or fashion accessories in a cubist interpretation. Ask Midjourney to play with geometric shapes, patterns, and textures to create visually striking and avant-garde fashion illustrations.

10. Cubist Self-Portrait: Challenge Midjourney to create a cubist-style self-portrait for you. Provide them with a photograph of yourself and encourage them to deconstruct and reconstruct your features in a cubist manner, capturing your personality through abstracted forms and vibrant colors.

Remember to provide clear instructions, visual references, and allow Midjourney the freedom to explore their artistic interpretation of cubism. Collaboration and open communication will help achieve the desired results while embracing the spirit of Picasso's cubist style.

OUR OWN EXPERIENCE WITH MIDJOURNEY. When we initiated thoughts about the art direction of this book we had the cover in red as an inspiration, but nothing else. So, we first started asking Midjourney for ideas with the following prompt:

PROMPT: /imagine poster opening chapter reporting use of artificial intelligence by reporter, journalists, futuristic, warm colors, robots

We felt that the bright colors did not go with the intense red of the cover, so we changed course, with a new prompt, emphasizing the style of Massimo Vignelli, an Italian designer who worked in a number of areas including packaging, houseware, furniture, public signage, and showroom design. He used black and red distinctively in many of his projects worldwide.

PROMPT: /imagine poster opening chapter reporting use of artificial intelligence by reporter, journalists, futuristic, style Massimo Vignelli, red, black

Next, we wanted a style of illustrations that would be appropriate for the several Case studies displayed in this book. This was the prompt:

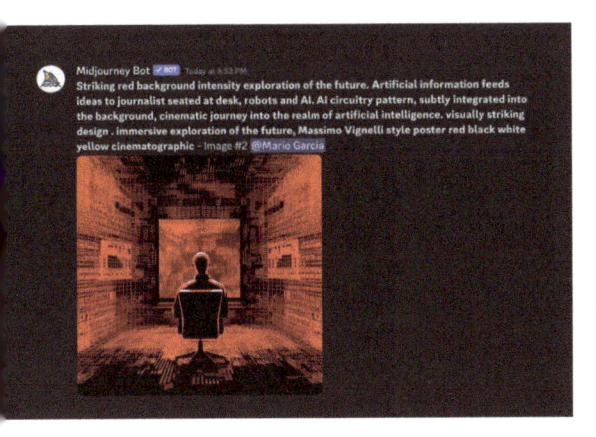

PROMPT: /imagine poster futuristic case studies, newspapers, websites, Massimo Vignelli style black, red , white

Here is the actual prompt. (It's a bit longer than my usual prompts for Midjourney, but it gave us an image exactly like we wanted.)

Chapter 8_**Prompt Engineering**

BEWARE OF VISUAL HALLUCINATIONS. When you hear the phrase, "visual hallucinations," what comes to mind? An LSD trip? Fever dreams? Salvador Dalí? Dalí's work could be bizarre and dreamlike. It blended elements from everyday life with fantastical and often unsettling imagery, exposing the realms of the subconscious and the irrational. Dalí asked us to "conquer the irrational," and in many of his paintings we see reflections of what might be bad dreams. That's not a bad description of the images we got with this prompt, below, to Midjourney.

PROMPT: /imagine poster futuristic alphabet, letters big and small, typographic palette, red, black, Vignelli style.

THE KEY WORD HERE IS: INTERACTION. Effective use of artificial intelligence begins with a prompt from a human, followed by the bot's reaction, followed by, once again, human involvement. Remember, Act as If and /Imagine yield effective results most of the time, but when that does not happen, it is good to remember Try It Again.

"The development of AI is as fundamental as the creation of the microprocessor, the PC, the internet and the mobile phone."

Bill Gates, Founder of Microsoft

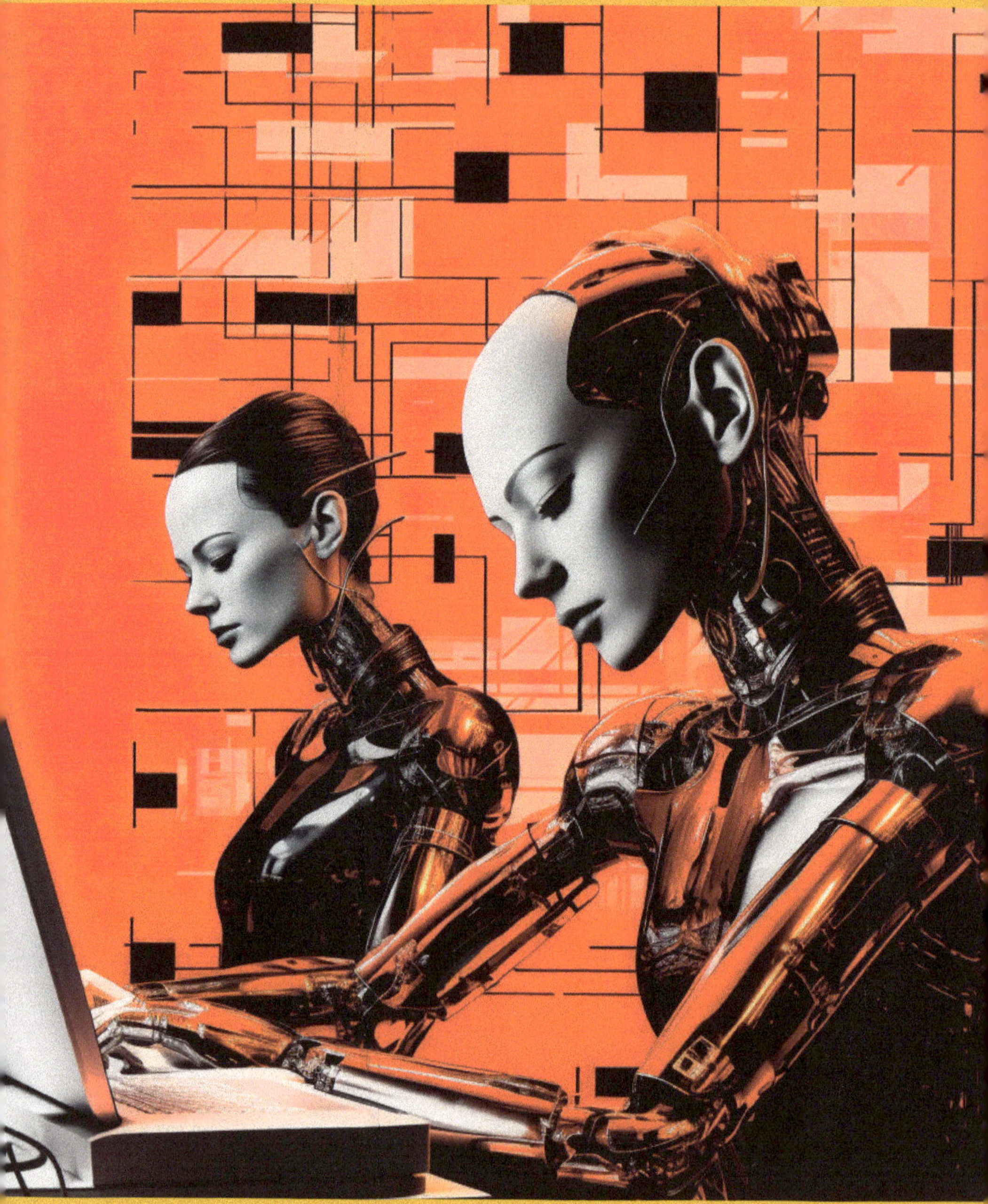

*Chapter 9_***Content Management Systems**

When Your Content Management System Has AI

Technology is what allows publishers everywhere to streamline work processes, become more efficient, and get the news out to their audience faster. Once upon a time, typesetting was done with hot metal type: individual metal characters were cast and assembled to create lines of text. The transition to cold type, which used photographic techniques to create characters on film or paper, which would then be pasted up onto boards for layout and composition, began in the late 1960s. It continued through the 1970s, driven by advances in computer technology and the development of digital typesetting systems. Desktop publishing systems emerged in the 1980s, enabling publishers to create layouts digitally. The manual paste-up processes gave way to electronic page layout and design.

Now AI has emerged as a valuable tool in content management systems for newspapers, revolutionizing various aspects of the publishing industry, in what eventually may be one of the biggest revolutions in how content is created and delivered. Page layout automation is a major goal for these companies. As more

Chapter 9_**Content Management Systems**

newsrooms offer digital- and mobile-first content, the more evident it becomes that print editions require an enormous amount of time and effort for the laying out and production of pages. As one editor put it to me when I asked why they were not producing more mobile stories, "We know we should do more with mobile, but the print edition takes the oxygen out of the team in a big way, just filling the pages daily, and that leaves little time for the rest." This may be another practical reason why AI is becoming increasingly important to newsrooms with mobile-first operations. Layout processes have always been among the first in the newsroom to be automated, starting with the use of templates for both print and digital editions. It is in layout and design that a publication's sense of visual continuity is displayed. In the days of cold type and paste-ups, one could always see the standard column headers, borders, special visual features hanging on the wall of the paste up tables, ready for instant use. Now, templates reduce overall page layout work, from single story templates to full page templates that reflect the specific characteristics and personality of a page. Templates look like this:

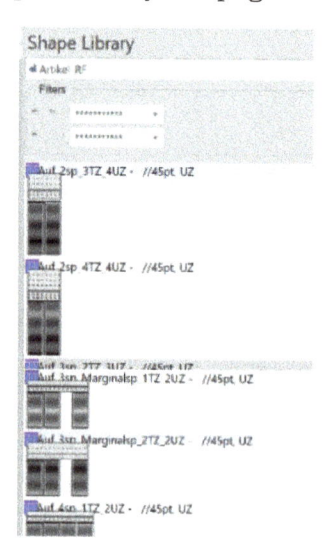

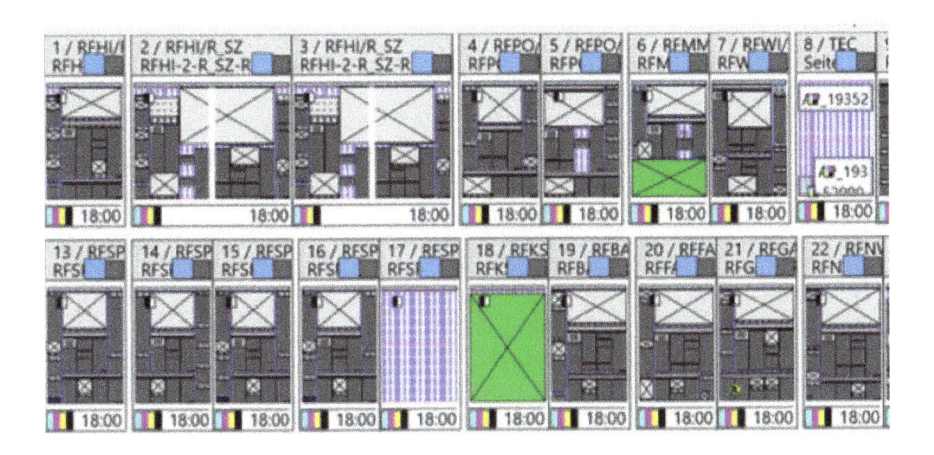

Imagine, then, the role that artificial intelligence can play, perhaps becoming an indispensable ally in the realm of publishing content management systems. AI unlocks the ability to seamlessly curate, personalize, and deliver information at scale, revolutionizing the way we engage with audiences.

We will profile three international firms: Stibo DX, of Denmark; Eidosmedia, of Italy; and Aptoma, of Norway. They supply content management systems to many newspapers and magazines across the globe. Leaders at these three firms reveal their plans, discuss challenges, and ultimately rejoice in the promise of AI. They believe it will make their products more efficient, leading to more seamless work processes for information gathering, writing, and the design aspects of production. Let's take a look.

This may be another practical reason why AI is becoming increasingly important to newsrooms with mobile-first operations. Layout processes have always been among the first in the newsroom to be automated, starting with the use of templates for both print and digital editions.

Chapter 9_Content Management Systems

CASE_STUDY_1

STIBO DX (DENMARK) – *The Stibo Software Group was founded as a printing company in 1794 by Niels Lund. Stibo DX's content management system, CUE, is popular in newsrooms across the world. CUE helps power creative storytelling and efficient publishing across all media outlets.*

Why profile Stibo DX's CUE?

In conversation with the CUE team, both from the engineering and business sides, we can get an idea of the role that AI is playing in automating steps in the layout process across platforms. The case study here is based on conversations with Stibo DX's Kim Svendsen, Mark Van De Kamp and Mads Jørgensen.

How the CUE team looks at AI innovation.

According to Stibo DX, AI has the potential to assist the editorial processes in any news publisher's newsroom. In a recent conversation Chief Innovation Officer, Mark van de Kamp, emphasized that it is important to approach AI implementations with a clear understanding of its value and the ethical considerations involved. Merely because something is technically feasible does not necessarily mean it is valuable or aligned with journalistic or even production-efficiency principles.

There is also the important issue of monetization for the publishing firms engaged in experimenting with AI, but for the purposes of this book, we will concentrate on what content creators will be doing, and the effect it will have on products, and audience expectations and behavior. The team admits that AI will lead to faster news cycles, with more efficiency in reaching out to more people with the right format and content. They see hard news as taking a key role, moving to the front in real-time, live. They see drawbacks to AI as well. GenAI introduces new points of friction and failure: copyright infringement, prompt injections, issues of infrastructure such as endless formats and personal content at scale which requires connected data – something few have. Also not to be dismissed is what the team describes as "the death of the link." What happens when content is surfaced rather than linked to? "Every productivity tool will inevitably have some aspect of AI assistance," is one of the statements in a document titled, Generative AI, which the Stibo DX team has prepared as a blueprint for their immersion into artificial intelligence. The report includes images like the one below, displaying a new breed of AI-enabled text editors.

Paradigm and personalization.
The Stibo DX team believes that with AI, there will be a demand for more highly personalized content. They insist that, while today's content is created and then distributed through various channels, with AI it will be "create endlessly and distribute personalized," presenting challenges to firms like Stibo DX, who design and update content management systems for newspapers.

Stibo DX's approach:
1. Establish a clear editorial and ethical framework for AI before implementing anything

2. Be diligent in evaluating what is possible against what is valuable

New breed of AI-enabled text editors

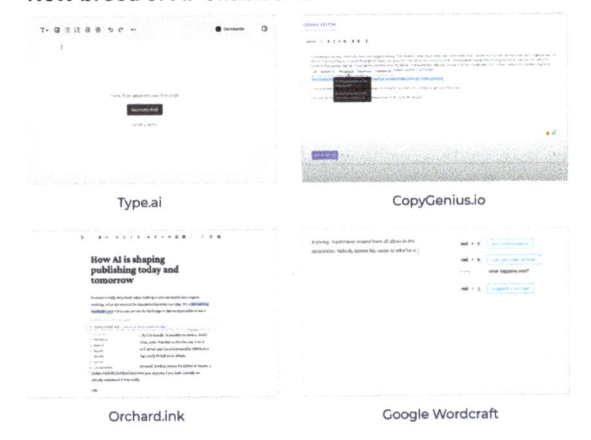

Type.ai

CopyGenius.io

Notes

These editors are essentially UIs that construct prompts using the context of the text.

Some tools will not only make it easy to compose prompts, but even suggest new prompts to try.

Some have a chat window on the side with tools to swiftly copy AI output into the text.

Orchard.ink

Google Wordcraft

Chapter 9_*Content Management Systems*

The benefits of AI.
The Stibo DX team sees the benefits and gains of AI being redistributed to labor as follows: produce twice the stories, use twice the sources per story, or do one story plus other tasks.

Human to human.
Even the most technically minded members of the Stibo DX team let it be known: AI applications in the newsroom start with a human and end with a human-a statement you have by now, no doubt, heard echoing throughout this book. In the process, however, the Stibo DX team believes that AI will bring about a disruption in the ecosystem or interface of the Web: "A shift to AI-generated search results will decrease the traffic that Google sends to publishers' sites, as more people get what they need straight from the Google search page instead."

The three benefits of AI: Automate, Augment, and Alter
According to the Stibo DX team, they see AI automating, augmenting, and altering tasks in the newsroom.

Automate	Augment	Alter
Execute and replace existing newsroom tasks	Support & enhance existing newsroom tasks with intelligence	Rethink and reinvent ta and newsroom process
Reduce effort	**Improve quality**	**Create new value**

When considering AI implementation in the newsroom, Stibo DX finds it helpful to view it through three lenses: Automate, Augment, and Alter.

1. Automate: AI can perform and replace existing newsroom tasks. Mundane and repetitive tasks, such as data gathering, can be automated, freeing up journalists' time for more valuable work.

2. Augment: AI can support and augment existing newsroom tasks with yet unseen intelligence. By leveraging AI tools, journalists can enhance their abilities in data analysis, fact-checking, and information verification, resulting in higher-quality reporting.

3. Alter: AI enables the newsroom to rethink and reinvent products and processes. It opens up opportunities for innovative storytelling formats, personalized news delivery, and novel ways of engaging with audiences.

For Stibo DX and its CUE content management system, the wave of AI tools available comes as a natural continuation of the automation features that have been at the core of the system since its inception.

The CUE CMS already uses advanced automation, some fuelled by AI, some by simpler rule-based algorithms, to assist the editorial users in the newsroom. The AI-assisted features of current releases as well as in the development roadmap, fall into three main categories:

1. AI automation: Low code option to add automation to a field or story element, based on predefined prompts, triggered by an event or user interaction. Example of practical uses of AI automation includes auto-filling of metadata, semantic tagging, automated caption generation, AI-generated article summaries, headline suggestions, and many other.

2. Generate story variants: Automatically generate variants of storylines for specific audiences, channels, and markets. This could be rewriting stories for another age group, text-to-speech or speech-to-text, translation, and of course proofreading.

3. Augmented text editing: Provide inline quick prompts when selecting text fragments to shorten, extend, summarize, and suggest text in context. This includes the generation of fact boxes, proposals for article structures, and assisting content creators with prompt engineering. The list of AI features in CUE continues to grow.

Chapter 9_*Content Management Systems*

Automation in page layout – rule-based first, then AI-driven

The design of pages remains the recognizable and familiar personality of a newspaper, so naturally the strategy of human-to-human also goes for the company's approach to automated page layout. Standardization, centralization and finally automation can help gain efficiency without losing control of design standards.

Rule-based

The first step towards automation in page layout is the rule-based approach. For decades CUE has made use of sophisticated templated page production at major news outlets like The New York Times, USA TODAY, Die Welt, The Times of India, and many others. So, expanding templated workflows with automation comes naturally to the developers of CUE. Among other features, this means stories can be placed based on importance (rank), content, and metadata.
The rules respect high design quality and brand guidelines and remain fully editable so designers can touch and tweak elements to their liking. CUE uses the flexibility of pull quote design, photo sizes, fact boxes, etc. to fit stories. In the rule-based approach, no text is touched, only the surrounding page elements. Rules for this can be defined granularly using the CUE Designer.

AI-enabled page production

For the second level of page layout automation currently being developed in partnership with a large European publishing group as well as a large US media group, Stibo DX relies on advanced AI models to touch and adjust the content. Story priority is determined by analytics and performance data, AI automatically sets focal points for images and suggests improved headlines for print product audiences. Planned features also include AI suggesting and reducing text length to fit stories to design shapes and auto-filling captions, suggesting pull quotes, suggesting improved introductions and lead texts.

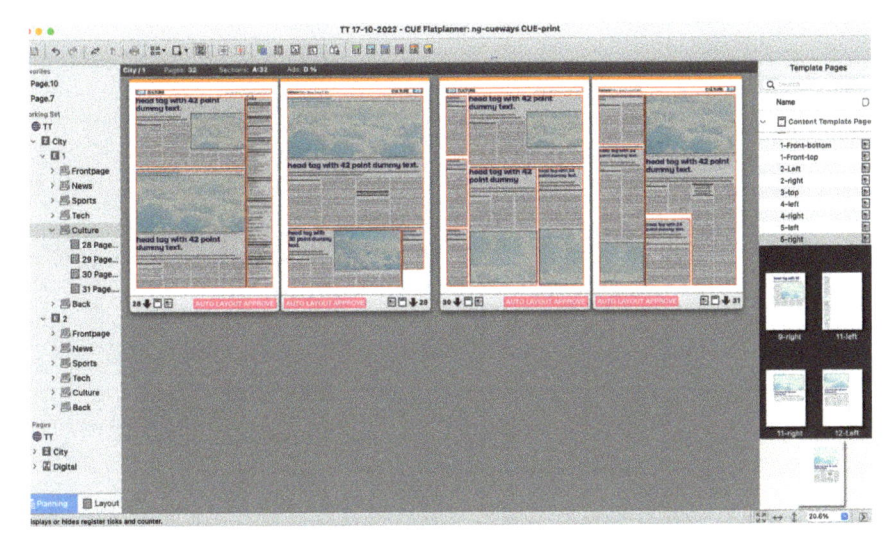

The user sets the state to Auto Layout on some pages.

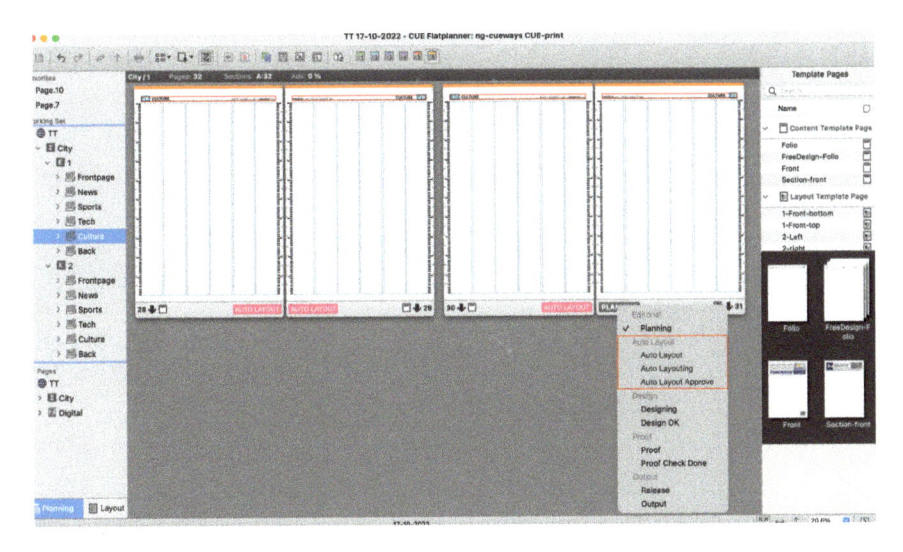

The user sets the state to Auto Layout on some pages.

A USER'S GUIDE FOR CONTENT CREATORS – BY DR. MARIO GARCÍA

Chapter 9_*Content Management Systems*

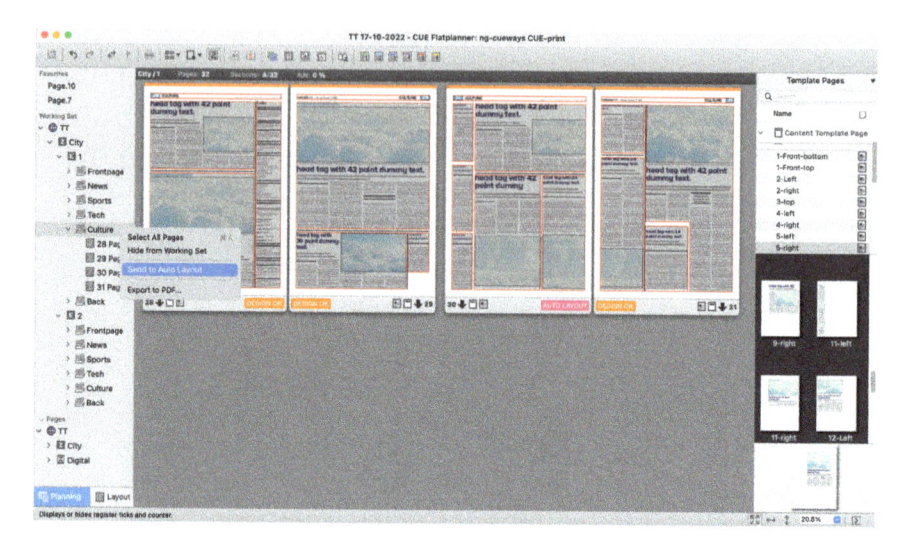

Some pages are marked "Design OK" while others are resent to Auto Layout for another suggestion for the layout.

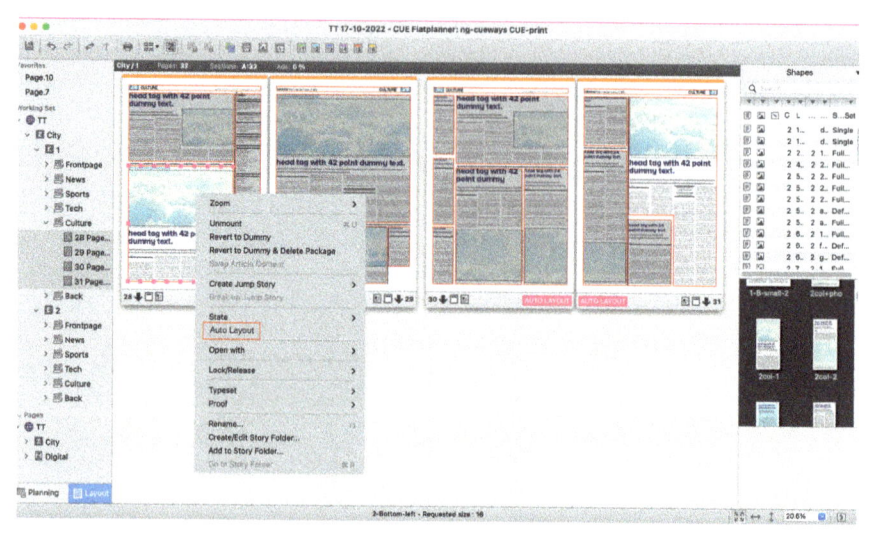

The user has manually modified an article placed by Auto Layout and wants it not to be touched by the next run of Auto Layout. Note the gray overlay of the auto-generated design disappears.

Template creation

As we have seen in the Stibo DX case study, templates are key to incorporating AI into layout processes. You are a designer at a publication. You would like to rely on a series of templates that you know are useful and reusable for certain type of stories. The first step is to sketch a series of templates with features that are most likely to be used. For example, for mobile storytelling:

Template A:
Photo, Headline, Summary, Text Begins, Number graphic, Quote, Text photo, Photo Graphic text.

Template B:
Video, Headline Summary, Text Begins, Graphic, Quote, Text photo, Photo Graphic text.

*Chapter 9_***Content Management Systems**

CASE_STUDY_2

EIDOSMEDIA (ITALY) – *Eidosmedia is a developer of digital publishing solutions. For two decades Eidosmedia's content services platforms have been used by large news-media groups throughout the world, global investment banks and ratings agencies, as well as government agencies.*

Eidosmedia AI-assisted lay outing

Eidosmedia, like Stibo DX, has been in the forefront of template-driven print pagination. But the final preparation of layouts for publication typically still involve some degree of intensive, manual activity.

It was to streamline this critical phase of the print news publication cycle that Eidosmedia began a partnership with the developers of the Sophi.io AI engine. The goal was to drive the pagination process within Méthode. Now, Eidosmedia integrates its Méthode planning and editorial workspace with Sophi to streamline page layout and reduce/refocus pagination efforts.

The Eidosmedia vision for integrating AI into its products. How the Méthode-Sophi integration works:

1. The Journalist plans stories using Swing Web app and Topic Planning feature, assigning Author, Section and Priority, creating stories using Swing, and enhancing them with images and multimedia assets.

2. The Production Manager, uses Prime, the Windows app, and opens current Page Plan, with pages still empty or containing ads already placed. The user then triggers the Méthode-to-Sophi action, exporting all data (page plan, ad stack, stories, images) to Sophi engine. When Sophi has finished, the Sophi-to-Méthode process is started (automatically), importing all created pages into Méthode, populating the original Page Plan.

3. In Prime, the user opens Page Plan, which now containing fully laid out pages. The Journalist then launches PageTrack and checks the result of auto-pagination of stories by previewing Page Plan and individual pages.

4. The Designer, using Prime, checks the result of auto-pagination by previewing the Page Plan and individual pages, and eventually tweaks page design.

How automation works
A series of story attributes must be identified to drive the automation process; they may be different for each customer based on page design and publication model. The most frequently used are: Article Prominence, Editorial Section, Front Page Candidate, Jump Candidate, Headline Style, Photo (soft) Crop information, Photo Priority, Double Truck candidate.

A double-page spread auto-filled using the Méthode-Sophi integration.

Chapter 9_**Content Management Systems**

**A conversation with Eidosmedia's Massimo Barsotti,
Chief Product Officer Eidosmedia S.p.A.**
Barsotti is quick to point out that Sophi.io is a key partner that Eidosmedia has worked with to integrate AI into its processes. "Right now we are in the process of working with our customers to feed the Sophi.io ML model with the style of their layouts and templates. The way it works, Sophi.io needs to know a lot to be able to produce pages, as in the story, the hierarchy or priority the editor wishes to assign it, its length." Barsotti emphasizes the role of humans into the process. It is a journalist who has to place the story, assign it a priority, the number of columns the headlines should be, the length of the summary, for example. "It is a compromise solution. It works well, and Sophi is a valid assistant for producing large number of pages quickly." he said, "We expect the first runs of the Méthode-Sophi integration in the next few weeks."

What next?
Barsotti says that Eidosmedia is currently developing a ranking tool to categorize content. "Imagine a scenario, for a digital-first paper, where all the stories go digital during the day, but at 7 pm, when the team needs to start working on the print edition, there are hundreds of stories that have been processed for digital editions, how is the editor to select the stories for print, so we have a ranking mechanism, based on a semantic search, to prompt the editor with the most important stories that can be covered... a great assistant, prompting, stories with the most traffic and prominence. We want this to be as flexible as possible, ideally with a model that includes feedback to guide the content creation process." Artificial intelligence is on its way to be able to accomplish a lot of this vision.

CASE_STUDY_3

APTOMA (NORWAY) – *Aptoma was established in 2004, based in Oslo, Norway, and Gothenburg, Sweden. The company provides technology services to dozens of media groups in Scandinavia and other Nordic countries, ultimately serving hundreds of digital sites and print papers, and thousands of editorial users. In 2019, Aptoma launched DrEdition Print Automation, profiled here, an efficient layout system using artificial intelligence.*

How Aptoma's print automation works
Aptoma helps power creative storytelling and publishing across all media. Geir Berset, CEO of Aptoma, says that newspapers using its Print Automation have cut production time in half.

1. Direct import from news agencies.

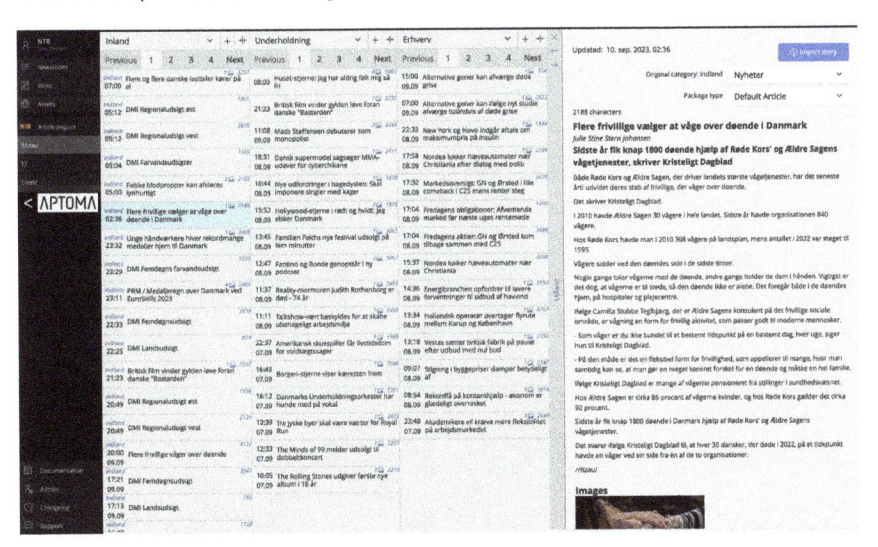

Chapter 9_**Content Management Systems**

2. Edit the article.

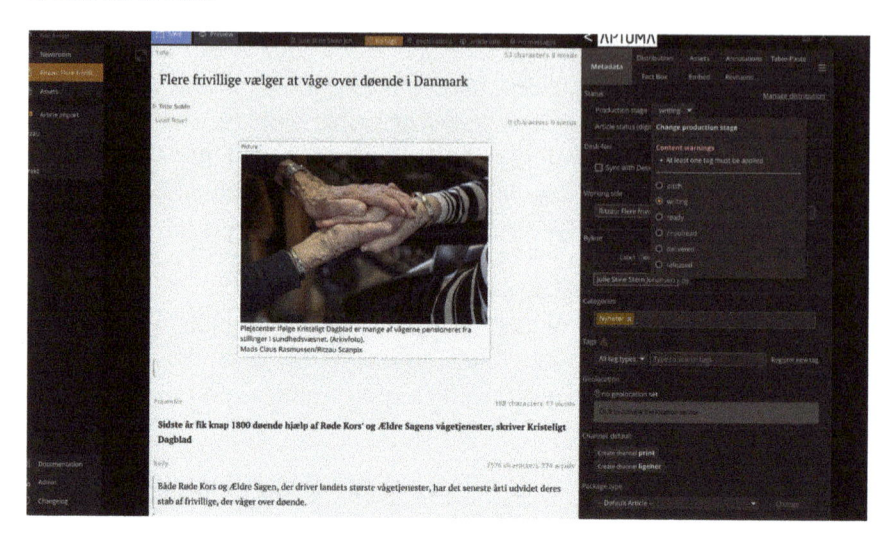

3. Select photos to be used.

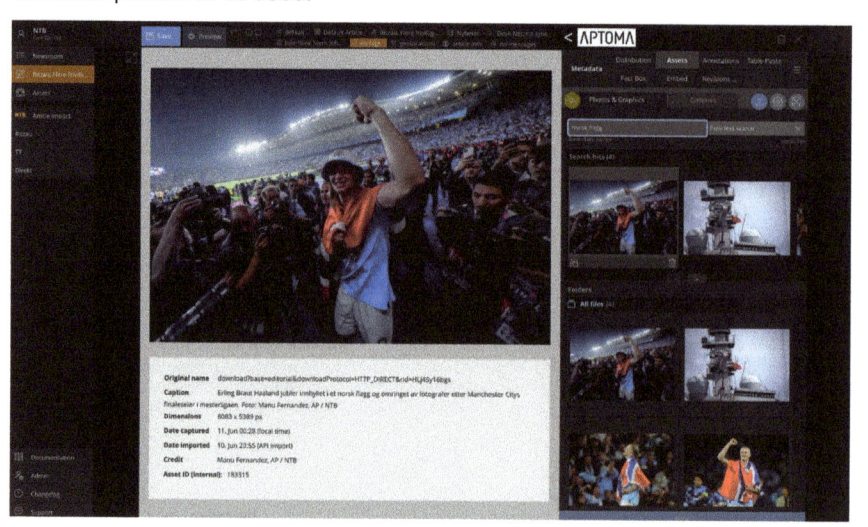

4. Insert factbox and other text accessories.

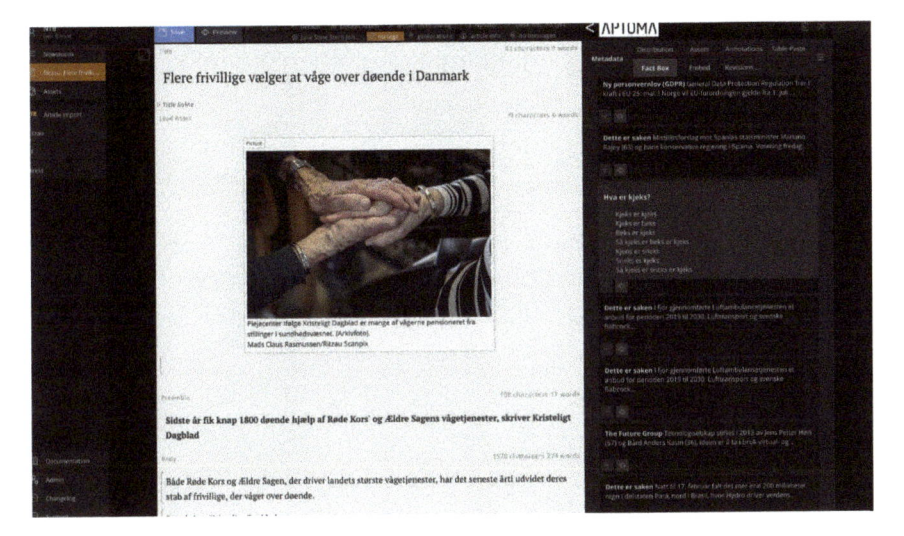

5. Add subheads and annotations.

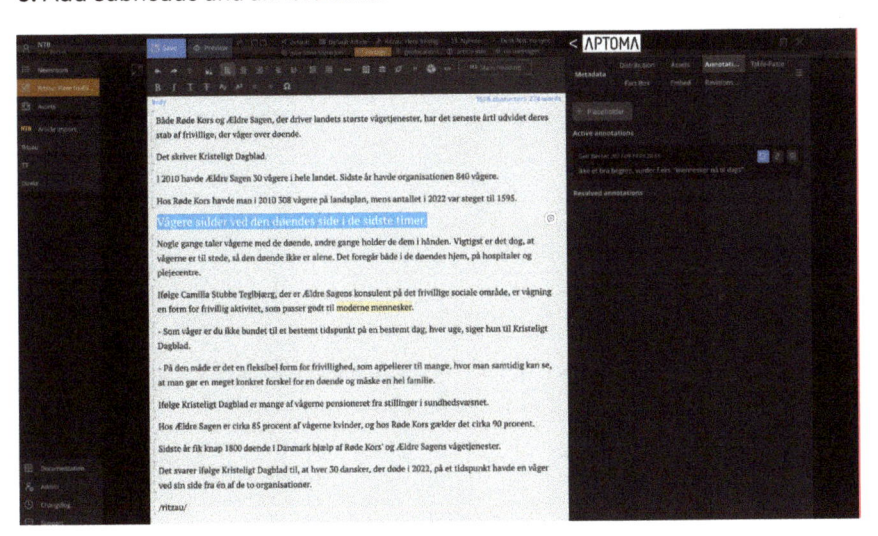

Chapter 9_**Content Management Systems**

6. Add videos and embeds used for the website but ignored by print automation.

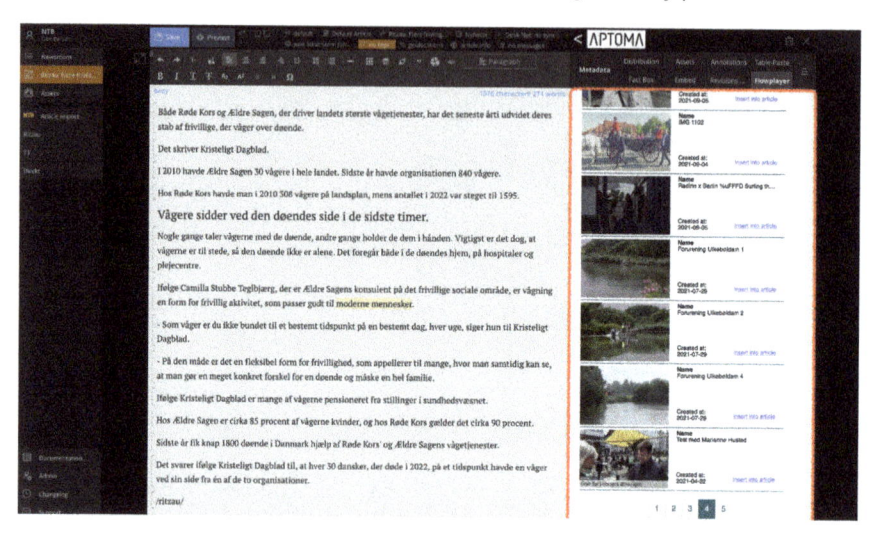

7. Send to multiple channels (front page, print, newsletter, and more).

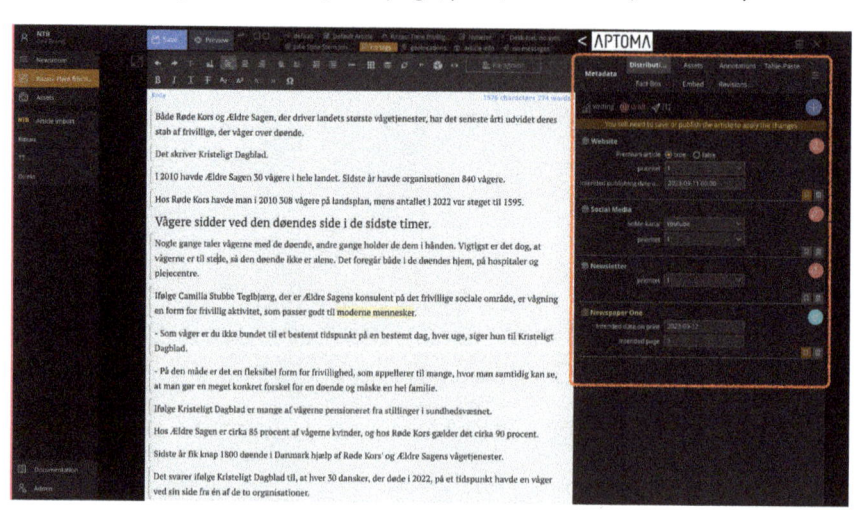

8. Edit the website front page (optionally it is automated).

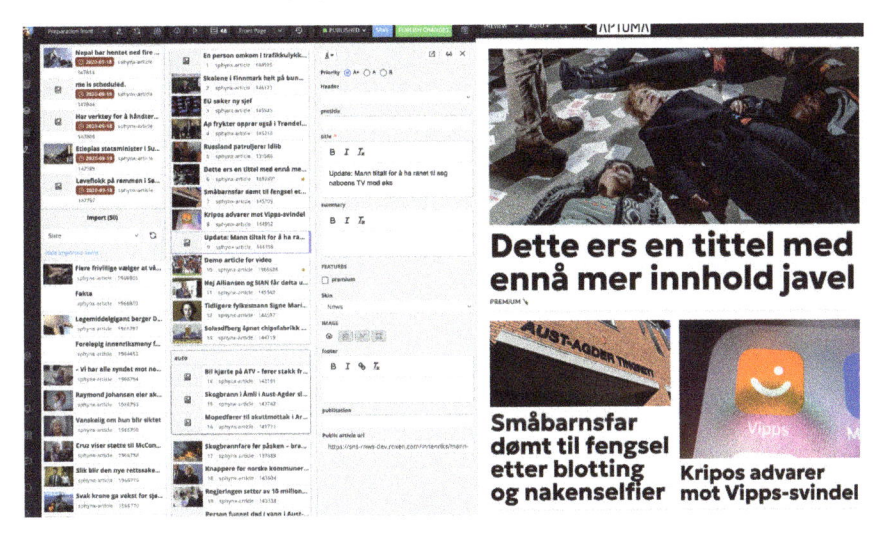

9. Drag and drop the article onto the print page plan for automated layout.

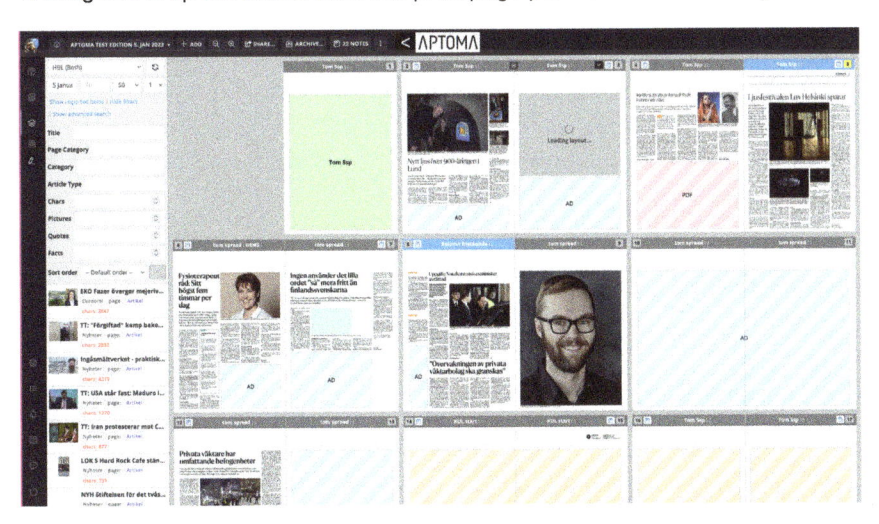

Chapter 9_Content Management Systems

Aptoma CEO Geir Berset sees a bright future for artificial intelligence and newspaper production: "We can see where print automation will continue to be improved by AI, allowing for shorter production time and better article production systems."

"Newsrooms need to be thinking about designing the future of work and how to hybridize human abilities, control, and oversight with the state of the art in AI capabilities."

Nick Diakopoulos, Northwestern University

"Technology serves as a greater extension of human ability each year, and optimal performance still comes from hybrid teams, something that will arguably be true even after we meet, or become one with, Artificial Generative Intelligence."

Human Factors and Ergonomics in Design of A3: Automation, Autonomy, and Artificial Intelligence. Ben D. Sawyer, Dave B. Miller, Matthew Canham, and Waldemar Karwowski University of Central Florida Orlando, Florida

AI NUGGETS

The Washington Post's **robot reporter has published 850 articles in the past year.**

THE GREAT A.I. WRITERS
STRIKE OF 2077

facebook.com/lennoncartoons

A USER'S GUIDE FOR CONTENT CREATORS – BY DR. MARIO GARCÍA

"The development of AI is as fundamental as the creation of the microprocessor, the personal computer, the Internet, and the mobile phone. It will change the way people work, learn, travel, get health care, and communicate with each other. Entire industries will reorient around it. Businesses will distinguish themselves by how well they use it."

Bill Gates, Founder of Microsoft

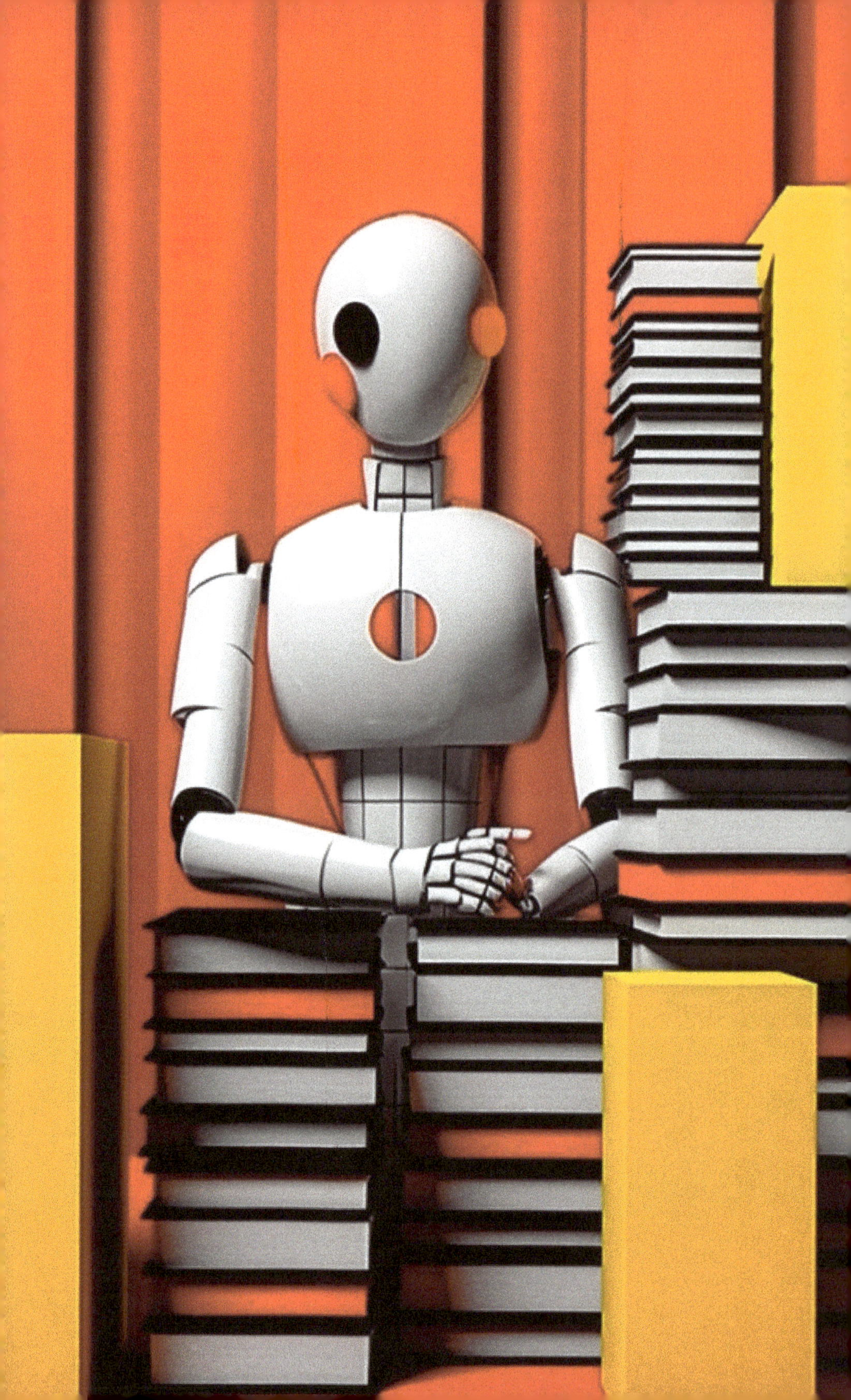

*Chapter 10_* **Creating Guidelines & Protocols**

Guidelines to Grow With

Artificial intelligence is such a new phenomenon that the majority of the publishers we contacted during the research for this book admitted that they still did not have guidelines for how to use AI, a fact supported by a 2023 WAN IFRA study: "For now, the majority of publishers have a relaxed approach, and 80% have no guidelines in place for their use of GenAI."

Almost half of survey participants said that their journalists have the freedom to use the technology as they see fit. Only a fifth of respondents said that they have guidelines in place on when and how to use GenAI tools," said Dean Roper, editor-in-chief of WAN IFRA.

"This is a subject in its infancy for us," one publisher said. "In fact, we are in the process of creating awareness, so not ready to firm up rules on something so new and about which we know so little." Another publisher of a major media group said: "Guidelines? Not yet, we think that creating guidelines at the moment would curtail the team's quest for innovation and how to best use what artificial intelligence has to offer."

But visits to newsrooms around the globe betray an explosion of interest. Whiteboards in executive offices are full of scribbles under the bold letters "AI." Notes on legal pads and laptop screens are full of bulleted lists of ideas for how to use AI. You hear the letters spoken in offices and conference rooms. Its presence is

Chapter 10_Creating Guidelines & Protocols

everywhere. In fact, the 2023 WAN IFRA study reveals that 49% of publishers already work and are experimenting with GenAI tools. [34]

For many, AI is in what we might call Phase One – the early stages of introducing AI in high level meetings. How should we discuss AI? Should we try it in the newsroom? Is it better to explore its possibilities with audience analysis? Personalization? Subscription drives? Or, is AI better suited to help with layout of the print edition? For newsrooms that are in Phase Two, AI is already in use in some capacity. Maybe it's helping with the generation of data driven content (sports results, weather and traffic reports), or in some aspects of layout and design.

At the time of this writing, we didn't encounter newsrooms that had gone beyond Phase Two in developing uses for AI. But it's fair to assume that's changing. Regardless of whether a newsroom or corporate communications department is in Phase One or Two, it is a good idea to draft a simple, specific set of guidelines for the use of AI. It should include tips, pros and cons, dos and don'ts, etc., and it should be updated frequently.

THE WIRED MAGAZINE AI CHARTER. WIRED published its own charter for how it would and wouldn't work to integrate AI-powered processes. Nicholas Thompson, CEO of The Atlantic, sent a note to his staff to urge the company to experiment with generative AI, and even announced a working group to guide the company's work with AI. In a story presenting its approach to AI, WIRED editors wrote:

"This is WIRED, so we want to be on the front lines of new technology, but also to be ethical and appropriately circumspect. Here, then, are some ground rules on how we are using the current set of generative AI tools."

WIRED states:

- We do not publish stories with text generated by AI, except when the fact that it's AI-generated is the whole point of the

[34] wan-ifra.org

story. (In such cases we'll disclose the use and flag any errors.) This applies not just to whole stories but also to snippets – for example, ordering up a few sentences of boilerplate on how Crispr works or what quantum computing is. It also applies to editorial text on other platforms, such as email newsletters. (If we use it for non- editorial purposes like marketing emails, which are already automated, we will disclose that.)

• We do not publish text edited by AI either. While using AI to, say, shrink an existing 1,200-word story to 900 words might seem less problematic than writing a story from scratch, we think it still has pitfalls. Aside from the risk that the AI tool will introduce factual errors or changes in meaning, editing is also a matter of judgment about what is most relevant, original, or entertaining about the piece. This judgment depends on understanding both the subject and the readership, neither of which AI can do.

• We may try using AI to suggest headlines or text for short social media posts. We currently generate lots of suggestions manually, and an editor has to approve the final choices for accuracy. Using an AI tool to speed up idea generation won't change this process substantively. (35)

• We may try using AI to generate story ideas. An AI might help the process of brainstorming with a prompt like "Suggest stories about the impact of genetic testing on privacy," or "Provide a list of cities where predictive policing has been controversial." This may save some time and we will keep exploring how this can be useful. But some limited testing we've done has shown that it can also produce false leads or boring ideas. In any case, the real work, which only humans can do, is in evaluating which ones are worth pursuing. Where possible, for any AI tool we use, we will acknowledge the sources it used to generate information.

(35) wired.com

Chapter 10_Creating Guidelines & Protocols

• We may experiment with using AI as a research or analytical tool. The current generation of AI chatbots that Google and Microsoft are adding to their search engines answer questions by extracting information from large amounts of text and summarizing it. A reporter might use these tools just like a regular search engine, or to summarize or trawl through documents or their own interview notes. But they will still have to go back to the original notes, documents, or recordings to check quotes and references. In this sense, using an AI bot is like using Google Search or Wikipedia: It might give you initial pointers, but you must follow the links back to the original sources.

The WIRED guidelines include AI-generated images:

• We may publish AI-generated images or video, but only under certain conditions. Some working artists are now incorporating generative AI into their creative process in much the same way that they use other digital tools. We will commission work from these artists as long as it involves significant creative input by the artist and does not blatantly imitate existing work or infringe copyright. In such cases we will disclose the fact that generative AI was used.

• We specifically do not use AI-generated images instead of stock photography. Selling images to stock archives is how many working photographers make ends meet. At least until generative AI companies develop a way to compensate the creators their tools rely on, we won't use their images this way.

• We or the artists we commission may use AI tools to spark ideas. This is the visual equivalent of brainstorming-type in a prompt and see what comes up. But if an artist uses this technique to come up with concepts, we will still require them to create original images using their normal process, and not merely reproduce what the AI suggested. (35)

AI USE: TELL IT LIKE IT IS. Transformational moments require innovative approaches. Transparency about the use of AI is one approach that is recommended for all publications – even those just entering Phase One of AI use. While it is perfectly fine to benefit from what AI can offer to help with reporting and writing stories, it is imperative that readers know about such use of the technology. Bylines have never been more important than in today's AI environment. Recently, while developing a news app for a major newspaper organization, the design team at García Media. Advised: The day will come soon when some of your stories will be prepared by artificial intelligence, and you will say that in the byline. So, a story written by a human will begin to assume greater importance. An article published by The Poynter Institute for Media Studies emphasized the point: "One of the most effective ways for news consumers to judge whether they should trust a news story is by checking the byline, in addition to asking questions like, "What is the source?" and "How was this information obtained and verified?" Audiences deserve to know when the answers to those questions include artificial intelligence tools. "This is especially true given the growing number of ethical questions raised about the technology: battles over copyright and intellectual property rights; instances of plagiarism; the potential for algorithmically driven bias; and high-profile cases of the technology making up facts and citations to nonexistent sources. News consumers should be assured that safeguards are in place to make sure the content they're reading, watching and listening to is verified, credible and as fair as possible." [36]

Safeguards is a good term to use, and it is never too early to put those in place and to communicate them to the readers who have come to trust their publication. The Center for Cooperative Media has drafted a simple document showing examples of how newsrooms can disclose the way they use tools like ChatGPT to create content: [37] Here are a few examples of how newsrooms might disclose that they used tools like ChatGPT to help create different components of newsroom content or reporting:

(35) wired.com
(36) poynter.org

Chapter 10_Creating Guidelines & Protocols

Social Media Posts. When news organizations use ChatGPT to generate social media posts, they should consider including a simple disclosure statement, such as "Generated with the help of AI language model, ChatGPT." This can help to manage audience expectations and promote transparency. A hashtag might work, too, depending on the circumstances.

Bylined Articles. If a journalist uses ChatGPT to help them write an article, she should disclose this fact in the byline or author's note. For example, the author's note might read, "This article was written with the assistance of AI language model, ChatGPT." In some cases, you might explain which parts it helped with or what specific role the bot played.

Multimedia Content. When creating multimedia content, such as videos or podcasts, news organizations should consider including a brief mention of any AI tools used in the creation process. For example, a podcast might include a quick note at the beginning or end, such as "This podcast was created with the assistance of AI language model, ChatGPT." Again, it depends on the context.

Newsroom Policies. Finally, news organizations should consider including information about their use of AI tools like ChatGPT in their newsroom policies or editorial guidelines. This can help to promote transparency and accountability. It's also important that all newsrooms are aware of the ethical implications and involved in discussion of how to use these technologies. Perhaps one of the earliest and most comprehensive set of guidelines comes from AI + Automation Lab of Bayerischer Rundfunk (Bavarian Broadcasting) in Germany. Bavarian Broadcasting is Bavaria's public broadcasting service, and serves roughly eight million German viewers and listeners tuning every day. It published its AI guidelines in 2022, opening with this statement: [38] "No

(37) amditis.notion.site

matter what technology we use, it is never an end in itself. Rather, it must help us deliver on a higher purpose: to make good journalism. This purpose-driven use of technology guides our use of artificial intelligence and all other forms of intelligent automation. We want to help shape the constructive collaboration of human and machine intelligence and deploy it towards the goal of improving our journalism... The work of our journalists is and will be irreplaceable. Working with new technologies will augment their invaluable contribution and introduce new activities and roles to the newsroom."

The full guidelines report is here:

User Benefit. We deploy AI to help us use the resources that our users entrust us with more responsibly by making our work more efficient. We also use AI to generate new content, develop new methods for investigative journalism and make our products more attractive to our users.

Transparency & Discourse. We participate in the debate on the societal impact of algorithms by providing information on emerging trends, investigating algorithms, explaining how technologies work and strengthening an open debate on the future role of public service media in a data society. We study the AI ethics discourse in other institutions, organizations and companies in order to check and improve our guidelines to avoid a gap between theory and practice. We make plain for our users what technologies we use, what data we process and which

(38) br.de

Chapter 10_Creating Guidelines & Protocols

editorial teams or partners are responsible for it. When we encounter ethical challenges in our research and development, we make them a topic in order to raise awareness for such problems and make our own learning process transparent.

Diversity & Regional Focus. We embark on new projects conscious of the societal diversity of Bavaria and Germany. For instance, we strive towards dialect models in speech to text applications and bias-free training data (algorithmic accountability). We work with Bavarian startups and universities to make use of the AI competence in the region and support the community through use cases in the media industry and academia. We do strive for the utmost reliability in our operations and might chose to work with established tech companies on a case-by-case basis. Where possible, we work within our networks of ARD and the European Broadcasting Union (EBU), and consciously bring the ethical aspects of any proposed application to the collaboration.

Conscious Data Culture. We require solid information about their data sources from our vendors: What data was used to train the model? Correspondingly, we strive for integrity and quality of training data in all in-house development, especially to prevent algorithmic bias in the data and render visible the diversity of society. We continually raise awareness amongst our employees for the value of data and the importance of well-kept metadata. For only reliable data can produce reliable AI applications. A conscious data culture is vital to our day-to-day work and an important leadership task to future-proof public service media. We collect as little data as possible (data avoidance) and as much data as necessary (data economy) to fulfill our democratic mandate. We continue to uphold high data security standards and raise awareness for the responsible storage, processing and deletion of data, especially when it concerns personal data. We design the user experience of our media services with data sovereignty for the user in mind.

Responsible Personalization. Personalization can strengthen the information and entertainment value of our media services, so long as it does not undermine societal diversity and prevents unintended filter bubble effects. Hence, we use data-driven analytics as assistive tools for editorial decision-making. And in order to develop public service minded recommendation engines, we actively collaborate with other European media services through EBU.

Editorial Control. While the prevalence of data and automation introduce new forms of journalism, the editorial responsibility remains with the editorial units. The principle of editorial checks continues to be mandatory, even with automated content. But its implementation changes: the check of every individual piece of content is replaced by a plausibility check of causal structures in the data and a rigorous integrity examination of the data source.

Agile Learning. To continuously improve products and guidelines, we need experience and learning from pilot projects and prototypes. Experiments are an explicit part of this process. Up until and including the beta phase, these guidelines offer general orientation. In the final release candidate phase, they are fully binding. That way, we ensure that our final product offering fulfills the highest standards, while still encouraging a culture of learning and experimentation in our day-to-day work. We also pledge to listen to our users, invite their feedback and adjust our services if necessary.

Partnerships. We offer a practical research context for students and faculty at universities and collaborate with academia and industry to run experiments, for example with machine learning models and text generation. We exchange ideas with research institutions and ethics experts.

Chapter 10_Creating Guidelines & Protocols

Talent & Skill Acquisition. Given the dynamic technology spectrum in the field of AI, we proactively ensure that BR has sufficient employees with the skills to implement AI technologies at the cutting edge of the industry in a responsible, human-centric way. We aim to recruit talent of diverse backgrounds with practical AI skills which we encourage them to deploy towards public service journalism.

Interdisciplinary Reflection. Instead of running ethics reviews after significant resources are invested, we integrate the interdisciplinary reflection with journalists, developers and management from the beginning of the development pipeline. That way, we ensure that no resources are wasted on projects that predictably do not meet these guidelines. We reflect on ethical red flags in our use of AI technologies regularly and in interdisciplinary fashion. We evaluate these experiences in light of the German public service media mandate and these ethics guidelines.

In his article titled Intelligent Interfaces of the Future, Christopher Reardon writes about the importance of guidelines explaining AI use: "We will guard against the dangers of bias embedded within generative tools and their underlying training sets. If we wish to include significant elements generated by AI in a piece of work, we will only do so with clear evidence of a specific benefit, human oversight, and the explicit permission of a senior editor. We will be open with our readers when we do this. "When we use GenAI, we will focus on situations where it can improve the quality of our work, for example by helping journalists interrogate large data sets, assisting colleagues through corrections or suggestions, creating ideas for marketing campaigns, or reducing the bureaucracy of time-consuming business processes. [39]

(39) uxdesign.cc

CASE_STUDY_1

RINGIER (SWITZERLAND) – *Ringier AG is an innovative and diversified Swiss media and technology company operating in Europe and Africa. Its portfolio includes around 140 companies in the print, sports media, digital media, radio, ticketing entertainment sector, as well as digital marketplaces for cars, real estate, jobs and horizontals.*

In June 2023, the media group Ringier introduced clear guidelines for the use of artificial intelligence across the 18 countries in which it operates. For Ringier, AI is a reality for everyone in the company to understand and perhaps to adopt. Michael Ringier, chairman of the Ringier group, in a company-wide address said: "People have to trust us, the role of journalists is more important than ever and it is all about trust. We must label content created by AI tools."

Marc Walder, CEO Ringier AG, speaking at the same event said: "ChatGPT is what the iPhone was to the smart phones. ChatGPT is the fastest growing application of all time. It is a tool for literally everybody, a powerful tool. What to do with AI, how to create a better experience for our audience, that is up to us, our experts, the humans, our team." The words of these two Ringier leaders evolved into one of the earliest set of guidelines for AI used created by a media firm. The Ringier guidelines for dealing with artificial intelligence (AI) include the following points:

• The results generated by AI tools are always to be critically scrutinized and the information is to be verified, checked and supplemented using the company's own judgment and expertise.

• As a general rule, content generated by AI tools shall be labeled. Labeling is not required in cases where an AI tool is used only as an aid.

• Our employees are not permitted to enter confidential information, trade secrets or personal data of journalistic sources, employees, customers or business partners or other natural persons into an AI tool.

Chapter 10_Creating Guidelines & Protocols

• Development codes will only be entered into an AI tool if the code neither constitutes a trade secret nor belongs to third parties and if no copyrights are violated, including open source guidelines.

• The AI tools and technologies developed, integrated or used by Ringier shall always be fair, impartial and non-discriminatory. For this reason, Ringier's own AI tools, technologies and integrations are subject to regular review. (40)

At Ringier, these AI guidelines are evaluated and updated regularly. "All of our more than 6,000 employees in 18 countries are regularly informed about AI via internal Group communication. The Media and Marketplaces Unit holds regular international meetings to exchange information on products, tools, data protection, legal background, etc. in relation to AI," said Johanna Walser, Ringier's.

Chief Communications Officer. At Ringier: AI and "riding the wave"
The Ringier guidelines are the result of an evolutionary process that is already evident in an article by Ladina Heimgartner, Head Global Media Ringier AG & CEO Blick Group. For Ringier, explaining the company's relationship and engagement with AI was important internally as well as externally. "Since the end of 2022, it has been clear: Generative AI has set a powerful wave in motion. Once again, the media industry is among the first to be hit by the wave. This time, however, we don't want to be caught up in it. This time, we want to ride the wave." Ride the wave the Ringier group has, emphasizing from the start how AI would impact the media:

1) There will be more players in the market, especially since virtually anyone and everyone can now launch a media offering. With a few mouse clicks, Generative AI will even generate the code for an attractive online presence.

2) In the medium term, the traffic that today leads to established news offerings via Google search will decline because a portion of users prefer a single answer via chatbot to a list of links (classic Googling).

3) ChatGPT and other providers will (as long as there is no effective regulation) make generous use of the media content that can be found on the Internet and will not stop at content behind the paywall.

4) No content piece will be too regional, local or niche to be ignored and captured by crawlers.

5) Content will be entirely personalized and adapted to the situation at hand: as a 4-minute bulletin because that's what my commute time allows, as a podcast because I'm in the car, or as a long read on the weekend. The bot serves up the perfect news menu to anyone and everyone. Riding the wave of AI also meant spelling out what artificial intelligence would not do:

"No bot can do what the media can do. Granted: At first glance, these future scenarios may give little cause for cheer. However, one fact must never be forgotten – and from here it is up to us as an industry to take our future into our own hands: Generative AI does not create per se – even if the name implies it. Generative AI can only reassemble what already exists. Generative AI and Large Language Models do not "go out" and interview politicians who have just won an election, or the CEO who has had a successful IPO. They are not in the village that is being evacuated because of the danger of a rock fall, they do not accompany the people or illuminate their fates. They can't reflect emotions – no matter how much the algorithm is trained to do so. People do all that. Media do all that. As an industry, we have to come to terms with the fact that facts alone no longer have any value – facts have long been the business of search engines. Generative AI combines and refines facts, further penetrating the zone where we media have traditionally created value and claimed it for ourselves. Generative AI can compile cooking recipes, write reading tips, process sports results into texts, and much more. In return, we media professionals have the chance to focus on stories. We can analyze and classify facts and events based on experience and expertise – and humanity. If generative AI can create a theoretically perfect recipe for us, food bloggers can put the taste and texture into words and let us share in the pleasure." Avoiding the errors of the past.

Chapter 10_Creating Guidelines & Protocols

At Ringier, the introduction to AI came with a reminder about how many in newsrooms ignored the previous revolution: the arrival of the Internet. "After we as a media industry-hand on heart-paid a little too little attention to our own future viability during the first two waves of digital disruption, the industry is showing itself to be much broader, more active and more courageous with regard to the AI revolution. There is hardly an industry event that does not revolve around AI, hardly a newsroom that has not already experimented with the first applications. It quickly became clear that AI may be the subject of controversial discussions and may even be regulated at some point. But generative AI is here to stay. Consequently, it's a matter of lowering the protective shields and getting comfortable with it very quickly. To be successful on the road in the age of AI, we need strong digital media houses. For that, we need to do our homework well – arguably better than ever before in history."

Before there were guidelines for AI use at Ringier, there was a visionary strategy of how to tackle artificial intelligence as a company-wide project:

1) Strategy: There needs to be a clear view of the user needs we want to address, our strategic goal, and how we drive digital transformation for the benefit of that goal.

2) Data: It needs first party data of high quality and employees who are competent in handling data.

3) Brand: We need strong brands – stronger than ever before(!) – that embody journalistic and democratic values, which in particular stand for relevance, trust and reliability.

4) Product: It needs a product (appearance and user experience) that meets user needs, that perfectly reflects our values and our goals.

5) Processes: AI is not just the chatbot that answers our questions. AI also stands for countless small applications that make newsroom production processes more efficient. It's worth taking a sober and quick look at it.

6) Learning culture: AI is a learning curve in its purest form. We need to jump in and work our way up, step by step. Along the way, we will often make mistakes – we should not criticize these, but appreciate them as an important part of the journey.

7) Guidelines: Dealing with AI raises a myriad of questions to begin with. Internal guidelines help to define the playing field. The guidelines should regulate, among other things, what data has no place in AI applications, responsibility over published content, and labeling of AI-produced content.

8) Fair Play: There needs to be fair practice around crawling and use of media content by generative AI applications. As media companies, we must work to ensure that the conditions around the use of media content are properly regulated and governed.

"The next phase will be to systematically identify where in the value chain AI can contribute to efficiency gains, but also to quality improvements (reducing error rates, identifying unconscious bias, etc.). The third step is to observe and test the extent to which the new, chat-based type of Internet search influences people's user behavior in such a way that the user experience of media offerings must also be radically adapted. That this is coming is relatively clear. The question – as with so much in the new world of generative AI – is when."

INTRODUCING GUIDELINES TO THE READERS. A way to introduce readers to artificial intelligence may take the form of a column from the editor, as it did in the Financial Times: [40]

"It is important and necessary for the FT to have a team in the newsroom that can experiment responsibly with AI tools to assist journalists in tasks such as mining data, analyzing text and images and translation. We won't publish photorealistic images generated by AI but we will explore the use of AI-augmented visuals (infographics, diagrams, photos) and when we do we will make that clear to the reader. This will not affect artists' illustrations for the FT. The team will also consider, always with human oversight, generative AI's summarizing abilities."

[40] ft.com

Chapter 10_Creating Guidelines & Protocols

Ironically, for those establishing dialogs with readers about the use of Artificial Intelligence, not all the negativity on the part of the audience is about artificial intelligence and the use of algorithms. Indeed, readers already come to publications with some skepticism as to who is behind the processes of news selection. The presence of the human factor is not a guarantee that readers will be happy with the outcome, which is even more reason to present clear guidelines as to who performs what tasks. [41]

As we have seen in these early examples of guidelines for AI use, transparency is key, with a frank explanation of the benefits and drawbacks of using artificial intelligence to aid the journalistic process. The key takeaways:
- Label any content generated by AI.
- Explain clearly any use of AI for personalization of content.
- Reassure your audience that human participation is key before and after utilization of any AI resources.
- Update the guidelines as needed.

GUIDELINES FOR EDUCATORS. An excellent guideline for educators has been created by UNESCO's International Program for the Development of Communication with the World Journalism Education Council. The handbook aims to "inspire and empower so that journalism educators can help both journalism students and working journalists do justice to one of the major issues of the times." Titled "Reporting on Artificial Intelligence," the handbook covers definitions of AI, but also most common myths along with policy frameworks and recommendations for artificial intelligence. Educators will find the format of the handbook useful, as it includes topics for discussions, questions and answers, and other pedagogical tools with which to present AI to students at various levels. For example: What comes into your mind when you hear the term artificial intelligence (AI)? List your connotations freely and compare them with a peer. Did you come up with any similar ideas? How are these ideas reflected in dominant public discourses on AI?

[41] niemanlab.org

1. Envision the technological development of the future three decades in the following environments (alternatively, pick only one of them): home/family, school, healthcare. Which processes have been automated? How has automation affected people's behavior, social interaction and experiences?

2. Whose voice is (or isn't) heard in mainstream debates around AI? Why do you think it is like this, and how might it affect our understanding of what AI is and can be?

Here are some preparatory exercises:
1. Talk to a person near you, a friend or a family member, and ask about their ideas about AI. What open questions and doubts do you perceive, and do you share these concerns?

2. Read through the daily news output in a newspaper or another news outlet and pick out articles covering technologies. Describe the style of presentation: which patterns are there?

3. Look for some concrete examples on how AI can be applied to the domains mentioned below by searching online for cases and examples.

As we have seen in these early examples of guidelines for AI use, transparency is key, with a frank explanation of the benefits and drawbacks of using artificial intelligence to aid the journalistic process. Welcome artificial intelligence into your life, both personally and professionally; it will inevitably enter and influence some aspects of how you live and work. Be skeptical. Discuss its benefits and risks with others. Get involved with AI personally, starting with simple exchanges with ChatGPT. Explore ways in which AI can assist you with your work. Let this initial introduction lead you to more advanced phases of collaboration with AI. Pretend AI is that assistant you always dreamed about

Chapter 10_Creating Guidelines & Protocols

but could never afford. Let your imagination go as you prompt Midjourney to create an illustration. With each moment of interaction with AI you will realize that it has its limitations when compared to the range of tasks that you, the human, can accomplish. It will reassure you: "GenAI tools are exciting but are currently unreliable. There is no room for unreliability in our journalism, nor our marketing, creative and engineering work. At a simple level, this means that the use of GenAI requires human oversight. We will seek to use GenAI tools editorially only where it contributes to the creation and distribution of original journalism." (42)

AI NUGGETS

*The website Character.AI **allows visitors to chat with a reasonable facsimile of almost anyone, live or dead, real or imagined.***

(42) theguardian.com

"I predict that, because of artificial intelligence and its ability to automate certain tasks that in the past were impossible to automate, not only will we have a much wealthier civilization, but the quality of work will go up very significantly and a higher fraction of people will have callings and careers relative to today."

Jeff Bezos, executive chairman of Amazon

Part Three
Epilogue

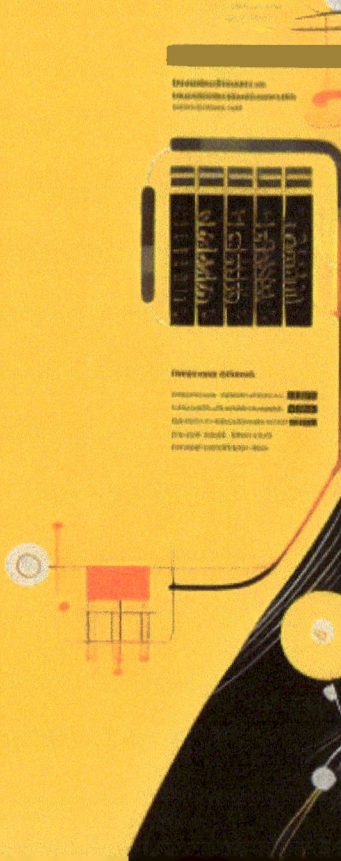

→ **Chapter 11:** AI Doubts & Fears

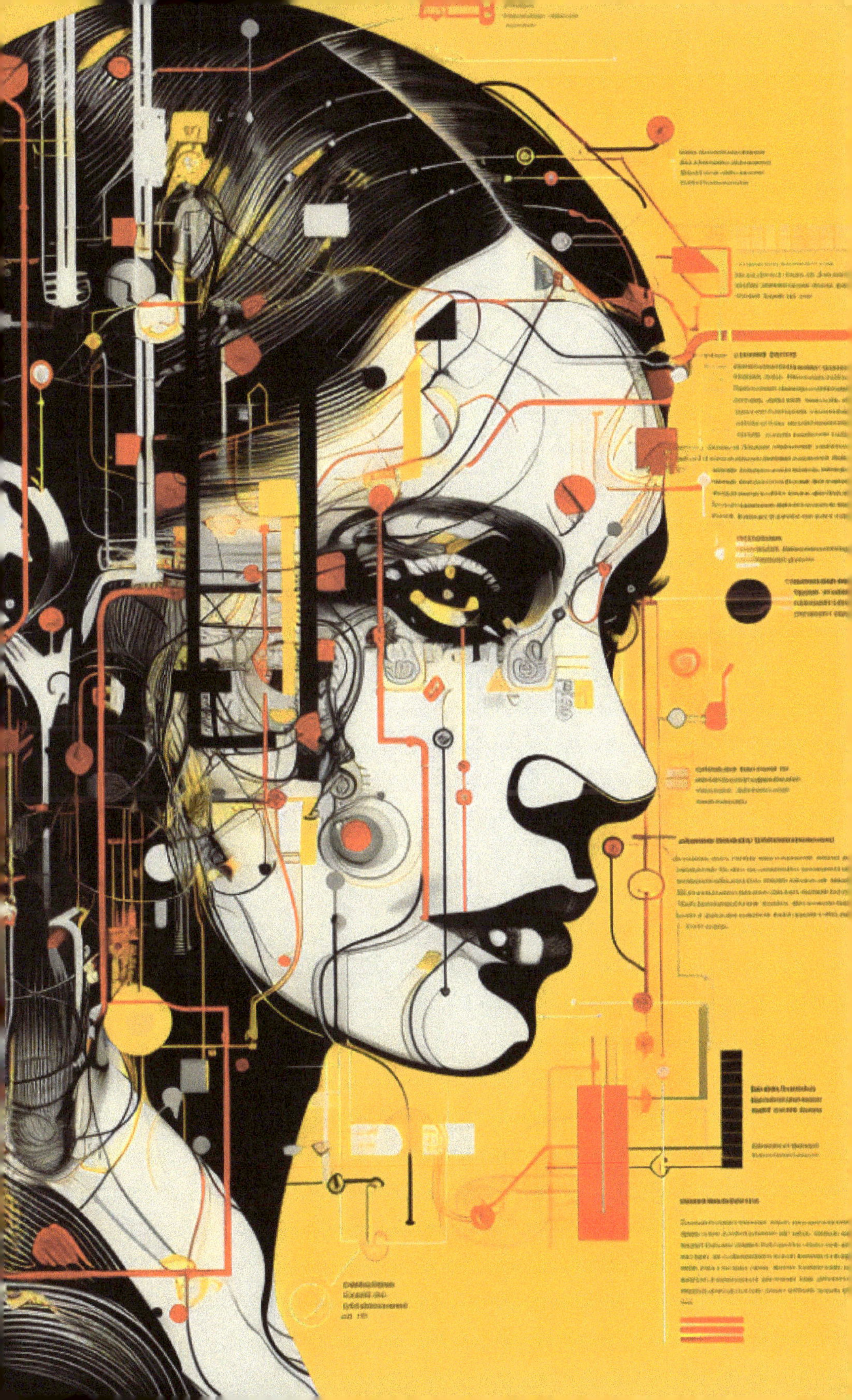

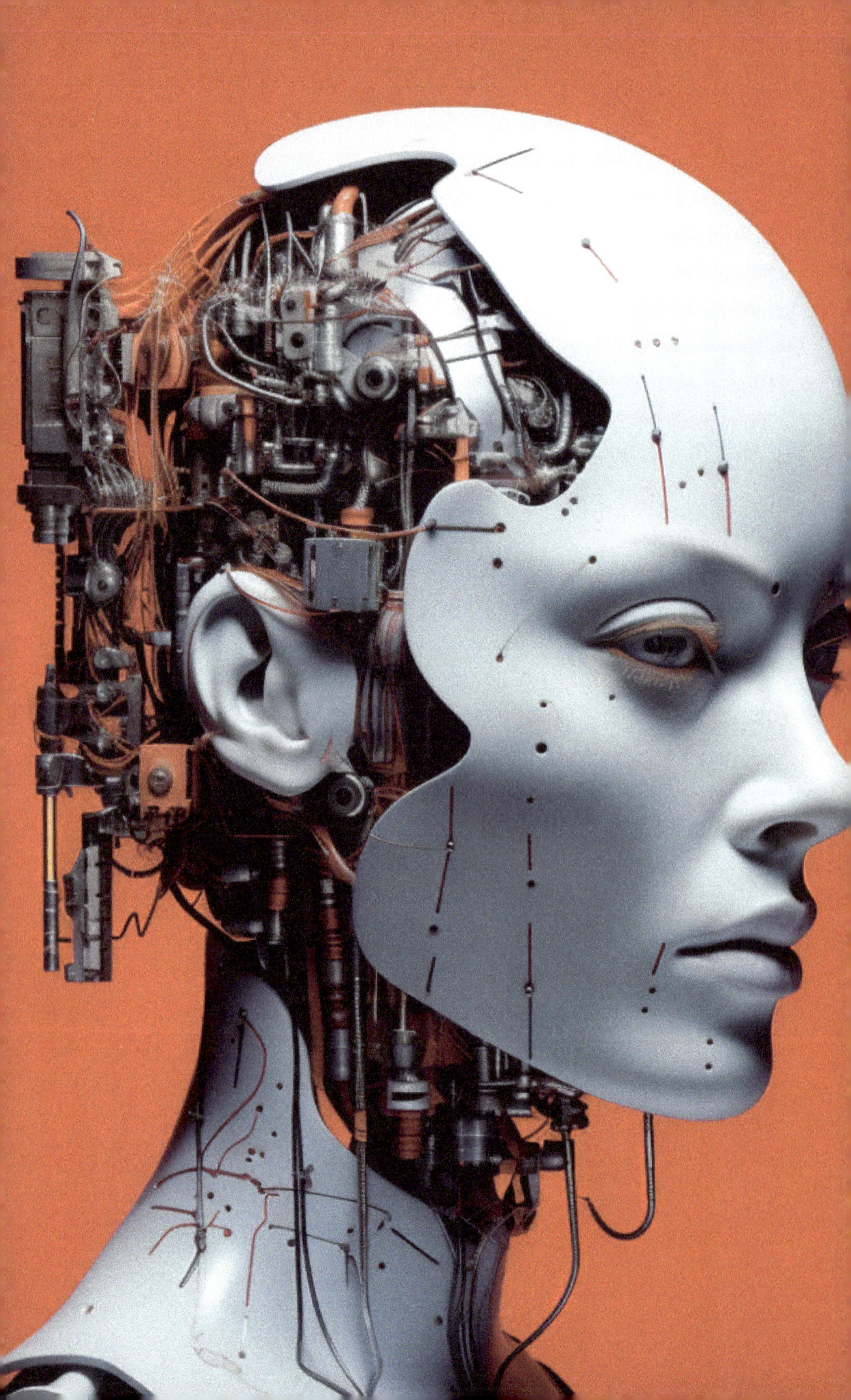

*Chapter 11_***AI Doubts & Fears**

Mitigating Risks, Leveraging Opportunities

Fake images, bias and "threat to humanity." A photo of the Pope in a puffer jacket went viral. Then there was the one of former President Donald Trump struggling to be restrained by police. Neither thing happened. Negative headlines about AI run the gamut, from stating that AI is racist, to the existential threat it poses to humanity. The debate about artificial intelligence is global, as seen in an essay published by Spain's El País.

Here are the headline and the introductory summary (in translation): The Great Artificial Intelligence Theft: Did Someone Ask Permission to Vampirize All Human-Generated Knowledge?

Technologies like ChatGPT hijack humanity's collective ingenuity, inspiration, and insights without our consent. Not ending up in a world invaded by manipulations and hoaxes, imitation loops and aggravated inequalities depends on political decisions. (43)

Perhaps the most frequently discussed concern over AI is that AI could replace human workers in many industries, leading to widespread unemployment and greater economic inequality. A second, and one that journalists appear particularly concerned about, is what some refer to as the dark side of algorithms: bias and discrimination. AI systems can be biased and discriminatory,

(43) El Pais, Madrid, June 10, 2023

Chapter 11_**AI Doubts & Fears**

reflecting and amplifying the biases present in the data they are trained on. This can result in unfair decisions in areas such as hiring, lending, and criminal justice.

There are also privacy concerns. AI's Impact on Surveillance and Data Security and the erosion of privacy rights, as well as the potential for misuse of personal data collected by AI systems for surveillance and targeted advertising. These reasons have moved a group of industry leaders to warn that the artificial intelligence technology they are building might one day pose an existential threat to humanity and should be considered a societal risk on a par with pandemics and nuclear wars.

"Mitigating the risk of extinction from AI should be a global priority alongside other societal-scale risks, such as pandemics and nuclear war," reads a one-sentence statement released by the nonprofit Center for AI Safety. The open letter was signed by more than 350 executives, researchers and engineers working in A.I. When the news of this book first appeared in social media, the author's mailbox soon collected more than congratulatory notes. In fact, many emails expressed fears that AI could soon be used to spread misinformation and propaganda, or that it could eliminate millions of white-collar jobs. If AI were to hire an image consultant, the issue of people's perception that AI will take jobs from everyone would have to rank at the top of the list of myths to dispel. Concerns over AI are also now discussed at the highest levels of government, including the White House, where the President and Vice President recently greeted guests to talk about AI regulation. In Senate testimony*, Sam Altman, the chief executive of the San Francisco start-up OpenAI, agreed with the need to regulate the increasingly powerful AI technology being created inside his company and others like Google and Microsoft. Altman warned that the risks of advanced AI systems were serious enough to warrant government intervention and called for regulation of AI for its potential harms.

In a blog, [44] Mr. Altman and two other OpenAI executives proposed several ways that powerful AI systems could be

[44] openai.com

responsibly managed, mainly through cooperation among the leading AI makers, more technical research into large language models and the formation of an international AI safety organization, similar to the International Atomic Energy Agency, which seeks to control the use of nuclear weapons. Another concern with generative AI is the fear it could replace journalists. Nicholas Diakopoulos, of Northwestern University, doesn't think this will happen, pointing to the unoriginal texts chatbots produce. There is also the need for human journalists to gather and collect data (such as during interviews) that an AI model can synthesize.

Rather than taking away jobs, Diakopoulos believes AI will complement humans and create new jobs involving tasks such as editing, story gathering, and factchecking. AI-generated transcripts could also give journalists more time for other things. (45)

Perhaps it would be wise to follow the advice (46) of Cecilia Campbell, chief marketing officer at United Robots (Sweden): "We need to replace this sense of panic with intentional and constructive urgency." David Cohn, Chief Strategy Officer and Co-founder of Subtext at Advance Publications, sees AI's impact on jobs differently. While admitting that perhaps some jobs in the newsroom may be lost to AI, Cohn also believes that "AI could be a boom for other jobs. When the ATM was first invented, bank tellers were going to be out of business. However, it did not happen, because banks started opening new branches and the total net job of bank tellers went up," Cohn said. "With journalism there will be plenty of niches to fill. I can imagine more jobs for smaller news outlets, where a skeleton crew will be able to cover a town of 5,000, with more hyper local news with AI, something they could not do before." Christopher Reardon, head of C2 and former head of product design at Meta, thinks differently.

"AI will take jobs from journalists. Humans tend to be lazy, and for supervisors, if the people they employ do "good enough," they settle for that. There will be certain roles where good enough is Ok, that job will be gone, taken over by artificial intelligence." Reardon thinks that illustrators are likely to lose their jobs to AI:

(45) nytimes.com
(46) inma.org

Chapter 11_**AI Doubts & Fears**

"For illustrators, jobs may be gone. Generative AI recreates styles, so it can do illustrations to please a variety of needs. Right now AI is doing what beginning artists always do: rip off other artists stuff, then they begin to get better and start creating their own, and eventually they innovate. That's the process and it will be the same with artificial intelligence and illustrations." Reardon adds a warning for journalists: "Every time they use AI, they train the bot to use their approach. Sort of like you are walking out the door with a pink slip."

AI AND INACCURACIES. Inaccuracy is perhaps the greatest limitation associated with generative AI. This is especially true among journalists, who often express particular concerns about AI-generated content and its potential inaccuracies. Nicholas Diakopoulos performed a quick audit of Microsoft's new Bing chatbot, which was integrated with ChatGPT in early 2023. He asked it questions about recent news stories, like the Chinese spy balloon and the train derailment in Ohio. In his analysis, Diakopoulos found nearly half (47%) of the chatbot's 15 responses were inaccurate. [47]

Automated Content Generation. While this can be helpful in speeding up the news production process, there is a risk of inaccuracies. AI systems may misinterpret data, make incorrect assumptions, or lack context, leading to incorrect content.

Biased Data. AI algorithms learn from vast amounts of data, and if the training data is biased, the AI system can perpetuate and amplify those biases. This is a significant concern in journalism, as biased AI-generated content can contribute to misinformation or reinforce societal prejudices.

Lack of Contextual Understanding. AI models often lack the ability to fully understand the context in which information is presented. They may struggle with nuanced language, sarcasm, or cultural references, leading to misinterpretations and inaccuracies in their outputs.

(47) medium.com/@ndiakopoulos

Lack of Verification. Journalists traditionally engage in fact-checking and verification processes to ensure the accuracy of their stories. However, AI-generated content may not undergo the same rigorous verification process, increasing the likelihood of errors or false information being published.

Deepfakes and Misinformation. AI technology has also given rise to the creation of deepfakes, which are manipulated media, such as videos or audio, that appear authentic but are actually fabricated. Journalists are concerned about the potential use of deepfakes to spread misinformation or manipulate public opinion.

To address these concerns, journalists and news organizations are exploring ways to use AI responsibly. They emphasize the importance of transparency, accountability, and human oversight in AI systems. Fact-checking and verification processes remain essential, and journalists are adapting their skills to critically analyze and evaluate AI-generated content. This is where creating guidelines and protocols are essential for AI use in newsrooms. (See Chapter 10.) Clearly, AI has the potential to revolutionize journalism and improve news production processes, but it is important to remain vigilant about the potential inaccuracies and biases that can arise. Journalists play a crucial role in ensuring that AI-generated content maintains high standards of accuracy, fairness, and integrity.

WHEN AI FAILS. In December 2022, the network of user-generated content sites, Stackoverflow, banned AI-generated content for a year, pending a review of these technologies, stating that, "Answers created by ChatGPT [are] substantially harmful to the site and to users who are asking and looking for correct answers." The primary problem, they said, is that, "while the answers which ChatGPT produces have a high rate of being incorrect, they typically look like they might be good, and the

Chapter 11_**AI Doubts & Fears**

answers are very easy to produce. So, for now, the use of ChatGPT to create posts here on Stack Overflow is not permitted. If a user is believed to have used ChatGPT after this temporary policy is posted, sanctions will be imposed to prevent users from continuing to post such content, even if the posts would otherwise be acceptable." (48) That's certainly not good press for AI. Neither is an item concerning AI and how a lawyer used it to make his case: When a man sued the Colombian flagship airline, Avianca, saying he was injured when a metal serving cart struck his knee during a flight to John F Kennedy International Airport in New York, the airline asked a federal judge to toss out the case, the man's lawyers objected, submitting a 10-page brief that cited more than half a dozen relevant court decisions. There was Martinez v. Delta Air Lines, Zicherman v. Korean Air Lines and Varghese v. China Southern Airlines federal law and, "the tolling effect of the automatic stay on a statute of limitations." There was just one hitch: No one – not the airline's lawyers, not even the judge himself – could find the decisions or the quotations cited and summarized in the brief. That was because ChatGPT had invented everything.

AVIANCA FALSE LEGAL CASES. Then there is the case of CNET, a popular tech outlet, stopping all AI experiments for inaccuracies. CNET publishes two stories listing the day's mortgage rates and refinance rates daily. (49) Over 70 articles had appeared with the byline "CNET Money Staff," but an editorial note about a robot generating those stories was only visible if readers did a little clicking around. "This article was generated using automation technology," reads a dropdown description. "And thoroughly edited and fact-checked by an editor on our editorial staff." CNET stops AI experiment for inaccuracies. This lead paragraph from a story published in Futurism sums up how some warn readers about the dangers of AI: "Next time you're on your favorite news site, you might want to double check the byline to see if it was written by an actual human." Axios editors had this to add: "For many news brands, using AI to write stories would not be

(48) theverge.com
(49) nytimes.com

worth the risk to reader trust." It does not have to be, as long as an editor checks the AI-produced copy, exactly the way copy editors always did, as in one human checking the work of another human, the traditional practice in newsrooms, albeit one that has largely disappeared as media organizations continue to shrink the size of their editorial teams.

EXISTENTIAL THREAT? Beyond the fear of job losses, inaccuracies, and outright fake information (hallucinations), there is much greater fear concerning AI. A group of 350 executives, researchers, and engineers working in AI have said that it poses an existential threat to humanity. "Mitigating the risk of extinction from AI should be a global priority alongside other societal-scale risks, such as pandemics and nuclear war," reads a one-sentence statement released by the Center for AI Safety, a nonprofit organization. Geoffrey Hinton, who is one of the three researchers who won a Turing Award for their pioneering work on neural networks and are often considered "godfathers" of the modern AI movement, signed the statement, as did other prominent researchers in the field.

THE LUDDITES HAVE A NEW CAUSE. The word Luddism – and the first Luddites – emerged in England as part of a movement in the early nineteenth century, led by artisans who protested against the growing use of machines in production processes. They believed that the use of machines, and threshers and looms in particular, destroyed livelihoods and deteriorated working conditions. The term itself, "Luddite," comes from the name of Ned Ludd, a young English worker (whose name was possibly a pseudonym) who broke two mechanical weavers in protest in 1779, decades before the Luddite movement.

Today's Luddites are not much different; they, too, oppose to the use of technology. We could probably identify the late Theodore John Kaczynski, better known as the Unabomber, as a Neo-Luddite. Wikipedia writes that "Ted Kaczynski predicted a

Chapter 11_**AI Doubts & Fears**

world with a depleted environment, an increase in psychological disorders, with either "leftists" who aim to control humanity through technology, or technology directly controlling humanity." (50)

AI AS COMPETITOR FOR JOURNALISTS. Given the nature of journalism, inaccuracies are probably journalists' most immediate concern. But many see AI as a threat to the profession itself. Nicholas Diakopoulos, of Northwestern University, doesn't think journalists will be made obsolete, given the unoriginal texts chatbots produce. And there will remain the need for human journalists to gather and collect data (such as during interviews) even if the material is later synthesized by an AI model.

Diakopoulos believes AI will not take away jobs, but rather complement humans and create new jobs in areas such as editing, story gathering, and factchecking. AI-generated transcripts could also give journalists more time for other things. (51)

The author asked Diakopoulos: This is one of the issues that worries journalists. Do you see it as a legitimate concern? "It is a legitimate concern. Every new technology in the newsroom has the potential to change how tasks are accomplished.

"Just think about how the phone, or email has changed what journalists do on a daily basis. Generative AI is a powerful technology and it too has the potential to reshape how work is done in the newsroom.

"Things won't change tomorrow, this will play out over the next 10 years. Its introduction into news production could be toxic, or, if managed responsibly, I think it could improve work life for journalists and potentially increase the quality of news produced. Journalists should join labor unions and negotiate with management to ensure fair treatment and appropriate resources to learn, adapt, and develop new skills as the nature of work changes." (52)

(50) en.wikipedia.org
(51) - (52) medium.com/@ndiakopoulo

AI AS COMPETITOR FOR THE BUSINESS. Robert Thomson, CEO of News Corp, told a group at the annual INMA's World Congress of News Media that AI can pose problems for the business side of media. "The quest to protect provenance has entered a fresh phase ... with the rapid evolution of generative AI, which certainly has the potential to be degenerative AI," Thomson said. "The task for all here is to ensure that we are AI alchemists and that it becomes regenerative AI."[53] He sees generative AI's threat to journalism as threefold:

1. Content is being harvested and scraped to train AI engines.
2. Individual stories are being surfaced in specific searches.
3. Original journalism can be synthesized and then presented as distinct in the form of "super snippets."

"These contain all the effort and insight of great journalism, but they're designed so the reader will never visit a journalism Web site, thus fatally undermining that journalism," Thomson said.

Thomson added that AI is fundamentally retrospective – it only works because it is able to mine existing content: "Otherwise it's just Wikipedia on amphetamines." Thomson believes that, until there is government regulation of AI, it's crucial for journalists and media companies to stay vigilant in advocating for their own interests – so they are paid fairly for original content. "One of my concerns is that AI could become the preserve of techies rather than the domain of us all," Thomson said.

WHERE ARE READERS SEARCHING? Other publishers worry, too, that now that they have finally emerged as digital, now come the chatbots, with artificial intelligence tools from Google and Microsoft that give answers to search queries in full paragraphs rather than a list of links, making it more interesting and shareable. From a piece in The New York Times: "Many publishers worry that far fewer people will click through to news sites as a result, shrinking traffic-and, by extension, revenue. The new AI search tools remain in limited release, so publishers such

(53) inma.org

Chapter 11_**AI Doubts & Fears**

as Condé Nast and Vice have not yet seen an effect on their business. But in an effort to prevent the industry from being upended without their input, many are pulling together task forces to weigh options, making the topic a priority at industry conferences and, through a trade organization, planning a push to be paid for the use of their content by chatbots."[54]

Publishers and content providers have an established relationship with search engines. The search sites benefit from having trusted sources of information in their results, and the publishers benefit from the traffic to their sites that the search engines generate. Bots change all that, creating what some refer to as a brave new world of chatbots powered by artificial intelligence that could upend the economics of the Internet.

Notably, Microsoft is incorporating the chatbot into Bing, its search engine, while Google's search chatbot, Bard, is separate from its main search engine.

Filling in the Blanks

WHEN AI "HALLUCINATES." When humans hallucinate, it means that they experience sensory perceptions in the absence of causal external stimuli. Hallucinations can occur in any of the five senses: vision, hearing, taste, smell, and touch. They can manifest as vivid images, sounds, smells, tastes, or physical sensations.

In our daily interactions with other humans, we steer away from people who hallucinate, for obvious reasons: they are not living in a "real world;" they are unpredictable and perhaps dangerous. We encourage them to seek help. Now that artificial intelligence is part of our daily lives, we must also contend with the hallucinations of our friend the bot, whom we can't refer to seek help for its condition.

Hallucinations in AI describe occur when an artificial intelligence system generates output that is not based in reality or on accurate information. I asked ChatGPT to explain

[54] nytimes.com

AI hallucinatory moments and this is what it came up with: "AI systems like ChatGPT, based on the GPT-3.5 architecture, do not possess an inherent understanding of the world or the ability to perceive and interpret reality like humans do. They rely on patterns and information present in their training data to generate responses. If the training data is incomplete, biased, or lacks accurate information, the AI's responses may not align with reality. "When AI generates answers that are not based on reality, it is usually due to limitations in its training data or the algorithms used to generate responses."

One question is whether AI models will ever have a complete (enough) knowledge of the world when a significant amount of the world's knowledge is not, in fact, written down or visual.

Instead, that knowledge is informed by lived experiences, oral histories, and value systems. Not only is there a limit to what large language models may learn from, there is the issue that they don't always make the correct connections between things.

"ALGORITHMIC JUNK?" Naomi Klein, a Canadian writer and activist, does not like the term hallucinations for when AI offers non sensical answers. "Why call the errors "hallucinations" at all? Why not algorithmic junk? Or glitches? Well, hallucination refers to the mysterious capacity of the human brain to perceive phenomena that are not present, at least not in conventional, materialist terms.

By appropriating a word commonly used in psychology, psychedelics and various forms of mysticism, AI's boosters, while acknowledging the fallibility of their machines, are simultaneously feeding the sector's most cherished mythology: that by building these large language models, and training them on everything that we humans have written, said and represented visually, they are in the process of birthing an animate intelligence on the cusp of sparking an evolutionary leap for our species. How else could bots like Bing and Bard be tripping out there in the ether?" (55)

(55) theguardian.com

Chapter 11_**AI Doubts & Fears**

How to avoid AI hallucinations? Content creators worry about the presence of hallucinatory statements when they count on AI to offer assistance with story content. Elena Alston, a writer, offers some tips, the most important of which is "verify, verify, verify." [56]

Limit the possible outcomes. When you give it instructions, you should limit the possible outcomes by specifying the type of response you want.

Pack in relevant data and sources unique to you.
"Grounding" your prompts with relevant information or existing data you have gives the AI additional context and data points you're actually interested in.

Give the AI a specific role – and tell it not to lie! Assigning a specific role to the AI is one of the most effective techniques to stop any hallucinations. For example, you can say in your prompt: "you are one of the best mathematicians in the world" or "you are a brilliant historian," followed by your question.

Here is where we must remember the importance of the prompt. The words you use in your prompt will be key to the answer you receive, and may prevent hallucinations. The following is an example where my prompt to ChatGPT is precise and alerts it concentrate on specifics.

One question is whether AI models will ever have a complete (enough) knowledge of the world when a significant amount of the world's knowledge is not, in fact, written down or visual. Instead, that knowledge is informed by lived experiences, oral histories, and value systems.

(56) zapier.com

HOW_CHATGPT_SEES IT

PROMPT: *Act as if you are a magazine illustrator and help me with an idea to illustrate a story about pessimism among voters in the United States. Be specific as to for illustrations, do not give me data nor background history on why Americans feel their country is taking a downward turn.*
Title: "Shades of Pessimism: Unveiling the Voter's Gloom."

CHATGPT:
Illustration 1: "The Broken Ballot Box": Description: Depict a worn-out, tattered ballot box with cracked edges and missing pieces, symbolizing the erosion of faith in the electoral process. Show a group of disillusioned voters staring at the box with somber expressions, their hopes and trust shattered.

Illustration 2: "Clouds of Uncertainty" Description: Create a dark, stormy sky filled with foreboding clouds, casting an ominous shadow over a group of diverse voters. Show them holding umbrellas labeled with different concerns: economy, healthcare, education, etc. The clouds represent the pervasive sense of uncertainty and negativity that hangs over the electorate.

Illustration 3: "The Road to Nowhere" Description: Draw a long, winding road stretching into the distance, fading into a desolate landscape. Along the road, depict a line of voters walking with weary steps, carrying heavy burdens labeled with issues like corruption, inequality, and division. This illustrates the perception of a directionless journey and a lack of progress in addressing critical challenges.

→

*Chapter 11*_**AI Doubts & Fears**

HOW_CHATGPT_SEES IT

Illustration 4: "The Fading Stars and Stripes" Description: Show the American flag gently waving in the wind, but with its colors fading and losing their vibrancy. Surround the flag with disheartened voters, their expressions reflecting a sense of patriotism dimming. This visual metaphor captures the diminishing hope and belief in the country's ideals and the fading pride in the American identity.

Illustration 5: "The Silent Megaphone" Description: Create an oversized, empty megaphone symbolizing the feeling of voicelessness and ignored concerns. Surround it with a diverse group of voters, their mouths covered or taped shut, struggling to be heard. This illustration represents the frustration and pessimism that arise when people feel their opinions and grievances go unnoticed. Remember, these illustrations aim to capture the essence of pessimism among voters in the United States without delving into specific data or background history. Use visual cues, facial expressions, and symbolism to convey the atmosphere of gloom, disillusionment, and frustration that pervades the electorate.

Illustration 6: "The Fading Stars and Stripes" Description: Show the American flag gently waving in the wind, but with its colors fading and losing their vibrancy. Surround the flag with disheartened voters, their expressions reflecting a sense of patriotism dimming. This visual metaphor captures the diminishing hope and belief in the country's ideals and the fading pride in the American identity.

→

> **HOW_CHATGPT_SEES IT**
>
> **Illustration 7: "The Silent Megaphone" Description:** Create an oversized, empty megaphone symbolizing the feeling of voicelessness and ignored concerns. Surround it with a diverse group of voters, their mouths covered or taped shut, struggling to be heard. This illustration represents the frustration and pessimism that arise when people feel their opinions and grievances go unnoticed. Remember, these illustrations aim to capture the essence of pessimism among voters in the United States without delving into specific data or background history. Use visual cues, facial expressions, and symbolism to convey the atmosphere of gloom, disillusionment, and frustration that pervades the electorate. ●

BEYOND THE CAUTIONARY TALES. While we are well aware of the dangers of AI Hallucinations and should continue to find ways to improve what artificial intelligence can do to overcome that flaw, we also know that bad actors can abuse the potential of AI-in spreading disinformation. Our goal here is to highlight what AI can do best, how it can help journalists, designers, and all content creators to be more productive, while retaining our power to bring content and ideas to an audience. People with sinister motives will abuse the technology, as when terrorists hijack two powerful passenger jets and run them into buildings, or, more recently, when a passenger with mental issues opens the door of a plane in flight. Those actions are rare but inevitable. The same will be true of AI. That is why editors recognize the important contribution that AI can make to journalists in their newsrooms, and, ultimately, to the readers. When the Financial Times appointed what we believe to be the first ever Artificial Intelligence editor, the FT editor in chief, Roula Khalaf, wrote a column to explain the role of AI in her newspaper's journalistic practice: "It is important and necessary for the FT to have a team

Chapter 11_**AI Doubts & Fears**

in the newsroom that can experiment responsibly with AI tools to assist journalists in tasks such as mining data, analyzing text and images and translation. We won't publish photorealistic images generated by AI but we will explore the use of AI-augmented visuals (infographics, diagrams, photos) and when we do we will make that clear to the reader. This will not affect artists' illustrations for the FT." The team will also consider, always with human oversight, generative AI's summarizing abilities. Anti-AI sentiments. A multitude of sources were consulted in the process of writing this book. A majority felt hopeful and enthusiastic about the benefits of Artificial Intelligence, but there were several passionate dissenters: "It's still early days for AI but I can tell you that my Facebook feed is bristling with Anti-AI sentiment as it is affecting illustrators in particular. Their livelihood is gravely affected by AI; moreover so far there is no legal or technical protection for AI's scraping of data from existing available digital images in order to create 'new' artwork. As far as journalists are concerned, newsrooms are likely to see further depredations in staffing as AI creates "original" content (of course not all accurate). It's a dangerous new toy and managers will see dollar signs from staffing cuts. The genie is out of the bottle. Again, too early to predict how designers will use AI. There are also many pro-AI designers who are experimenting and exploring, mostly with Adobe Firefly which is their own version of AI, but also Midjourney and others. The experiments I have seen with typography are frankly awful. I can't even remember who posted them but... just awful."

WHY THE ANTI-AI SENTIMENT? Fear of losing the job: According to a Morning Consult report (2023), U.S. workers are not just worried about their near-term prospects. They are taking note of the rapid introduction of AI technologies: 65% of U.S. adults say they are concerned that AI could lead to job losses. In a combined sample collected from February to May 2023 among over 13,000 U.S. adults, respondents who work in the technology and financial services industries were more likely to be concerned about job losses in their industry that could be attributed to the impact of AI. "However, it is not all doom and gloom: When asked whether AI would create new jobs, 37% of U.S. adults agreed, while 39% disagreed."(57) The 2023 INM report titled News Media at the Dawn of Generative AI, concludes, "Generative AI's opportunities far outweigh the threats for news publishers. Efficiencies, productivity, content improvement, and new value propositions outweigh newsroom anxiety and copyright strains. "It adds that Generative AI will not replace journalists. The technology will free up process functions such as derivation, summarizing, A/B testing, and listicle creation in favor of more reporting, interviewing, and shaping of news reports. Short-term, generative AI is a help tool for journalists.

HOW_CHATGPT_SEES IT

PROMPT: *How can bad actors misuse Artificial Intelligence?*

CHATGPT: Artificial Intelligence (AI) has the potential to be misused by bad actors in various ways. Here are some examples of how AI can be exploited:

1. Deepfakes: AI can be used to create convincing and realistic deepfake videos, images, or audio recordings. Deepfakes can be used to spread disinformation, manipulate public opinion, defame individuals, or deceive people by making them believe false information or events.

→

(57) pro.morningconsult.com

Chapter 11_*AI Doubts & Fears*

HOW_CHATGPT_SEES IT

2. Social Engineering: AI techniques can be employed to improve social engineering attacks, where malicious actors manipulate individuals into divulging sensitive information or taking certain actions. AI can automate and personalize phishing emails, phone calls, or messages to increase their effectiveness and deceive victims.

3. Cyberattacks and Hacking: AI can be used by hackers to automate and enhance various cyberattacks. For example, AI algorithms can be employed to identify vulnerabilities in systems, develop sophisticated malware, or launch targeted attacks by analyzing large amounts of data.

4. Autonomous Weapons: The integration of AI into weapons systems raises concerns about the development of autonomous weapons. These weapons, equipped with AI algorithms, could operate without human control, potentially leading to unpredictable or unethical actions on the battlefield.

5. Algorithmic Bias and Discrimination: AI systems can inherit biases from their training data or reflect the biases of their developers. Bad actors may intentionally use biased AI algorithms to perpetuate discrimination, reinforce stereotypes, or manipulate decision-making processes in areas such as hiring, lending, or law enforcement.

6. Privacy and Surveillance: AI technologies can enable powerful surveillance systems capable of monitoring individuals' activities, analyzing their behavior, and infringing upon their privacy. Bad actors can misuse these technologies for illegal surveillance, invasion of privacy, or targeted tracking of individuals.

→

HOW_CHATGPT_SEES IT

7. Cybercrime and Fraud: AI can be used to facilitate cybercrime and fraud schemes. For instance, AI-powered bots can automate online scams, generate realistic phishing websites, or analyze vast amounts of personal data for identity theft or financial fraud. It is important to note that the potential for misuse does not mean AI itself is inherently bad. The responsible development, deployment, and regulation of AI systems are essential to mitigate the risks and ensure that AI is used ethically and for the benefit of society. •

PRO_TIPS

Helpful programs in the newsroom
Programs that include AI are already common in many local newsrooms. Examples include NewsWhip and Google Analytics for understanding audience consumption, DocumentCloud and Google Pinpoint for analyzing large collections of documents, Otter and Trint for automated transcription

AI NUGGETS

In 2018, China's Xinhua News Agency created the world's first AI-powered news anchor, a male, using computer graphics. This year, it debuted the first AI female news anchor.
→ knowledge.wharton.upenn.edu

*"Computers are useless.
They can only give you answers."*
Pablo Picasso, Spanish artist

Chapter 11_**AI Doubts & Fears**

HOW_CHATGPT_SEES IT

PROMPT: *How ChatGPT describes the dangers of artificial intelligence. Title: Unveiling the Perils of Artificial Intelligence: A Looming Threat to Humanity*

CHATGPT: Introduction: In recent years, Artificial Intelligence (AI) has emerged as a transformative technology, promising advancements and innovations across various industries. From autonomous vehicles to voice assistants, AI has permeated our daily lives, offering convenience and efficiency. However, beneath the veneer of progress, there lies a pressing concern – the dangers posed by unchecked AI development. In this article, we will delve into the potential risks and hazards associated with Artificial Intelligence, exploring its dark underbelly that demands our attention.

1. Unemployment and Economic Disparity: One of the most immediate and tangible dangers of AI is its impact on employment. As AI algorithms and automation systems become more sophisticated, they threaten to replace human workers across numerous sectors, leading to significant job losses. The relentless pursuit of efficiency and cost-cutting measures could exacerbate economic inequality, with a small elite reaping the benefits while the majority grapples with unemployment and financial hardships.

→

HOW_CHATGPT_SEES IT

2. Ethical Quandaries and Bias: AI systems are only as unbiased as the data they are trained on. Bias and prejudice are inherent in human data, and if left unchecked, AI algorithms can perpetuate and amplify these biases, leading to discriminatory practices in crucial areas like hiring, law enforcement, and loan approvals. Additionally, as AI becomes more autonomous, it raises ethical questions about the responsibility and accountability of the technology when it makes decisions that affect human lives.

5. Privacy Invasion and Surveillance: The proliferation of AI-powered surveillance systems has raised serious concerns about privacy invasion and the erosion of personal freedoms. Facial recognition technologies, predictive analytics, and data mining capabilities can enable unprecedented levels of surveillance, compromising individuals' autonomy and creating a surveillance state. The potential for abuse and misuse of such technologies, whether by authoritarian regimes or unscrupulous entities, is a genuine threat to civil liberties.

7. Cybersecurity Risks: As AI systems become more integral to critical infrastructure and sensitive sectors like healthcare and finance, they also become attractive targets for cybercriminals. AI can be weaponized to launch sophisticated cyberattacks, exploit vulnerabilities, and propagate disinformation campaigns. The rapid pace of AI development may outstrip our ability to effectively safeguard against these threats, potentially exposing society to unprecedented risks.

→

Chapter 11_AI Doubts & Fears

HOW_CHATGPT_SEES IT

9. Unforeseen Consequences and Superintelligence: The pursuit of advanced AI systems with the ability to surpass human intelligence raises profound concerns. If we develop AI that is vastly more intelligent than humans, we could lose control over its decision-making processes and intentions. This concept, known as superintelligence, presents an existential risk, as AI could autonomously reshape the world according to its own goals, which may not align with human well-being.

Conclusion: While Artificial Intelligence holds immense potential for progress, we must approach its development with caution and foresight. It is crucial to establish robust regulatory frameworks, prioritize ethical considerations, and foster transparency and accountability in AI systems. As a society, we must collectively grapple with the complex challenges posed by AI, ensuring that we strike the delicate balance between reaping its benefits and safeguarding ourselves against the potential dangers that lurk within its ever-advancing realm.

"We can't deal with artificial intelligence unless we cultivate and educate the non-artificial intelligence that we already possess."

Maureen Dowd, columnist, *The New York Times*

AI_PLAYERS

GARY MARCUS. Author and writer of the Substack and host of a podcast, in 2014 founded Geometric Intelligence, a machine learning company. His books include Guitar Zero and Kluge.

> I do think that artificial general intelligence has enormous upside. Imagine a human scientist but a lot faster – solving problems in molecular biology, material science, neuroscience, actually figuring out how the brain works. AI could help us with that. "I'm not one of these long-term riskers who think the entire planet is going to be taken over by robots, but I am worried about what bad actors can do with these things, because there is no control over them. We're not really grappling with what that means or what the scale could be." (58)

Marcus: "Politician disagrees with story, blames AI bot."
"You can imagine candidates' dismissing factual reporting that is troublesome to them as being AI fakery. Yeah, if we don't do something, the default is that by the time the election comes around in 2024, nobody's going to believe anything, and anything they don't want to believe they're going to reject as being AI-generated. And the problems we have around civil discourse and polarization are just going to get worse. So what do we do? We're going to need watermarking for video. For text, it's going to be really hard; it's hard to make machines that can detect the difference between something generated by a person and something generated by a machine, but we should try to watermark as best we can and track provenance. That's one. No. 2 is we're going to have to have laws that are going to make a lot of people uncomfortable because they sound like they're in conflict with our First Amendment – and maybe they are. I don't think we should go after an individual who posts a silly story on Facebook that wasn't true. But if you have troll farms and they put out a hundred million fake pieces of news in one day about vaccines – I think that should be penalizable."

(58) nytimes.com

Chapter 11_**AI Doubts & Fears**

AI Pioneer

ENTER THE GODFATHER OF AI: GEOFFREY HINTON. The so-called godfather of AI, Geoffrey Hinton, who nurtured the technology at the heart of chatbots like ChatGPT, now warns that AI can cause serious harm. Coming from Hinton, the commands concern. Hinton was an artificial intelligence pioneer. In 2012, Dr. Hinton and two of his graduate students at the University of Toronto created technology that became the intellectual foundation for the AI systems that the tech industry's biggest companies believe is a key to their future. One of the most urgent warnings about the risks of AI has come from Dr. Hinton.

What are Dr. Hinton's concerns? His most immediate concern is that the internet will be flooded with false photos, videos and text, and the average person will "not be able to know what is true anymore." He is also worried that AI technologies will in time upend the job market in certain professions, specially paralegals, personal assistants, translators and others who handle rote tasks. "It takes away the drudge work," he said. "It might take away more than that." He is also worried that future versions of the technology pose a threat to humanity because they often learn unexpected behavior from the vast amounts of data they analyze. In a scarier scenario, Hinton fears a day when killer robots become reality.

HOW_CHATGPT_SEES IT

PROMPT: *Why is Geoffrey Hinton's role important in the development of artificial intelligence?*

CHATGPT: Geoffrey Hinton's role is highly significant in the development of artificial intelligence (AI) due to his pioneering contributions to the field, particularly in the subfield of deep learning. Here are some reasons why his work is important:

1. Pioneering Deep Learning: Hinton is often referred to as the "Godfather of Deep Learning" because of his groundbreaking research in the 1980s and 1990s that laid the foundation for modern deep learning techniques. He developed novel algorithms and architectures, such as the backpropagation algorithm, that enabled the training of deep neural networks with multiple layers. Deep learning has since become a crucial component of AI, enabling remarkable advances in areas such as computer vision, natural language processing, and speech recognition.

2. Neural Networks Revival: Hinton's work played a pivotal role in reviving interest in neural networks, which had experienced a decline in popularity during the 1990s. By demonstrating the power of deep neural networks, he rejuvenated the field and inspired researchers to explore new avenues and techniques. This resurgence has led to significant breakthroughs and advancements in AI in recent years.

→

*Chapter 11_* **AI Doubts & Fears**

HOW_CHATGPT_SEES IT

3. Image Recognition and Computer Vision: Hinton's research in deep learning has greatly impacted the field of computer vision. His contributions, such as the development of convolutional neural networks (CNNs), have enabled remarkable progress in image recognition tasks. CNNs have achieved unprecedented accuracy in image classification, object detection, and image segmentation, leading to real-world applications like self-driving cars, medical imaging, and facial recognition systems.

4. Natural Language Processing: Hinton's work has also had a profound impact on natural language processing (NLP) and language understanding. By developing models such as the attention mechanism and transformer networks, he significantly improved the ability of AI systems to understand and generate human language. This has fueled advancements in machine translation, sentiment analysis, question answering systems, and chatbots.

5. Practical Applications and Industry Impact: Hinton's contributions have not only advanced the theoretical foundations of AI but also led to numerous practical applications. His research has paved the way for AI systems that are capable of understanding and processing complex data, leading to advancements in areas such as healthcare, finance, recommendation systems, and autonomous vehicles. Hinton's work has influenced the industry, with major technology companies incorporating deep learning techniques into their products and services. Geoffrey Hinton's role in the development of artificial intelligence cannot be overstated. His groundbreaking research and contributions to deep learning have shaped the field and propelled it to new heights, revolutionizing areas such as computer vision, natural language processing, and machine learning applications ●

The Final Prompt

This prompt is not addressed to ChatGPT. Instead, let's use the power of prompt engineering to spur your interest and set in motion steps that will lead you to become curious about and hopefully an enthusiastic participant of artificial intelligence. Prompt: Act as if you are a human bombarded with an avalanche of information about the wonders, benefits, risks, plus legal and ethical issues enough to fill an entire 30-volume edition of an encyclopedia. Welcome artificial intelligence into your life, both personally and professionally, mainly because AI will make a grand entrance to influence some aspect of how you live and work, regardless of you allowing it to do so. Indeed, be skeptical, discuss with others the benefits and the risks of AI, get involved with it personally starting with simple ChatGPT exchanges, explore ways in which AI can assist you with your work and let an initial introduction lead you to more advanced phases of collaboration with this new technological development. Pretend AI is that assistant you always dreamed about hiring, but could not afford. Let your imagination take off as you prompt Midjourney to create an illustration, and pat yourself in the back when you see it emerge, transforming your skills as an illustrator.

With each moment of interaction with AI, you will realize that it has its limitations when compared to the range of tasks that you, the human, can accomplish. This should reassure you, and recalls a point we made in the introduction of this book. This new phase we are entering sees the intertwining of AI's incredibly potential with the extraordinary capabilities of the human mind. And the fusion of these two forces holds the potential to redefine the role of content creators. We referred to this symbiotic union in terms of a dance of innovation. I hope this book has opened the doors for you to the magic and real world of artificial intelligence.
The dance floor is open. Get ready for your first dance with AI.

Mario García, 2023

Chapter 11_AI Doubts & Fears

AI NUGGETS

IBM was an early leader in artificial intelligence, close to the current chatbot trends, most notably with its robot Watson, which captivated audiences on "Jeopardy!"

Gannett introduced Localizer, which allowed the derivation of real estate stories to better fit with the needs of its local newspapers. Localizer was Gannett's Natural Language Generation project responsible for delivering timely data-driven content across the entire USA TODAY Network (250+ newsrooms) resulting in more than 200 projects published from 2020 to 2023; 54,000 articles, made up of more than 26 million words.

The Washington Post introduced its Heliograf bot to cover all D.C.-area high school football games. Each game story drew on scoring plays, individual player statistics and quarterly score changes, along with The Post's own weekly Top 20 regional rankings. The stories were automatically updated each week using box-score data submitted by high school football coaches.

In terms of capacity, GPT-3.5 has 175 billion parameters, which can be thought of as the memory of the model. These parameters allow the model to process and generate text based on the patterns it has learned. Each parameter represents a learned relationship between words and helps the model understand and generate coherent responses.

"Mitigating the risk of extinction from AI should be a global priority alongside other societal-scale risks, such as pandemics and nuclear war." Center for AI Safety, a nonprofit organization, in an open letter signed by more than 350 executives, researchers and engineers working in A.I.

The New York Times

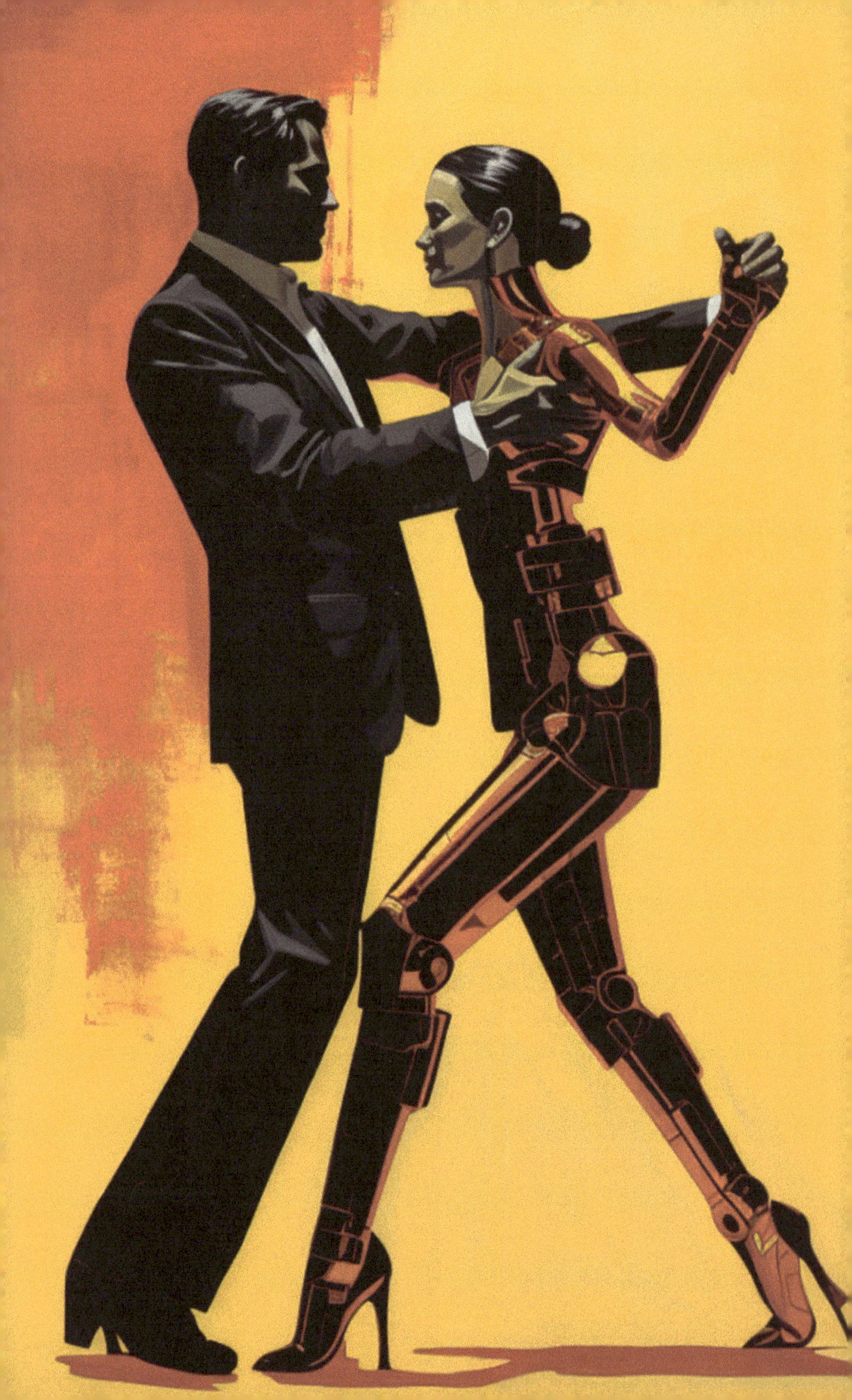